PENGUIN BOOKS

CANADA AT WAR

Maclean's

John Bayne Maclean published his first general-interest magazine in October 1905 as *The Business Magazine*. It was renamed *The Busy Man's Magazine* before the year was out and in March 1911 became known as *Maclean's Magazine*. From a circulation of five thousand copies in 1905, readership has grown to more than 2 million each week. The magazine's archives have revealed themselves to be a treasure trove of writing about Canadians at war.

Michael Benedict

Michael Benedict, a member of the *Maclean's* Board of Editors, has been with the newsmagazine in a variety of roles since 1986. In 1994, he conceived and oversaw the production of the June 6 special issue commemorating the 50th anniversary of the D-Day landing. It was that project that gave him the idea of collecting in one volume the best war stories that have appeared in *Maclean's* throughout its nearly one hundred years of publication.

Beginning his journalist's career as a copy boy at the CBC newsroom in Montreal, he went on to reporting jobs with the *St. John's Evening Telegram*, and in Ottawa's Parliamentary Press Gallery for *The Toronto Star* and CTV. In 1980, he moved to Toronto and worked in communications for the Government of Ontario and Canada Post before returning to his first love, journalism, with *Maclean's*.

CANADA AT WAR

edited by
MICHAEL BENEDICT

Penguin Books

PENGUIN BOOKS
Published by the Penguin Group
Penguin Books Canada Ltd, 10 Alcorn Avenue, Toronto, Ontario,
Canada M4V 3B2
Penguin Books Ltd, 27 Wrights Lane, London W8 5TZ, England
Penguin Putnam Inc., 375 Hudson Street, New York, New York 10014, U.S.A.
Penguin Books Australia Ltd, Ringwood, Victoria, Australia
Penguin Books (NZ) Ltd, cnr Rosedale and Airborne Roads, Albany,
Auckland 1310, New Zealand

Penguin Books Ltd, Registered Offices: Harmondsworth,
Middlesex, England

First published in Viking by Penguin Books Canada Limited, 1997
Published in Penguin Books, 1998

10 9 8 7 6 5 4 3 2 1

Manufactured in Canada.

Canadian Cataloguing in Publication Data

Main entry under title:
Canada at war
Collection of articles originally published in *Maclean's*.

ISBN 0-14-026474-4

1. Canada – History, Military – 20th century.*
2. Canada – Armed Forces – Biography. I. Benedict, Michael, 1947–

FC603.C34 1998   355'.00971'0904   C97-930427-X
F1028.C362 1998

Visit Penguin Canada's web site at **www.penguin.ca**

CONTENTS

FOREWORD

Major-General Lewis MacKenzie

AS I READ WITH interest the *Maclean's* articles from the First World War onward, I was impressed by the magazine's unique Canadian style of reporting. When describing war, other nations' journalists tend to report the success or failure of large military operations. Massive arrows drawn on small maps accompanied by a narrative explain allied operations. *Maclean's* reporting on the other hand, and much to its credit, concentrates on the human element—the individual soldier's story. In the final analysis, it is the actions of individual soldiers or small groups of soldiers that win or lose the battle.

In times of crisis, Canadians have consistently rallied to the cause for the very best of reasons: God, King, Queen, country, freedom and, dare I say, adventure. However, once on the battlefield, in dangerous skies or on unforgiving seas, they risk their lives for a much more personal and tangible reason—their comrades, their buddies. The flow of adrenaline generated by a combination of fear and excitement creates a form of tunnel vision. In actual battle, your world of interest shrinks dramatically and you are only aware, in vivid detail, of things that are happening in your immediate vicinity. All that matters to you in the world is within earshot, and your fellow soldiers a few metres on either side of you are the most important people on the face of the earth. At that moment, Queen and country are rather remote. Wars are best understood by studying the actions of individuals, not the large formations to which they belong.

At the individual level, war has changed very little over the past century. During the Gulf War, a perception was created that combat was now more similar to an arcade game than its gruesome predecessors. Regrettably, for the soldier, such is not the case. In the comfort of our living room, our television screen might show a missile disappearing into a bunker accompanied by a silent flash as it explodes. What it doesn't show is the disintegration of the 20 or so human beings inside the bunker. It doesn't show the follow-up ground assault troops picking through the bits and pieces of enemy body parts, looking for anything that might be of use to the intelligence folks. It doesn't show hardened soldiers unashamedly vomiting in front of their comrades or breaking down emotionally at the sight and the smell of the carnage. This common aspect of war, as clearly demonstrated in the *Maclean's* collection, has not changed between Vimy Ridge in 1917 and the UN's battle for the Medak pocket in Croatia in 1993.

If there is one combat skill that is virtually timeless compared to any other, it is that of the sniper, captured so brilliantly in the December 1917 article by Corporal R.N. Siddle about his adventures and those of his buddy Adam Crookshanks. Snipers, then and now, must possess uniquely high standards of skills that virtually define the ideal soldier, sailor or airman: stealth, endurance, marksmanship and above all the courage to be patient. A single sniper can and has stopped, delayed and deflected the movement of thousands of enemy troops. His is a very personal war. In the majority of cases, he can see the facial features and expressions of the person he is about to kill. While he studies his potential victim, he suffers. Wind, rain, sleet, cold and body-stiffening immobility are his lot. The more miserable the conditions, the more vulnerable his target. Discussions of large battles rarely mention the snipers in spite of their significant impact on the outcome.

For a nation that is constantly referred to by its citizens as "non-military," our record for doing more than our share when the trumpet sounds is, quite frankly, second to none. Protected by three oceans and a friendly neighbour to the south, we did not have to go to war at any time during this century. We could have stayed at home when Germany swaggered forth with her military might in 1914. We could have ignored Europe's crisis in 1939, and it would have been easy to turn our back on South Korea in 1950 and the Gulf in 1991. It would have been shameful and embarrassing, and our international reputation would have been sullied, but all these wars would have been won without us—albeit with

Foreword

significantly greater sacrifices by our allies. Nevertheless, we could have stayed home and we would still be a nation today.

Canada fought in four wars in this century and we have participated in more UN peacekeeping missions than any other country in the world, not because we were threatened but because it was the right thing to do. I believe that a nation's obligations abroad are somewhat proportional to its blessings at home. That being the case, Canada has a fairly significant offshore debt and it has been paid in full, with interest, by our servicemen and servicewomen throughout this century. Their dedication and selflessness, which continues today, is all too often taken for granted.

Mind you, there is nothing new about that. However, as we bask in the outstanding reputation our military has earned for us in some of the most miserable and dangerous locations in the world, let's pause occasionally and consider our men and women in uniform and their sacrifices which have made us so respected as a nation. God bless each and every one of them, particularly those who made the ultimate sacrifice and never made it home to this magnificent country.

Maj.-Gen. Lewis MacKenzie MSC, CD
First UN Commander in Sarajevo (1992)

PREFACE

IN ITS NEARLY 100 years of publication, *Maclean's* has featured some of the finest writers in Canada and from around the world. The magazine's archives are a treasure trove, ranging from works by Stephen Leacock during the First World War through Lionel Shapiro and Scott Young in the Second World War and, in more recent times, Pierre Berton, Peter Gzowski, Peter C. Newman and Mordecai Richler. Some of those names appear in this collection of articles about "ordinary" Canadians who displayed extraordinary courage in battle, from the muddy trenches of the First World War to the muddy hills in the former Yugoslavia. Many of their stories—all originally published in *Maclean's*—are hair-raising and horrific, such as the epic survival of RCAF pilot John Shanahan, downed by a Junkers 88 over the Mediterranean Sea.

Other, equally dramatic articles reflect the magazine's news orientation. *Maclean's* was the first publication anywhere, in its November 1, 1945, edition, to record the heroic details of what later became known through books and movies as The Great Escape. Flt.-Lieut. Tony Pengelly, a self-taught document forger from Truro, N.S., stayed behind on a wintry night in March 1944, to provide a final check on the phony papers carried by more than 80 of his fellow prisoners who crawled out under Stalag Luft III. Most were captured and summarily executed. Shortly after his liberation and the end of the war, Pengelly told writer Scott Young about the dramatic prison break-out.

Escape and imprisonment are common threads connecting the wartime experiences of Canadians for more than 75 years. Whether fleeing the Japanese after the fall of Hong Kong or being imprisoned in German camps, in both world wars, and then by the Serbs in 1994, the soldiers' stories are remarkably similar.

CANADA AT WAR

The articles on the following pages cover the First World War, the Second World War, the Korean War, the Gulf War and peace-keeping in Cyprus, Somalia and the former Yugoslavia. The range of Canadian military activity reflected in the collection is astounding. Indeed, Canada's fighting men—and women—participated in war theatres usually not associated with this country, such as the partisan fighting in Yugoslavia, the Pacific battles of the Second World War and the Mesopotamian campaign of the First World War. Canadians also proudly took part in the mostly forgotten post-Bolshevik Allied invasion of Siberia in 1919. Throughout, they fought bravely on land and sea and in the air. While warfare has undergone revolutionary change from the trenches of the First World War to the high-tech wizardry of the Gulf War, the articles show that the experiences of the ordinary fighting man and woman remain surprisingly constant.

Most of the articles were shortened, but otherwise they underwent very little editing. Strenuous efforts were made to locate the Cana-dians—or their families—featured in these articles, as well as the writers who set down their deeds. Where successful, the informa-tion is noted at the end of the piece. *Maclean's* received invaluable assistance in this effort from Bill Wood, head of the Personnel Records Unit, Researcher Services Division of the National Archives of Canada.

There were many others who worked assiduously to bring this collection together. They include *Maclean's* associate photo editor Kristine Ryall, who spent a week in Ottawa at the Archives, and many days thereafter finding and organizing the historic and per-sonal photographs to accompany the articles. Tanya Davies and Joanne Spence helped bring the articles from the pages of the mag-azine into book form. David North, who has written an in-house history of *Maclean's*, was a fount of background knowledge.

Special thanks go to *Maclean's* researcher-reporter Ruth Abramson, who tracked down Canadian war heroes all over the world, fact-checked all new material and responded cheerfully and helpfully to every request for further information.

A final word of gratitude to the man who inspired this pro-

Preface

ject—Charlie Martin, one of the first to land on the Normandy beaches on D-Day, more than half a century ago. He allowed *Maclean's* to accompany him on an emotional 50th anniversary return visit in 1994, which is recorded in this collection. A typical Canadian war hero, both modest and self-deprecating, Martin's story and the quiet force of his character prompted the search for similar tales in the pages of *Maclean's*. The result was a gold mine.

Michael Benedict
Editorial Director, New Ventures
Maclean's
Toronto

FIRST WORLD WAR

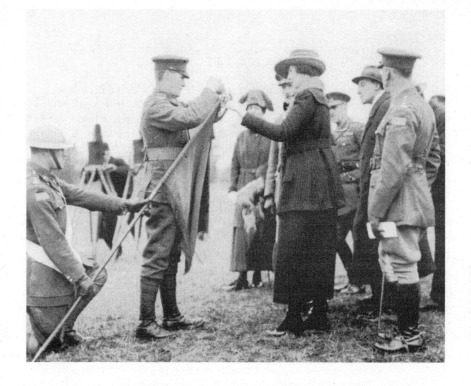

THE CANADIANS IN HOSPITAL

—May 1916—
Private George Eustace Pearson

The writer of this article was with the original "Princess Pats" and served for five months in the trenches of Flanders. He became ill during the latter days of the heavy fighting around Ypres and was removed to England, where he had the opportunity of observing all phases of life in military hospitals. In the accompanying article, he tells what happens to the wounded or sick soldier from the time that he is taken from the trenches to the day he is discharged or returned to duty.
—The Editor, 1916

Princess Patricia reviewing the Princess Patricia's Canadian Light Infantry at Bramshatt, England, in 1919.

It was Netley, that great British military hospital, which received the largest part of the Canadian wounded after Ypres. It dropped its staff military formality for the nonce and as those men of Flanders trooped in through the open gate, mud-bespattered, soggy of shoe and with coats cut to suit all variety of barbaric taste, the whole staff—doctors, nurses and orderlies—pressed upon them, cheering and weeping, shaking them by the hand, even the stretcher cases, in a wild hysteria of gratitude for the men who had saved Ypres and the gate to England.

These men had come promptly from the firing line through a chain of happy circumstance. Cases have been known, many of them, of men leaving England early in the week, going up the line promptly and getting their "Blighty"—a trip to England, wounded—before the week was out.

Usually, however, the patient may depend upon a long series of vicissitudes before he arrives in an English hospital. There are all degrees of haste and slowness, efficiency and lack of it. All depends upon the degree of stress of the moment and the ability of the individuals concerned to handle a situation.

A man may be wounded in the morning and lie all day in a crowded trench, occasionally walked on and continually exposed to the perpetual rain, or partially neglected in a wet dugout. These possibilities become certainties if there is no communication trench that may safely be used in daylight hours, or unless the case is so desperate that the stretcher-bearers are justified in risking German fire by making a run for it across the open ground. With the night, however, under ordinary conditions the wounded man is at once taken to the regimental dressing station a few hundred yards, or a thousand of them, in the rear. His comrades have already given him first-aid treatment with the aid of the package each soldier carries, so there is nothing to be done at the dressing station but to give him adequate shelter, rest and a hot drink. And then he goes to sleep, always, even though he is dying. He is so tired. Always.

Every night, shortly after dark, there comes the motor ambulance from the nearest clearing hospital, which is usually a few miles away. So the stay at the dressing station may be a very brief one, and very rarely exceeds twenty-four hours. A short ride to the clearing hospital and the first treatment and real attention is received. The soldier is moved on as soon as this is done, usually in a few hours' time to the stationary hospital at Bailleul, St. Omer, or similar points another five or ten miles back. Here he may remain for a day, a week or a month. In any event he will now begin to receive regular attention, and will probably live—else he would have died long before from lack of attention.

In times of great stress, however, such, for instance, as occurred during the Battle of Ypres, all these arrangements are upset. Every road then overflows with wounded, walking and crawling and carried and wheeled in all manner of conveyance at all hours and in all sorts of places. Dugouts, ditches, roads and dressing stations are littered indiscriminately with dead and dying. It is at such times as this that men lie out unattended for days, fired on by friend and foe, dying painful deaths.

From this first stationary hospital the soldier may go into another of a similar character further down the line in order to make room for the constant influx of newly wounded. This may occur once or twice or thrice before he reaches one of the base hospitals, or the sea at Boulogne or Le Havre en route for "Blighty." Unless his wound is of so light a nature that he goes to a convalescent hospital in France, then to the base camp at Rouen, and eventually the trenches again.

The length of the stay at the base port hospital depends upon bed space in English and French hospitals, the patient's condition and other factors buried deep in the dullness of the official mind; for red tape still stultifies action to a very large degree in any branch of the army which is out of the reach of the front. Conditions there will not allow any supremacy of officialdom, and action reigns supreme.

The next stage of the journey is of all the happiest for the soldier. Technically he is shipped to the military hospital nearest his home; actually he may be taken to any part of Great Britain or Ireland. And at each hospital coming in and going out he undergoes the same monotonous ordeal of questioning as to his antecedents, the color of his hair and his religious persuasion. This last is of particular and paramount importance, if the eagerness of official curiosity is any indication, and has a definite bearing on the patient's chances of recovery.

It was thus the Canadian soldiers came to Netley.

There is more room for time and sentiment in the hospital than out there. The mind reverts back to what it has seen and seeks sentiment in quick relief.

Those who had seen the most talked the least of war. The net result of the continual strain, of the monotonous hardship and incessant fighting had made such an ineradicable impression on the minds of those who had experienced it week in and week out for months at a time that they turned from the thought of it in distaste, and found their wildest adventure in the innocent ravishing of a blackberry bush of its luscious fruit. The war has become so commonplace in its horrors that they could not adequately describe it. To do that one must have witnessed only the fringe of action. To plunge into the vortex of it was to have lost all perspective and all vividness of impression.

Princess Patricia's Canadian Light Infantry on parade, July 1917.

The Canadians in Hospital

Underneath all the reversion to childish things to which the men turned for the sheer contrast of it, lay an undercurrent of deep and serious thought that was most apt to rear its head in the surprising discussions that centred about the nightly campfire when the kingdoms of the earth were reconstructed. For these men of Flanders and of Gallipoli were now asking themselves the why and wherefore of this and that, and the reason why published accounts did not always tally with their observations of events.

As soldiers they had had little time to think. Further, it was dangerous to their peace of mind. Now they had little else to do and much food for thought. Memories. The process was more critical than constructive. There is now gestating within this Empire, more particularly in its armies, a process of thought that may bear strange fruit in days to come.

They were strong for conscription, Canadian troops and all, and insisted that the conscript army must be made to wear a distinctive badge. They were not at all anxious to get back to the lines; a condition of mind imposed, probably, by the sick and wearied condition of the body.

Swan, a Tommy, had been called up as a reservist at the outbreak of war and had seen as much of it as one man could hope for. This feeling of dread was very general in the hospital. Later, as they recovered their strength, they became reconciled to returning because their duty lay that way. But not because they liked it.

Swan suffered from the same affliction as myself, with the difference that his was a light case that showed alarming symptoms of an early return to health and the trenches whilst I was still bothered by an infinite quantity of weaknesses. He came to me in frank distress and inquired as to the location and operation of my various disabilities in order that he might emulate them. He was partially successful. Months afterwards he was in receipt of privileges that were denied me as being less in need than he was. But one day the *Aquitania* came sliding past us down the Solent with her four thousand odd of men from the Dardenelles. The hospital was cleared to make room for them. My last memory of Swan is that of his disconsolate figure as he sat, head in hands, waiting for the train that was to take him to a convalescent home; heart-broken as

7

he saw his rosy edifice of ill health crumbling and himself that much nearer the fatal day of "out there" again.

And the wounded Canadian, let it be here recorded, received the kindest treatment and most wide consideration. The women of the vicinity, irrespective of class, were insistent in their kindness. Like the medical officers, they felt a rush of personal gratitude to every wounded soldier and doubly so to Canadians. These they spoil. Their imagination had grasped the vital points of the worst side of this war more readily than the male civilians had done. The failure of the latter to do so caused common remark in the free-masonry of wounded soldier circles. "Blimey, them blokes don't know they's a war on." "Not awf," I said.

There was a great bond of sympathy between Australians, New Zealanders and Canadians. If their speech differed their mentation did not. The men from the antipodes were more nearly like the British in the modulations of their voices. But they thought in dif-ferent vein. They had that sense of humor and that breadth of vision that comes with a young civilization that has been swaddled in big places.

There were some Australian bullockys, the equivalent to our muleskinners, and equally proficient in profanity, in another ward. They found, as most men do, that although one must either be wounded or else in a dying condition from disease to gain admit-tance to hospital in France, one must be possessed of persuasive pow-ers to an unusual degree to get out of one in England. This irritated the bullockys. They felt quite fit. So they set aside precedent and upset convention. Blue-clad as they were, they scattered on French leave. The hospital staff was shocked, astounded, and finally wound up by being pleased. The incident vastly tickled a countryman of theirs, an elderly major on the hospital staff. He actually taunted mere New Zealanders and Canadians with it.

But woe betide the poor Tommy who sought to emulate these brave deeds. They had just cause for complaint. Even women visi-tors impulsively fell into the kindly error of singling out Colonials, more particularly Canadians, for especial favors.

"Blimey, it's a bit thick," Swan used to say. "When she says, 'Oh, are you a Canoydien? Won't you please 'ave some cigarettes?'

The Canadians in Hospital

Then, 'Oh, you're not a Canoydien!' and takes 'er bleedin' fags away. Bit thick I calls it."

The soldiers of all countries were warm in their admiration of the Canadian nurses. The press and public incline to a praise of Canadian soldiers that is probably as far removed from the truth as some of their ante-Ypres criticisms were; but praise of the nurses springs from the hearts of individuals and is more to be trusted.

Each day saw its influx or departure of old friends. They came from the far-flung Franco-Flemish front, Alexandria, Cairo and Gallipoli. One detachment from the latter place had participated in the combined Japanese-British campaign in China. Of the departing ones, some went at once on their seven-day leave, at the expiration of which they would report at their regimental depot ready for active service again. Others, less fit, went to convalescent homes for a period that must not exceed six weeks, after which they too received leave and then reported for duty. Others led nomadic lives that included frequent changes of hospitals for reasons they despairingly called on the powers above to elucidate. No one ever knew, but the thing must be done because it was an order. In this way some unfortunates became authorities on hospitals after having been in as many as twelve or eighteen different institutions. At some they only stop a day or two, at some a week, and always there is that momentous question: "What church do you belong to?"

There were Indian soldiers here also. They had their own mess, and all the many perquisites of their various castes. There was a man of one caste to cook their food, one of another to shave their bodies and so on ad infinitum. Their mental attitude towards their British officers was quite different to that commonly reported. Instead of adoring him as their father and their mother, they sometimes spat at the mention of his name, and turned loose a flood of picturesque invective. For their own high-caste Indian officers they professed the greatest love. "As for caste," they said, "you mock at us. You are worse." They pointed at the cemetery. "Here are your officers, your high caste. There are your common soldiers, your low caste. Even we do not do this thing."

It is to the Canadian Convalescent Camp at Lord Rosebery's

estate near the famous course at Epsom Downs that all Canadian soldiers must go before scattering on leave and later settling down to soldiering again at Shorncliffe. By a combination of easier discipline and the display of individual initiative they usually manage to stretch their single seven-day leave into several of them, by wiring for extensions, and in general insure themselves an adequate holiday.

Trust Tommy Canuck for that.

At the large convalescent camp at Epsom Downs even the British nurses forsook all attempt at decorum and openly romped with their charges. A nurse holds commissioned rank in the army. But at Epsom, as the night grew on, it was no unusual sight to see a skirted officer hugging the shadows of the wall as she gave a leg up to each individual of a long queue of convalescent Canadians returning from an evening's deviltry in the town. And these officers usually giggled in a very unsoldier-like manner.

At Shorncliffe the final sorting is done. Those fit for the front are placed in the company of newly arrived recruits and with them usually go through an extended course of training before going to France again. Cases have been known, though, of men leaving hospital one week and finding themselves in the trenches in the course of the following week. The remainder are placed in the Casualty Company, which is composed of the vets, the lame and the halt, and there by a lengthy process of elimination and repetition are sub-divided into those fit for light staff work in England or Canada, and those disabled and ready for discharge. The medical boards become the wounded soldier's bug-bear. His medical history papers are invariably lost and, at each place and for each fresh decision or reconsideration, all the facts of his case must be compiled again. Apparently no Napoleonic mind has conceived of the possibility of making out the data in duplicate so that the individual's original history may accompany him in his aimless Governmental wanderings up and down the length of Britain.

And if he is off "for Canada," he knows no sweeter joy and his comrade no greater envy than this. Of course, the future of the bloody memories and the mangled body must be faced. But at least in time, after the Canadian authorities at Quebec, Toronto or whatnot have had their fling, he may look forward to a future serene and happy in the dear knowledge that at last his duty to his country has been done, and that dull official curiosity has been satisfied. They now know to which church he belongs.

Before volunteering, Pearson worked for Hardware & Metal, *a Maclean Publishing Co. magazine, and after the war he returned to the publishing company as Montreal editor of the weekly* Financial Post. *He continued to write about the war for* Maclean's *and other publications until he died in 1928.*

CLOSING THE EYES OF THE HUN

—December 1917—
Corporal R.N. Siddle

Corporal Siddle enlisted in London, Ont., with the 18th Battalion. He served as a sniper for sixteen months and at the end of that time had a well-earned reputation as one of the crack snipers with the Canadian forces. He had been through the battles of Ypres and St. Eloi and at the Somme, and had to his knowledge accounted for 24 Germans. During the Battle of the Somme he was buried by a shell and narrowly escaped death. He was later invalided home. No one is in a better position to tell the story of the sniper and the hazardous work that falls to his lot. —The Editor, 1917

Canadian soldier hiding during the October 1918 advance on Arras, France.

Closing the Eyes of the Hun

We were "going up." It was an unusually dark night and we stumbled along the shell-pitted road as best we could. Suddenly one of our fellows pitched forward with a deep-wrung groan; and did not get up. A quick examination by those nearest revealed the fact that he had been hit—and *behind* the shoulder at that.

A few moments later another fellow emitted a sharp cry of pain. "I'm hit!" he exclaimed. "They've handed me one in the leg."

Almost before the words were out of his mouth another pellet came winging out of the blackness and nipped the arm of a sergeant. There was no longer any doubt as to what was happening. Somewhere in the darkness behind us, a "sniper" was concealed.

The 18th Battalion had not been long at the front and we were a little disturbed at this form of attack. The sniper had probably directed his aim by the sound of our tramping. Certainly he could not have seen us. For our part we had about one chance in twenty of locating him. He might be anywhere around us and there was plenty of cover. But, oddly enough, we managed to get the beggar, after all. One of our fellows chanced to catch a slight flash far off to the east of the road just as a bullet sang past his ear. The word was passed along the line and we began a cautious advance on the spot from all directions. As we drew closer the outline of a small shed became discernible in the darkness. Sure that we had our man cornered, we rushed the shed from three sides.

He had hardly a chance to emit a squeak before we had him out, rifle and all. He was caught red-handed, a venomous little spy who spat shrill curses at us as we lined him up against the side of the shed. This incident, which occurred early in September 1915, illustrates the gravity of the danger from snipers. The sniper has become just as necessary a part of the army organization as the sapper or the stretcher-bearer.

The sniper has many duties, but the first and all-important one is to prevent the enemy from making observations. In queer, unusual places, behind or in front of the line, the sniper lies patiently in wait, rifle leveled and ready. If anything shows above the line of the enemy trench he puts a bullet through it. If a periscope is shoved over the sandbags—whut! The sniper can hit almost anything within sighting distance.

It has become a post of honor and distinction. Only the best marksmen are used for this service. It requires, in addition, a very cool nerve and unusual powers of endurance.

There is little to choose between the two armies in regard to the thoroughness of their sniping arrangements but, individually, man for man, we have it over the Germans. Fritz is a good fighting man with his officers to direct him and army regulations to tell him what to do next. But get him alone out on No Man's Land with only his rifle for defence and his own wits to guide him and he is no match for the Canadian or the British Tommy.

Snipers are recruited from the best marksmen in a company. I had always been a good shot and succeeded during the course of training in hanging up some pretty fair records. I wasn't surprised, therefore, when Sgt. Major Walker called me over the first day we got up near the line.

"Siddle, you've been picked for the snipers," he said.

We had arrived the night before and were camped about three miles back of the front line. It was expected that we would go up any time and the roar of the guns had worked us up to a fine pitch of excitement. After so many months in training camps the prospect of active service was alluring. I imagine that every man in the battalion was itching for a sight of the trenches. Certainly I was delighted to hear that I had been picked as a sniper. It promised extra chances.

"That's all right," I said. "Who's to be with me?"

"Crookshanks," replied the S.M.

That bit of news made me completely satisfied with my appointment. Adam Crookshanks was from my own home town of Fordwich, Ont. He was a fine fellow, big and husky, and good natured and as straight as the day is long. We had enlisted together and had been the closest of chums all through training.

We worked together as a sniper team for over a year. When men lie side by side sometimes for sixteen hours at a stretch, when they get out on No Man's Land together day after day, they come to understand and know each other pretty well. I want to say that a better man than Adam Crookshanks never donned the khaki.

14

Closing the Eyes of the Hun

Snipers share a mess at battalion headquarters with the patrol men. The patrol have the most dangerous and least desirable part of all. Like the owls, they only come out at night and their work is to keep the enemy from bringing anything off under cover of darkness. They go out on No Man's Land and crawl up and down the line. When a star shell bursts they lie perfectly still; a move would bring a shower of bullets. Dead bodies in all stages of decomposition strew the path. It is generally raining so they crawl through water more than half the time. Work for real men, this.

Snipers work on their own. Each night they go back to battalion headquarters and get a hot meal. They need it. Before daybreak they sally out, always in pairs, to the post they have elected to occupy for the day. They carry rifles with special sights, steel plates, gas masks, steel helmets, fifty rounds of ammunition and a day's rations consisting of two biscuits and a tin of bully beef. They do not take their bayonets. The gas masks are very necessary, for gas hugs the ground and penetrates any shelter.

The post occupied is generally behind the front line trenches and elevated so that it commands a view of the enemy line. Sometimes refuge is found in a ruined building or in a tree, but this is not often the case. Hardly one brick is left standing on another where the guns have been at work and such seared stumps of trees as might still stand would be too shining a mark for the enemy guns.

The first day that I sailed out it was raining with a depressing steadiness. I found a post behind a ridge, a little above the front line trenches. The German line was three hundred yards beyond and Fritz was in a canny mood that day. I watched eagerly and got one or two chances but don't believe that I hit anything. In the meantime, the rain continued to come down and as I was lying full length in a hollowed-out space, it was not long before I was literally immersed in it. The cold water crept up over my legs and finally reached to my armpits. My teeth chattered, my body became number, my elbows sank down into the mud until I could hardly move them. I could barely lift my rifle, let alone make a clean shot with it.

Crookshanks was lying about ten feet off and in quite as desperate a plight as I was. He was mud from head to foot and,

15

whenever the guns let up, I could hear his teeth rattle.

"Can't stand this!" I said, finally. "I'm going to get a dry place or I'll be frozen stiff."

So we moved along the ridge, looking for dry spots. There weren't any. It was just mud and water and mostly pretty well exposed to view. Finally we went back to our first posts and settled down into the water again. We had twelve hours of this.

The sniper had no special equipment. He built up such shelter as he could with old boxes, sandbags and such. Gradually, however, more scientific methods were evolved and some hints also were picked up from the Germans. Special steel plates were made and supplied to us. Each night we would take our plates out to the spot we had picked for next day's post and would proceed to bank them up with earth in front. This plate is about two feet wide and a foot and a half high and quarter of an inch thick with a round hole in the centre big enough for sitting and firing through. The earth in front is arranged so as to cover the plate but leave the "peep hole" open. A flap of canvas is attached to the top and sides of the plate. It is big enough to cover a man crouching behind the plate. Then the canvas is covered with earth.

Before daybreak we would return to this post and crawl under our canvases. If the "camouflaging" had been well done we could hardly be detected at a distance of a few yards.

Snipers were doing this all along the Western front. When daylight spread over the trenches, the men in both lines knew that somewhere facing them were a number of these cleverly contrived sniping posts and that keen eyes were sweeping the line of the parapets. A hand exposed, a hasty movement, would bring a bullet.

Crookshanks and I worked by turns. One of us would watch with a telescope while the other lay ready to take a pot shot at anything that offered. Then we would reverse the order. We kept this up all day and there would hardly be a moment that a telescope would not be trained on the enemy line. Sometimes we would not get more than half a dozen shots between us all day. Needless to state we never blazed away promiscuously. The danger of being seen was too great. And at that most of the shots we got would be at periscopes. Fritz has so wholesome a respect for the "Englander" sniper that he does most of his observing through these handy devices.

Sometimes we would while away the hours at our posts by reading, but this wasn't always possible. We had to keep too sharp a watch. We knew, of course, that the other fellows were trying to find us out and that any moment a trench mortar might poke its muzzle up over the way and send a "Rum jar" in our direction. They are wicked instruments, those trench mortars, and a shot placed anywhere close to our post would have spelled a speedy and complete finish for us.

Once located we were tied to our post for as long as the daylight lasted. In the first place, it was a matter of duty and, in the second, it would be courting death to move. In order to get a clear view of the enemy trenches he must necessarily be exposed himself. To leave the post would mean a retreat in full view. Only when we became certain that Fritz had spotted us would we take a chance on moving.

Sometimes we took up our station on No Man's Land. This, of course, was possible only when the trenches were quite a distance apart. We would go out during the night, pick our spot and plant our equipment. Before daybreak we would navigate a tunnel leading out through the sandbags and crawl to our post.

Our first six months of service were spent in the Ypres region and we went through the Battle of St. Eloi. Nothing that occurred afterward, not even the Somme, could compare for sheer horror with St. Eloi. We hadn't the artillery then that we have now and the pounding the Germans gave us was terrific. We faced it in shallow trenches and just hung on, flesh and blood against gun-powder and steel. Crookshanks and I saw it through and we got back something of what our fellows were getting up in the front line. I accounted for fifteen Germans in three weeks. Most of them were picked off during the charges and countercharges that marked the struggle for this bloody corner of the salient.

Shortly afterwards we were moved along the line and figured in another period of delirious struggle. The Germans launched a sudden attack, in overwhelming numbers, on the section of the line we held. We were in rest billets after a hard spell in the trenches when the word came that the Boche had broken our line. It was two o'clock in the morning and ordinarily we would have cursed our luck at being thus cheated of our turn to rest. But I guess we realized that the situation was pretty black. We got into our equipment in ominous silence and fell into line in record time.

Then began a battle that lasted continuously for 36 days and we fought it through without rest or moment of respite. For 36 days not a man in our battalion got a chance to take off his clothes. We snatched odd moments of sleep during brief lulls in the fighting and ate whenever food could be brought up to us. The Germans never left us alone for a full hour. It was just one attack after another, and through it all the guns rained shells on us.

Nevertheless we managed to hold them and finally beat them back to the positions they held when the offensive started. Then reliefs came and we went back to rest billets again, such as were left of us. Most of our fellows were worn to the bone—lousy scarecrows, covered with the filth of weeks, their uniforms in tatters and caked with blood.

Then we were moved down to the Somme. The business of sniping took on many new phases there. No longer did we stop at one post for a whole day, watching an immovable enemy line. We became flying wings on a line that moved ever forward, getting its "yards" every time. The great offensive was in full swing when we arrived and the first big attack in which we figured saw the initial appearance of the "tanks."

Of course, this new form of attack meant a lot to the snipers. It was pretty generally expected that Fritz would have an attack of the nerves when he saw an armored train coming against him and we snipers were to be ready to deal with any bolt from the trenches that might develop. We were out and safely ensconced on No Man's Land long before daylight.

It was just at daybreak that the first tank crossed our trenches. It went over with a grunting and a rattle of machinery that could be heard for half a mile around. The opposite trenches came to life with a start and a roar of musketry spread along the front.

Pea-shooters would have been just as effective. The monster

went through the barbed wire entanglements like so much paper and then creaked and rattled on its way over No Man's Land, flame spurting from every corner. I guess the Germans thought that some engine from hell had been conjured up against them. In the grey of early dawn it was a fearsome looking thing; and it was just as deadly as it looked. It straddled the German trench and machine gun fire was directed up and down it, a flail of death from which no one could escape. But many of the Germans had not waited for this. They had bolted. They dropped their rifles and scrambled out of the trenches, bleating like sheep. They ran toward us with their arms up, and yelling "Kamerade." We took over 2,000 prisoners that morning and advanced 1,200 yards.

From that time on it was a steady advance. We snipers were kept busy as never before and our casualties were heavy. Each advance carried us far beyond the trenches and the only shelter we could find was in shell craters and "funk holes" and we never had much time to dig in. It rained steadily and the shell holes were nothing but lakes of water. Many a time we lay all day in mud and water with only our heads and shoulders clear.

Both Adam and I had many close shaves, but the narrowest squeak of all came one day when, by some evil chance, we discerned the stump of a willow tree that had withstood the bombardment. It was about seven feet high and hollowed out at the top. It was in the evening that we discovered this ideal nest and we agreed at once that next day we would make the tree our habitation. So we placed a couple of sandbags on the top, criss-crossing them to make a peephole, and next morning were back there bright and early. I took the first watch and clambered up into the stump. Crookshanks sat on the ground behind it.

Careless of the fact that the stump made a grand mark for the gunners, I looked around and saw a group about five hundred yards behind the German lines. I took a pot at them and they scurried promptly to cover.

"Broke up one party," I chuckled for the benefit of my partner who, of course, had to sit tight and couldn't see anything.

And almost immediately it seemed there was a roar and a cloud of flying sod not twenty-five yards in front of us. The smoke had hardly cleared away when another came over and landed about the same distance the other side. There was no mistaking what this portended. The Boches had our range. I scrambled out of the tree and the two of us broke for cover. We had barely gone twenty yards when a third shell landed squarely on that stump and blew it into millions of pieces.

The next day was misty so I went back and dug up that shell. I brought back the pieces as a souvenir.

In the fighting at the Somme, the snipers would go "over the top" with the rest whenever a charge was ordered, but would then skirt out to the flanks of the fighting area, taking post there to prevent any attempt at "flanking" on the part of the Germans. It was seldom that we held the same ground for more than a few days and this meant that we were occupying shallow trenches without proper communications and that the danger from counter-attacks was very great. So the snipers had a harder time of it than ever.

Neither Crookshanks nor I had been wounded up to this time. But the new style of fighting at the Somme brought us in for one long day of special adventure at the end of which poor Crookshanks lay under six feet of sod. It was early in October and the word was passed along one night that we were to "go over" again at daybreak. The Germans had been shoved back repeatedly at this point, but the general staff needed another push at this part of the line. The men tightened their belts and prepared for the worst. No man ever "went over" at the Somme expecting to come back.

It drizzled a little during the night, but just before daybreak it cleared off and a cold wind blew in from the north. The men shivered as they stood along the firing ledge, waiting for the word. Adam and I were at one end. He was in splendid spirits that morning.

"Going to be a fine day," he said. "I've an idea this team is going to distinguish itself. I'm keen to get started."

Strangely enough I felt depressed and gloomy myself. I had a vague sort of premonition of something impending. But my mood did not communicate itself to my pal, who jigged first on one foot then on the other to keep warm and whistled under his breath.

Then we went over. Crookshanks and I skirted off to the right according to orders. The Germans had been expecting the attack—they were always expecting it at the Somme, for we didn't give the beggars a moment's rest—and the rattle of machine gun fire drowned out the desultory yell of our fellows as they charged across. We got about half way across and took possession of a shell hole. We had not, so far as we could tell, been observed; although a bullet zipped over us once in a while. I dug my toes into the mud and managed to hoist myself into a position where I could command a view of the German trench. I did not dare fire, however, for fear of hitting our own men. Suddenly I felt Adam clutch my sleeve. "Look!" he said. "To the right! What did I tell you?"

Our chance had come right enough. A German machine gun squad had slipped out and taken possession of a shell hole about forty yards to our right. Here they were in a position to sweep the area between the trenches and wipe out our men as they charged across. The snout of the gun had just been swung into position and a Boche with a great bald head was bending over it. A moment later and death would have been let loose in the Canadian ranks. I blazed away almost blindly and the bald-headed gunner crumpled up out of sight. Adam's rifle spoke at about the same moment and another of the squad went down.

The lay-out was very favorable to us. A clump of grass hid us from the Germans and in the hideous din they could not detect us from the sound. They knew, of course, that snipers somewhere had spotted them and that it meant death to show themselves. But they were game. A big fellow with a reddish beard sprang to take the bald-headed one's place. It made a clear target, that reddish beard, so down he went. They kept coming and we picked them off as they came. It was terrible work but, if we had not been there, that machine gun would have spat messengers of death into the Canadian ranks at the rate of sixty a minute.

"Four," said Adam, as he accounted for another German who had stepped into the breach.

"Five," I replied, taking the next in line.

"Six" and "seven" followed soon after. We were panting with excitement and blazing away as fast as the grey-green uniforms showed, determined that not a shot should be fired from that machine gun. And not one revolution did it make. There were nine Germans in the squad and we got them all.

And then something happened that caused Adam and I to suddenly duck down under cover. A bullet ripped along within a few inches of my head, grooving the soil and splattering me with mud. It had come apparently from off to the right.

"Sniper," I said; and Adam nodded.

Any doubts that we might have had were dispelled by a regular procession of shots. The German systematically pumped lead over our heads. We found ourselves as good as prisoners in that slimy hole and unable to see anything that was happening.

Judging from the sounds the attack was going well. We squirmed around and cursed the sniper and all his generation. Here we were tied up and out of it all.

"We've got to be in at the finish," said Adam. "Can't stay here all day, just because of one measly German sniper!"

A moment later he started to brace himself to climb up the slippery side again. "Got to see what's going on," he called to me.

It was over almost before I had time to shout a warning. My chum raised his head above the level for just one moment and then rolled back into the hole. His body lay limp and twisted, his face in a pool of water. He never spoke.

Death was probably instantaneous. The German had shot him in the neck.

I was too stunned to even think for a time. Adam and I had bunked and fought together for over a year. We had lain together under snow for hours at a time when I could see nothing of him but his face; and even under those circumstances it had always been lighted up with a cheerful grin. We had been trapped by shell fire in spots where even a clump of grass looked good; we had charged together and starved together. And through everything he had been staunch and cheerful and game to the core.

I buried him where he lay in the shell hole. The German batteries had taken the range of their own trenches which I knew we must now be holding. Shells were coming down like hail and it would have been impossible to carry him back to what had formerly been our own lines. Besides, I had work to do farther on.

Closing the Eyes of the Hun

A captured German sniper's post, 1917.

In the meantime our sniper had disappeared. Finding himself too far inside the new British lines he had probably beaten a retreat; or perhaps one of the German shells had done him in. That is a danger the sniper always faces; he is in advance of his own guns.

So I moved on up, still keeping on the flank. Then the second big chance of the day presented itself. The Germans had been surrendering in batches all along the line, coming out from dugouts with their hands in the air. As I passed the first German line six of them came out, five men and an officer. The latter fumbled at his belt and drew a revolver when he saw me. I covered him and sharply commanded "Hands up!" Up went five pairs of hands to the accompaniment of a shrill chorus of "Kamerade!" But the officer swung his arm around and, in self-defence, I had to shoot. He went down at the first shot and the men, frightened to death, ran forward, jabbering their anxiety to give in.

I went through them all, made sure that they were not carrying arms and then ordered them to keep on going back. They followed my instructions, holding their hands above their heads and shouting "Kamerade!" at intervals. Someone farther back probably took them in hand and got the credit for capturing them.

I got "mine" a few days later. We snipers were often used for the conveying of messages during an action. It was on October 6, I think, that the Colonel sent me up to the front line with some instructions. We were occupying a shallow line in newly won territory. Back of the trench was an open space without a communicating trench of any kind. To hold up reinforcements, the German batteries were shelling all the territory back to headquarters. It was across this open space that I had had to advance. My message delivered, I started back the same way. The bombardment had increased in fury. Shells burst all around me and the air was filled with an indescribable roar. I ran like mad, making no effort to pick my way. Finally the bombardment became so terrific that I took shelter in a shallow funk hole. It seemed sure death to stay there. But if possible it was more dangerous to go on. So I elected to rest.

I had been there scarcely a moment when it seemed as though suddenly the whole earth had been turned upside down. A great weight fell upon me, wrenching and grinding me with unbelievable violence. The pain was terrible. I realized almost at once what had happened. A shell had struck just the other side of the hole and had buried me. What puzzled me at first was that total darkness had not descended. But, when the blinding, sulphurous dust had lifted, I found that part of my head was clear of the earth. I could still see and breath.

I was in a truly terrible position. Any moment another shell might land and complete the job of the first or perhaps bowl me over to a new position, which would have meant tearing me to pieces, encased as I was in the heavy earth. I could not move hand or foot. But I could see. That was perhaps the worst part of it all. I could see the shells bursting around me and could not even duck my head. I was wedged in too firmly.

Then a miracle happened. Two of the sniping squad, Blake and Darlington, were also on their way back and happened to see me. It looked like sure death for them to pause a moment. But they came over to me, of course.

"Suppose the rest of him's there?" Blake asked.

"We'll dig him out anyway," returned Darlington.

And they did. For ten minutes they stood out in full sight of the enemy and proceeded to dig me out. Then they carried me—for I was wracked and badly twisted—back to the dressing station. It was a miracle that none of us were hit. But we all three came through safely.

If ever men deserved reward it was Blake and Darlington. It did not look as though they could possibly save me and it was almost equally sure death for them to remain. They should have gone on and left me there until such time as the inevitable shell arrived. But they stayed. Unfortunately no one was there to see it. It was just one of the thousands of heroic deeds that go unrewarded, even unknown. Both Blake and Darlington I hear are now in hospital in "Blighty."

It may be remarked here that the sniper seldom comes in for official recognition. This, of course, is to be expected. He works by himself and there is no one around to see what he does. Even the manner of his death is seldom learned for he "goes out" somewhere beyond the lines. Seldom, indeed, is his body found. He is recorded "missing" and another man sallies forth with plate and rifle to take up the lonely work.

THE CANADIANS IN MESOPOTAMIA

—March 1918—
William Byron

Although no Canadian battalions have taken part in the Mesopotamian Campaign, the Dominion has earned its share of the credit for the successful outcome of the drive on Baghdad. Many Canadians figured in the campaign. There were about sixty in the medical corps, perhaps an equal number in the various branches of the engineering service—and the capture of Baghdad was an engineering feat in the final analysis—and quite a number of Canadian girls serving as nurses.

The story of the second Mesopotamian Campaign is the story of rout turned into brilliant victory, of chaos turned into perfect order and efficiency. The first campaign, bungled hopelessly by the Indian Office, had ended in the capture of General Townsend's forces at Kut-el-Amara. The Mesopotamian report issued last year has revealed all the mistakes of that frightful fiasco. Then the Imperial Government took charge and a rapid change came over the scene. Perhaps in no theatre of the war has better management and generalship been shown than in the second campaign on the Tigris. It has been the good fortune of the body of Canadian offi- cers already mentioned to assist in this transformation.

The Indian Office relinquished control of Mesopotamian affairs in July 1916, and the following month the first party of Canadians arrived consisting of twenty-one medical officers. They went first to Bombay and then trans-shipped to Basra, the sun- blistered port at the mouth of the Tigris River which has served as the base of the Mesopotamian Campaign. It was 120 in the shade the day they landed, a paralyzing heat that rendered the newcomers absolutely helpless. It struck through the pith helmets they wore with a numbing effect; it reflected up from the baked clay streets and the mud walls of Basra and filled the vision with delirious fantasies of color. None of the party will ever be able to forget that first day in Mesopotamia.

They were billeted in native palaces which had been turned into hospitals. Evening came on with a welcome degree of coolness and some of the new arrivals took advantage of it to have a look around.

They found Basra in a condition of peculiar turmoil. Ordinarily a very sleepy, dirty and odorous city of moderate size, it was rapidly growing to metropolitan proportions. At that time the population had swelled to well over 100,000 and today it probably runs as high as 150,000. Cities of the Orient are not adapted to rapid growth. The sanitary facilities are not adequate at any time; the streets are narrow, rough and crooked; the water and food supply is restricted; hotel accommodation is almost nil. Basra in the throes of growth was not good to look upon. The Canadian officers found tangible evidence of both the old order and the new. The old order was represented by long rows of straw thatched huts, where the wounded and sick were kept. They found these huts crowded with very miserable soldiers suffering from wounds, and dysentery and heat stroke.

"It is inconceivable what these places must be like in the middle of the day!" said a Canadian, as he emerged from one hut where the air had hung about the cots in foetid, stifling heaviness.

The new order was seen in the engineering work which was under way on every hand. Splendid new piers were being erected. A railway line was being started and already the steel was stretching out from Basra which would carry up the troops needed to push the Turk from his intrenched lines before Kut. New hospitals were in course of erection—well ventilated structures with every convenience and as much protection as could be obtained by mechanical means from the blistering sun of Mesopotamia.

The party met a young Canadian engineer who had been engaged on the pier work for a month or more. He was as brown as a berry and seemed pretty well acclimatized already. He was cheerful and even enthusiastic.

"You fellows are just in time to see a miracle," he exclaimed, pointing to the harbor. "That's the first evidence of it over there. They'll be able to bring their transport ships up soon and unload troops by the hundreds of thousands. Then we'll have the railroad built and plenty of ships to ply up and down the river—and some day soon something will land on Johnny Turk like a ton of bricks!"

In a very short time the miracle that the young engineer had predicted began to unfold. Transport ships steamed up to the new wharves and disgorged troops and tremendous piles of supplies. The railroad, ingeniously laid with three rails to accommodate rolling stock from both Britain and India, crept further and further up the banks of the Tigris. Flat-bottomed boats for transport upstream kept arriving until there were 150 in all at work. There was a machine-like regularity about it all that suggested a wonderfully well worked out plan.

The men slept under nets which kept the mosquitoes at bay, but the sand flies, which were small and venomous, easily found their way through all varieties of nets. In the morning a man awoke—if he had slept at all—with his body red and swollen from the activities of these nocturnal visitors. It became so bad finally that the engineers put oil in all the low-lying lands around the army lines. After that there was less discomfort, but at no stage could unbroken rest be enjoyed.

The work of preparation for the new drive went forward without any hostility on the part of the inhabitants of the country who were for the most part Arabs. At the same time the natives did not show any great cordiality. The Arab is a calculating person with a wholesome fear of his master, the Turk. The result of the first campaign had left seeds of doubt in the Arab mind. He expected that some day the British would leave Basra and the Turk would come back; and it would not do on that black day for the powers of the Porte to be able to say that the inhabitants had helped the invaders. So there was no enthusiasm and no cooperation. Later, when the Turkish troops were driven back from Kut, the attitude of the inhabitants began to change. When Baghdad fell, Basra came off the fence and from that time on has been actively and openly pro-British.

The Arab from the desert, the Bedouin, was a different problem again. A waif, a friend of no man and a thief of marvellous cunning, the Bedouin had to be carefully watched. Wherever the British tents were erected came these prowlers of the desert and, no matter how close the vigilance displayed, goods immediately began to disappear.

One night a party of three Canadian medical officers went to sleep in a tent. They wakened up to find the sun peeping over the eastern horizon and striking directly on them.

"What the—!" exclaimed the first one to roll over. "What's happened to our tent?"

Half of it was gone. One whole side had magically disappeared. The reason was guessed at when it was found that a sharp knife had ripped the canvas away. A Bedouin—may his tribe not increase— had been in need of canvas for some purpose or other, perhaps for a new robe, and had taken as much as he required from the tent as they slept.

A few nights later a still more daring feat was carried out. Some Arabs stole through the sentry lines and carried off several sets of mule harness. The officer in charge, again a Canadian, was at first very much wrought up. Finally, however, he began to see a comic side to it and he walked over to the medical headquarters to share the joke with his fellow countrymen there.

"This is a good one on friend Arab," he said. "They had donkeys only and they'll never be able to use the mule harness. It's too big. So they've had their trouble for nothing."

The next night the Arabs came back and stole the mules that went with the harness!

The Canadians mixed very freely with the natives, sometimes rather to the wonderment of their British comrades. Several of them used cameras extensively and the zest for pictures took them into all sorts of queer corners. One young medical officer had the unique distinction of photographing an Arabian woman of high rank. The wives of the better class Arabians never appear in public with more than their eyes showing. There is something peculiarly fascinating about these dusky-orbed daughters of the desert peeping out from shadowy lattices or gliding by with their graceful drapes and their faces hidden by veils which leave only the eyes free. One day this officer met a very important man, indeed, a date producer who had a large establishment in Basra. The Arab had one of his wives along and did not demur when the Canadian suggested he would photograph them.

"Tell the lady to remove the veil," said the latter. The Arab caught his meaning and told his wife to reveal her charms. She did. "After all," said the Canadian, "it would have been a much better picture the other way."

He went back to his quarters thoroughly disillusioned. Arabian women look better with their veils on.

The "front" when the campaign opened was on the east bank of the Tigris before Kut-el-Amara, and was similar in many respects to the front in France. It was, of course, trench warfare. The trenches were shallow owing to the sandy nature of the soil and there was no evidence of the complicated systems of communication trenches found on the Western front. There was comparatively little artillery fire and the number of airplanes was limited on both sides so that the approach to the front line was not fraught with the same hazards. On the other hand, however, such fighting as occurred was even more sanguinary. An attack was not preceded by heavy artillery fire calculated to wipe out the opposing line and had to be brought off across open ground swept by machine gun fire. There was much heavy hand-to-hand fighting and the British troops found the Turks hard antagonists at close range. They could not stand up to British attacks when it was a case of man to man, but they fought well and like gentlemen. They used their prisoners well, and consequently the British did not fear capture as they do on the Western front.

The campaign opened actively in the cool season; in other words, the season of rain and mud. Soldiers who had seen every variety of mud and had come through campaigns in Flanders swore with all the fluency of old campaigners that they had never seen the equal of Mesopotamian mud. It was heavy and clammy and everywhere. It stuck to the feet of the marching troops and made every step a muscular effort. After marching fifty yards through a muddy stretch, a man's legs began to ache and sweat beads of sheer agony stood out all over him. A mile was enough to kill the sturdiest. Sometimes attacks had to be made across a No Man's Land of such mud!

It was soon found that Turkish lines on the east bank were too strong to be carried. Under the direction of German officers the Turks had dug themselves in so strongly that to carry the lines by assault would have been too expensive an operation. So a large force was thrown across the river to the western flank. In the meantime a heavy artillery fire was kept up on the eastern side and the Turks did not detect the flanking movement until it was too late. Their troops on the west bank gave way before the attacking force, and the British pushed up the west bank of the Tigris without difficulty.

The flanking movement was a complete success, but crossing the river was found to be a serious problem. Realizing that they were trapped if the British crossed, the Turks fought desperately against all attempts. Finally the flanking movement carried the British above Kut on the west bank. A surprise attack by cavalry and the use of pontoon bridges finally effected a landing on the east side. It was a sanguinary struggle, however, and the British losses were heavy before the defending forces were driven back.

A Canadian medical officer, Lieut. Renton, of London, Ont., distinguished himself in the crossing of the Tigris. He was in charge of the Red Cross work and was under fire during the whole engagement. So heavy was the fire that all his stretcher-bearers were killed, and he himself was in continual danger. The work was so well carried out, however, that Lieut. Renton was again placed in charge when a similar crossing was successfully made above Baghdad.

The medical service, the weakest point in the first campaign, was well nigh perfect in the second. Contagious diseases were kept down and the wounded and sick got prompt and splendid attention. Ninety percent of the cases were medical—cholera, dysentery, malaria and heat stroke. The weather was a more deadly enemy than Johnny Turk at all stages of the campaign.

A Canadian officer was placed in charge of a hospital ship

31

which had been one of the original ten in the first campaign. The captain had served right through and was still seething with memories of the mistakes made by the Indian command. The Mesopotamian report was out by this time and some word as to the nature of it had leaked through the censor.

"It doesn't cover the case," grunted the captain, one evening as he paced the deck with the doctor. "I remember once during the hardest fighting they loaded this boat with wounded troops. Some of them hadn't even received first aid. They were in bad shape. So many had to be put on the boat that they were lying everywhere— out on the deck in the hot sun without covering and between decks where the heat was stifling. There wasn't a medical man sent along—none could be spared. It took us a week to get down stream to the hospital base and many of the men died on the way. All we could do was to drop them overboard with a bit of prayer."

The campaign moved rapidly after the capture of the Turks at Kut. This smashing blow had broken the back of the Ottoman force and little difficulty was experienced in shoving them back on Baghdad.

The entry into Baghdad was a tremendous and picturesque event. Baghdad to-day is, of course, a far different city from the Baghdad of the Arabian nights. It is modern in the Oriental sense—a sprawly city of noisy bazaars and crumbling minarets and unnecessary walls. Fully 50,000 of the inhabitants are Jews and Armenians who have suffered long under Turkish rule. The reception they gave the British troops was one of heart-felt enthusiasm. The rest of the population, Arabs, mostly, showed a degree of restraint at the time, but later—when they became convinced that the British were there to stay—they gathered enthusiasm rapidly.

The Canadians who have returned from that front declare that Mesopotamia is well worth keeping. They believe it can be made into a fertile, productive country. The great necessity is a broad sys- tem of irrigation.

At present Mesopotamia is a date growing country. Practically all its wealth emanates from the shipping of dates, and before the war Basra was monopolized by the date interests.

The climate, however, makes three crops a year a certainty in all cereals and vegetables. The Canadian officers, finding the army fare monotonous and at times insufficient, started to raise vegetables in little plots of ground back of the hospitals. The results were marvellous. Vegetables, all vegetables, shot up out of the earth and reached an early and fine maturity. It was necessary to keep them watered and the intense Mesopotamian sun did the rest. These Canadians assert that all grains, even wheat, could be grown there; provided, of course, that proper irrigation plans are carried out.

It will be recalled that the Garden of Eden was supposed to have been located somewhere near the junction of the Tigris and the Euphrates. Under Turkish misrule and the indolence of its inhabitants, Mesopotamia has become a country of parched land and desert stretches. A decade of progressive rule, British rule, will suffice to establish again a tropical Eden all the way from Baghdad to the sea.

SIXTEEN MONTHS IN GERMANY

—*March 1918*—
Private John Evans

I was in Germany as a prisoner of war from June 1916 to September 1917, and during the greater part of that time I worked in the coal mines of Westphalia. I rubbed shoulders with the German civilians who worked the mines and in time acquired sufficient intimacy with them and with their language to learn what they thought, what they liked and disliked, what they hoped and feared. The impression I brought away with me was that of a people repressed and mutinous, half-starved, overworked, longing for peace and hoping to see a universal strike that would sweep governments and kings into the discard; a people who muttered in groups but responded almost docilely to the voice of authority, who had given up hope of German victory, but still had enough national spirit left to enthuse over stories of German success. My experience was entirely with the mining class and I cannot say whether the feeling prevailing there was general throughout the German Empire. I feel sure, however, that among the poorer classes, at least, the conditions I found in Westphalia must be general.

The German laboring man is really interested today in one subject only—food! A peck of potatoes is more important to him than a victory on the Western front.

My story starts with the third battle of Ypres. The 4th Canadian Mounted Rifles were in the front line of Zillebeke and we had been pretty severely pounded. The morning of June 2 dawned clear and beautiful after a night of hideous anxiety and alarms; and about 5:30 I turned in for a little sleep with four other fellows who made up the machine gun crew with me. Lance-Corporal Wedgewood, who was in charge of the gun, elected to remain up and clean it. I had just nicely fallen off to sleep when it seemed as though the whole crust of the earth was torn asunder. I wakened to find myself buried under loose earth and sandbags. By a miracle I was not hurt and I finally managed to burrow out. A shell, I found, had blown up our dugout. Two of the crew were killed, but the fourth man had shared my luck. He was without a scratch.

"We're in for it," said Wedgewood. "They'll keep this up for a while and then they'll come over. We must get the gun out."

The gun had been buried by the explosion, but we managed to get it out and were cleaning it up again when another trench mortar shell came over. It destroyed all our ammunition but 300 rounds. Then the bombardment started in earnest. Shells rained on us like hail stones. The German artillery started a barrage behind us that looked like a wall of flame; so we knew that there was no hope whatever of help reaching us.

Our men dropped off one by one. The walls of our trench were battered to greasy sand heaps. The dead lay everywhere. Pretty soon only Wedgewood and myself were left.

"They've cleaned us out now. The whole battalion's gone," said Wedgewood. As far as we could see along the line there was nothing left, not even trenches—just churned up earth and mutilated bodies. The gallant Fourth had stood its ground in the face of probably the worst hell that had yet visited the Canadian lines and had been wiped out!

So we decided to get over to the next machine gun where there might be more ammunition. Taking what was left of our own, we started off down the line, scrambling over dead bodies and dashing through machine gun fire at places where no protection was left. We finally reached the next gun. Not a man was left alive there and the ammunition had been blown up.

We decided to keep on to the next gun, but after going fifty yards or so we reached the end of things. Beyond that point the trenches had been absolutely leveled out and there were few signs even of the unfortunate fellows who had held that section. They had been buried away from sight. Wedgewood and I were alone— and the time for the German charge was getting near.

It wasn't long before a trench mortar shell buried us to our waists. We managed to pull ourselves out and crept back a little farther. Here we were joined by two other survivors. We had no idea where they had come from and they were too far gone to bother about explanations. One of them said he had been buried four times. He was dirt and blood from head to foot and so weak that he could only lie in the loose earth and gasp. The other man suggested that we go back and take our chances with the barrage. Wedgewood looked at me and said something, but in the tumult of sound I could not catch what it was. I judged he was asking me what I thought and shook my head. He smiled back at me. We decided to stick it out.

We got back to the second gun and found that about eight yards of trench was left. We climbed in and waited. The bombardment was so heavy at this time that nearly all of our fellows who survived or were captured were deaf for months. This I heard afterwards from prisoners. At the same time I learned that roll call after the battle showed only 59 men left in the battalion.

It was not long before one of our party was finished by a piece of shrapnel, the poor fellow who had been buried four times. It was just as well. I was wounded in the back with a splinter from a shell which broke overhead and then another got me in the knee. I bled freely, but luckily neither wound was serious. About 1:30 we saw a star shell go up over the German lines.

"Coming!" cried Wedgewood and jumped to the gun.

The Germans were about seventy-five yards off when we got the gun trained on them. We gave them our 300 rounds and did considerable damage, but the oncoming line was barely checked. It wavered a little and the front line crumpled up, but the rest came on.

What followed does not remain very clearly in my mind. We started back, the three of us. Every move was agony for me. We did not go far, however. Some of the Germans had got around us and we ran right into four of them. We doubled back and found ourselves completely surrounded. A ring of steel and fierce, pitiless eyes! I expected they would butcher us, there and then. The worst we got, however, was a series of kicks as we were marched through the lines in the German communication trenches. I tripped up one

German who had aimed a kick at me and would probably have been clubbed to death had not an officer come along and ordered my assailant off.

We were given quick treatment at a dressing station and escorted with other prisoners back to Menin by Uhlands. The wounded were made to get along as best they could. We passed through several small towns where the Belgian people tried to give us food. The Uhlands rode along and thrust them back with their lances in the most cold-blooded way. We reached Menin about 10 o'clock that night and were given black bread and coffee—or something that passed by that name. The night was spent in a horse stable with guards all around us with fixed bayonets. The next day we were lined up before a group of German officers at what I imagined must be military headquarters. They asked us questions about the numbers and disposition of the British forces, and we lied extravagantly in our answers. They knew we were lying and gave us up finally. Leaving headquarters that night in cattle trucks we sang "Tipperary" as loud as our weakened condition would permit.

During the next day and a half we had one meal, a bowl of soup. It was weak and nauseating. We took it gratefully, however, for we were nearly starved by this time.

Finally we arrived at Dulmen camp, where I was kept two months and where the treatment was not unduly rigorous. The food was bad, of course, and very, very scanty. For breakfast we had black bread and coffee, for dinner soup (I can shudder at the thought of turnip soup still) and sometimes a bit of dog meat, for supper a gritty, tasteless porridge which we called "sand storm." We used to sit around with our bowls of this concoction and extract a grim comfort from the hope that some day Kaiser Bill would be in captivity, and we might be able to send him a meal of "sand storm."

While I was at Dulmen we had quite a few visitors and one day who should come in but Mr. Gerard, the American Ambassador. He looked us over with very apparent concern and asked us a number of questions. "Is there anything I can do for you?" he asked, as he was leaving.

"See if you can get them to give us more food," spoke up one of us.

"I shall speak to the camp commander about it," said Mr. Gerard.

I do not doubt that he did—but there was no change in the menu, and no increase in the quantities served. Visitors were never permitted to visit us at the place we were finally shipped to—that torture place known as Kommando 47 and referred to among prisoners as the "Black Hole of Germany." I want to make it clear that prisoners as a rule are not treated as badly as we were at Kommando 47.

However, after two months of it at Dulmen we got word that we were to be sent to work on a farm. It sounded good. We conjured up visions of open fields and fresh air and clean straw to sleep in and perhaps even real food to eat. They loaded fifty of us into one car and sent us off and when we reached our farm we found it was a coal mine!

As we tumbled off the train, stiff and weary and disappointed, we were curiously regarded by a small group of people who quite patently worked in the mines. They were a heavy-looking lot— oldish men with beards and dull, stolid women. They regarded us with sullen hostility, but there was no fire in their antagonism. Some of the men spat and muttered "Schweinhunds!" That was all.

We were marched off to the "Black Hole." It was a large camp with large frame buildings which had been erected especially for the purpose. There was one building for the French prisoners, one for the Russians and one for the British and Canadian contingent. Barbed wire entanglements surrounded the camp and there were sentries with drawn bayonets everywhere.

We were greeted with considerable interest by the other prisoners. There were about two hundred of our own there and all of them seemed in bad shape. They had been subjected to the heaviest kind of work on the slenderest rations and were pretty well worn out.

"Hope you like coal mining as a steady thing!" said one of them to me. "I've had six months of it."

"I'll refuse to work," I told him.

"No, you won't," he said. "I tried that. It doesn't get you anywhere. Better knuckle under at the start. They'll simply starve you."

I talked it over with the rest who had come up with me and we decided that this advice was sound. So, when we were lined up next day and told what was ahead of us, we made no protest. Some of us were selected for the mine and some were taken off for coke making which, as we soon learned, was sheer unadulterated hell. I was selected for the coal mine and put in three days at it—three days of smarting eyes and burning lungs, of aching and weary muscles. Then my chum Billy Flanagan was buried under an avalanche of falling coal and killed. There were no proper safeguards in the mine and the same accident might occur again at any time. So we struck.

The officers took it coolly and as a matter of course. We were lined up and ordered to stand to attention. No food was served and not even a glass of water was allowed us. We stood there for thirty-six hours. Man after man fainted from sheer exhaustion. When one of us dropped he was dragged out of the ranks to a corner where a bucket of water was thrown over him and, as soon as consciousness returned, he was yanked to his feet and forced to return to the line. All this time sentries marched up and down and if one of us moved we got a jab with the butt end of a gun. Every half hour an officer would come along and bark out at us:

"Are you for work ready now?"

Finally, we gave in. It was not until some of our fellows were on the verge of insanity, however. We stuck it out to a man and then gave in in a body.

After that things settled down into a steady and dull routine. We were routed out at 4 o'clock in the morning. The sentries would come in and beat the butts of their rifles on the wooden floor and roar "Raus!" at the tops of their voices. If any sleep-sodden prisoners lingered a second, they were roughly hauled out and kicked into active obedience. Then a cup of black coffee was served and at 5 we were marched to the mines. There was a dressing room at the mine where we stripped off our prisoners' garb and donned working clothes. We stayed in the mines until 3:30 in the afternoon and the "staggers"—our pet name for the foremen—saw to it that we had a busy time of it. Then we changed back into our prison clothes and marched back to barracks where a bowl of

39

turnip soup was given us and a half-pound of bread. We were supposed to save some of the bread to eat with our coffee in the morning. Our hunger was so great, however, that there was rarely any of
the bread left in the morning. At 7 o'clock we received another
bowl of turnip soup and were then supposed to go to bed.

If it had not been for the parcels that we received from friends
at home and from the Red Cross we would certainly have starved.
We were able to eke out our prison fare by carefully husbanding the
food that came from the outside.

At first our intercourse with the German civilians in the mine
was very limited. For the first few weeks I did not understand a
word of German and I made no effort to get on friendly terms with
them. I controlled my temper under the most aggravating forms of
persecution as best I could. And in the meantime I studied them
closely.

The men working in the mines when I first arrived were mostly
middle-aged. Many were quite venerable in appearance and of little actual use. It seems an axiom in Germany, however, that all
must work. To do the people justice I don't know that I heard any
complaints on that score. They were willing enough to work and
work hard; what they complained about was the lack of food. It was
not only lack of food from which they suffered. Clothing was very
scarce. Leather was almost unobtainable. Many of the people in
the mine went barefoot and most of them came to work that way.
I had a pair of good army boots that had been practically new when
the Fourth went up to Ypres and which served me all through my
term of imprisonment. I have thought since it was strange that I
was not held up and forcibly dispossessed of them. I had plenty of
offers for them, running all the way up to 150 marks, but, knowing
that I possessed a treasure, I refused to sell.

The German miners were quite as much at the mercy of the
"staggers" as we were. Discipline was very rigid and they were
"strafed" for any infraction of rules; that is, they were subjected to
cuts in pay. Lateness, laziness or insubordination were punished by
the deduction of so many marks from their weekly earnings and all
on the say-so of the "staffer" in charge of the squad. The first few
days I was puzzled at one custom. At a certain hour each day an

official would come around and hand each civilian a slip. It was an important matter, apparently, for the men put great store in those slips. I asked one of my companions, a British Tommy, who had been in the mine for a year or more and had picked up quite a smattering of German, what it was all about.

"Bread ticket," he explained. "If they don't turn up for work they don't get their bread tickets and have to go hungry. "

It was quite effective. It made regularity a necessity as well as a virtue. The same rule applied to the women who worked around the head of the mine, pushing carts and loading the coal. I often used to stop for a moment or so on my way to or from the pit-head and watch these poor women at work. Some went barefoot, but most of them wore wooden shoes. They appeared to be pretty much of one class, uneducated, dull and just about as ruggedly built as their men. They seemed quite capable of handling the heavy work given them. There were exceptions, however. Here and there among the grey-clad groups I could pick out women of a slenderer mould, women who seemed to suggest different associations. I made some enquiries after and found that quite a few women from neighboring towns, particularly from Recklinghausen, came out to the mines to work. Some of them were women of refinement and good education who had been compelled to turn to any class of work to feed their children. Their husbands and sons were at the front; perhaps they had already been killed.

I have often wished that the opportunity had presented itself of talking to some of these women. Their viewpoint would have been interesting, I think. But, of course, this was quite impossible. For one thing, the women about the mine were always very bitter towards the prisoners. We could get on more or less intimate terms with most of the men, but the women spat at us impartially, and called us "Schwein!" I can imagine that the bitterness of a woman of good position who had been forced to seek work in the mines because of the death or absence at the front of her husband would be very deep-seated toward us, the hated English, and perhaps also toward the German authorities.

I know this, that the food restrictions caused bitterness among all the mine workers. In the early days, when I had not picked up enough German to understand what was going on around us, I could tell that my fellow-workers were in a continual state of unrest. There were angry discussions whenever a group of them got together. For several days this became very marked.

The very next day, as we marched up to work in the dull grey of the early morning, we found noisy crowds of men and women around the buildings at the mine. A ring of sentries had been placed all around.

"Strike's on! There's a bread strike all through the mining country." The news ran down the line of prisoners, starting I don't know where. But it was right enough. We were delighted, of course, because it meant that we would have a holiday. The authorities did not dare to let us go into the mines with the civilians out; they were afraid we might wreck it. So we were marched back to camp and allowed to stay there until the strike was over. We did not have a chance on that account to see what was going on. Apparently, however, there was plenty of excitement.

The strike ended finally and the people came back to work jubilant. They had won their point, it seemed. Just what it was they had been granted I am not sure, but it had to do with the question of more food. The authorities had given in for two reasons as far as we could judge. The first was the dire need of coal which made any interruption of work at the mines a calamity. The second was the fact that food riots were occurring in many parts and it was deemed wise to placate the people.

I found that the active leaders in the strike shortly afterwards disappeared from the mine. Those who could possibly be passed for military service were drafted into the army. This was intended as an intimation to the rest that they must "be good" in future. The fear of being drafted for the army hung over them all like a thunder cloud which might burst at any moment. They knew what it meant and they feared it above everything.

When I first arrived at the mine there were quite a few able-bodied men and boys around 16 and 17 years of age at work there. Gradually they were weeded out for the army. When I left none were there but the oldest men and those who could not possibly qualify for any branch of the service. The dragnet had been of the

42

finest variety. No fish had escaped.

In the latter stages of my experience at the mine I was able to talk more or less freely with my fellow-workers. I had picked up quite a bit of German with the help of some of the other prisoners who had been there longer and who in one or two cases had spoken German before. A few of the Germans had for their part picked up a little English. There was one old fellow who had a son in the United States and who knew about as much English as I knew German and the two of us were able as a result to talk freely. If I did not know the "Deutsch" for what I wanted to say he generally could understand it in English. He was a creaky, rheumatic old codger with very bad eyes, but a genial disposition in spite of his many infirmities. He was very prone to terrific indictments of the German government, but at bottom he was intensely patriotic to the Fatherland. He hated England with a degree of hatred that caused him to splutter and get purple in the face whenever it was necessary to mention "the tight little island." But he could find it in his heart to be decent to isolated specimens of Englishmen. I shall call him Fritz, though that was not his name.

I first got talking with Fritz one day when the papers had announced the repulse of a British attack on the Western front.

"It's always the same. They are always attacking," he was muttering. "Of course, it's true that we repulse them. They are but English and they can't break the German army. But how are we to win the war if it is always the English who attack?"

I made this much out of what he was saying. So I broke in with a question: "Do you still think Germany can win?"

"No!" he fairly spat at me. "We can't beat you now. But you can't beat us! This war will go on until your pig-headed Lloyd George gives in."

"Or," I suggested, gently, "until your pig-headed Junker Government gives in."

"They never will!" he said a little proudly, but sadly too. "Every man will be killed in the army—my two sons, all—and we will starve before it is all over!"

I soon found that this impression was pretty general. They had given up hope of being able to score the big victory that was in

43

every mind when the war started. What the outcome would be did not seem to be clear to them. All they knew was that the work meant misery for them and that, as far as they could see, this misery would continue on and on indefinitely. Stories of victory had lost their power to rouse the people, at any rate the people of the mines. They had lost confidence in the newspapers. This, of course, was never acknowledged to us, but it was plain to be seen that the stereotyped rubber-stamped kind of official news that got into the papers did not begin to satisfy the people. Also there was a growing impatience with reference to the Royal Family. Many's the time I heard bitter anathemas heaped upon the Hohenzollerns by lips that were limp and white from malnutrition. There was no love among the miners for the glitter and pomp of Potsdam. They were socialists out and out. They hated war, they hated warmakers, they hated the English—and they were beginning to hate the war element in their own land. There was much excitement among them when early in 1917 the news spread that unrestricted submarine warfare was to be resumed. Old Fritz came over to me with a newspaper in his hand and his eyes fairly popping with excitement.

"This will end it!" he declared. "We are going to starve you out, you English. Submarines—that's it!"

"You'll bring America in," I told him.

"No, no!" he said, quite confidently. "The Yankees won't come in. They are making too much money as it is. They won't fight. See, here it is in the paper. It is stated clearly here that the United States will not fight."

"Then you still believe what the newspapers say?"

Fritz did not answer. He was poring over the paper in the dull light of a lantern and chuckling to himself. But when the news came that the United States had actually declared war, they were a very quiet lot. They stood around and discussed the situation quietly and, I thought, furtively. There was no bombast about them that day. I took the first opportunity to pump old Fritz about the views of his companions.

"It is bad, bad," he said shaking his head dolefully.

"Then you are afraid of the Americans after all?" I said.

Fritz laughed, with a short, contemptuous note. "No, it is not that," he said. "England will be starved out before the Americans can come in and then it will all be over. But—just between us, you and me—most of us here were intending to go to America after the war. We have had enough of wars and sufferings like this. We wanted to go to a land where we would be free from all this. But— now the United States won't let us in after the war!"

Bitterness grew among them from that time on. At first the news of the sinking of ships created some degree of satisfaction, but the impression had been general that a few months would see the end of it all. As month after month passed and nothing developed they began to get restless and impatient. They could not under- stand it. Fritz confided to me several times that England must be on the verge of giving in and that the good news would come all of a sudden; but he did not seem very confident about it. Finally the idea prevailed that the submarines had failed as all the other much heralded coups had done in the past, and from that time on solid gloom was the order of things.

It was about this time that I began to hear talk of strikes. The idea of a universal strike was a favorite one. They talked of a strike all over the world, the workers to arise and throw off their govern- ments simultaneously and settle the war. When it was given out that an international conference was to be held at Stockholm there was great excitement and jubilation.

"It is coming the great day!" said Fritz. "When the people, the workers get together what must be the result. Peace—new things— no more capital and nobility to grind us down."

"Do you think anything can come of this conference?" I asked him.

"Something must," he said. "It is the last hope."

I shall never forget the day that the papers announced the refusal of the English labor delegates to go to Stockholm. One excited miner struck me across the face with the open newspaper in his hand and hurled a jumble of objurgation at me. "Always, always the same!" he almost screamed. "The English block every- thing. They will not join and what good can come now of the conference? They will not be content and the war must go on!"

45

The last experiences I had with civilians that are worth record-ing have to do with the food shortage which reached a crisis about the time my happy chance to escape occurred. Sometimes when the people took their bread tickets to the stores they found that supplies had been exhausted and that there was nothing to be obtained. Prices had gone sky high. Bacon, for instance, was 10 marks a pound—$2.50. A cake of soap cost $3\frac{1}{2}$ marks. Cleanliness ceased to be a virtue and became a luxury.

At this time our parcels from England were coming along fair-ly regularly and I believe we were no worse off for food than the Germans themselves. Owing to the long shift we were compelled to do in the mines we fell into the habit of "hoarding" our food parcels and carrying a small lunch to the mines each day. These lunches had to be carefully secreted or the Germans would steal them. They could not understand how it was that starving England could send food abroad to us. The sight of these lunches helped to undermine their faith in the truth of the official information they read in the newspapers.

The lot of the prisoners of war at the mines is a hard one. It is in fact almost unendurable. We were supposed to receive four and a half marks (90 cents) a week for our labor, but there was contin-ual "strafing" to reduce the amount. If we looked sideways at a "staffer" we were likely to receive a welt with a pick handle and a strafe of several marks. Sometimes we only received a mark or two for a week's work. Most of this we spent for soap. It was impossible to work in the mines and not become indescribably dirty and so soap became an absolute necessity.

I feel in duty bound to record one incident that redounds to the credit of at least one German and shows that there is still some conception of justice in that country, even where the detested "Tommies" are concerned. I had been more or less of a thorn in the side of the "staffers" all through and they watched me closely. One day three of them found me taking a rest in a worked-out end of the mine, and they proceeded at once to give me a severe beating. I sprang up and swung around a mining lamp that I happened to be holding, catching one of them in the side. They backed off then, but had me hauled up that afternoon before the military authorities, who gave me six days "black"—that is, solitary confinement on bread and water. When I came out I was handed over to the civil courts on a charge of assaulting civilians. They took me to stand my trial at Recklinghausen.

The judge was an elderly man with a rather kindly face and I thought there was a trace of concern in his eye as he looked me over. So, when the evidence against me had been put in, I decided to make an appeal to him. The charge against me was that I had hit one of the "staffers" in the face with my lantern and hurt him seriously. I spoke up in English.

"Your Honor, this is a court of justice. Are you prepared to give a British soldier the same chance as a German citizen?"

This was translated and the magistrate replied rather severely that, "Certainly, I would have the same chance."

Then I asked: "Is there anyone in court who knows anything about a miner's lamp?"

A man came forward from the back who had worked in a mine and I asked him: "Would it be possible to hit a man in the face with a miner's lamp without breaking his jaw or marking him up?" The man hesitated and then answered reluctantly, "No."

The magistrate acquitted me at once.

We lived under conditions of great discomfort in the camp. As I stated before all the British and colonial prisoners were kept in one building—250 of us in all. There were two stoves in the building in which coke was burned and in winter the place was terribly cold. The walls at all seasons were so damp that pictures tacked up on them mildewed in a short time. Our bunks contained straw which was never replenished and we all became infested with fleas. Some nights it was impossible to sleep on account of the activity of these pests. On account of the dampness and the cold we always slept in our clothes.

Discipline was rigorous and cruel. We were knocked around and given terms of solitary confinement and made to stand at attention for hours on the least provocation. It became more than flesh and blood could stand. One day seven of us got together and made a solemn compact to escape. We would keep at it, we decided, no matter what happened until we got away. Six of us are now safely at home. The seventh, my chum J.W. Nicholson, of Winnipeg, is still a prisoner. Poor Nick was the most determined and resourceful of the lot of us, I think. Together we saw the Dutch frontier a few yards ahead only to be caught as we made our last sprint for liberty. It was the hardest of luck that robbed us of our chance that time. Luck was with me later, and not with Nick.

I made four attempts to escape before I finally succeeded. The first time a group of us made a tunnel out under the barricade, starting beneath the flooring of the barracks. We crawled out at night and had put fifteen miles between us and the camp before we were finally caught. I got seven days' "black" that time.

The second attempt was again by means of a tunnel. A close chum of mine, William Raesides, who had come over with the 8th C.M.R.s was my companion that time. We were caught after twenty miles and they gave us ten days' "black."

The third attempt was made in company with my chum Nicholson and we planned it out very carefully. Friends in England sent through suits of civilian clothes to us. We got a hint in advance that they were coming. The procedure with reference to the distribution of parcels was this: We would be summoned to headquarters where the parcels would be heaped up on a long table. The Kommandant would then have a prisoner call out the names on each parcel and a couple of soldiers would open the parcels for examination before handing them on. On the day I thought our suits were about due to arrive I pressed forward for the job of reading the addresses. They let me go ahead without any suspicion.

Sure enough there were parcels for us which looked sufficiently bulky and I was able to slip them unobserved to one of the other fellows. In that way we secured our civilian clothes.

The next day we dressed for the attempt by putting on our "civvies" first and then drawing the prisoner's uniform on over them. When we got to the mine we took off the uniform and slipped the mining clothes on over the others. We worked all day. Coming up from work in the late afternoon, Nick and I held back until every one else had gone. We went up alone in the hoist and tore off our mining clothes as we ascended, dropping each piece back into the pit as we discarded it.

It was fairly dark when we got out of the hoist and the guards did not pay much attention to us. There was a small building at the mine head where we prisoners washed and dressed after work and a separate exit for the civilians. Nick and I took the civilian exit and walked out into the street without any interference.

We could both speak enough German to pass so we boldly struck out for the Dutch border, which was 75 km from Kommando 47, travelling only during the night. We had a map that a miner had sold to us for a cake of soap and we guided our course carefully by it. We got to the border line without any trouble whatever.

The line, we knew, was very carefully guarded. There were three lines of sentries to be broken through, and on the last line they were stationed but fifty yards apart. It was, therefore, necessary to wait until night before making the attempt. We were caught through over-confidence due to a mistake in the map. Close to the line was a mile post indicating that a certain Dutch town was two miles west. Now the map indicated that this town was four miles within the Dutch border.

"We're over!" we almost shouted when we saw that welcome mile post. Throwing caution aside we marched boldly forward right into a couple of sentries with fixed bayonets.

It was two weeks' "black" they meted out to us that time. The Kommandant's eyes snapped as he passed sentence. I knew he would have been much more strict on me as the three-time offender had it not been that the need for coal was so dire that labor, even the labor of a recalcitrant prisoner, was valuable.

"No prisoner has yet escaped from this Kommando!" he declared, "and none shall. Any further attempts will be punished with the utmost severity."

Nevertheless they took the precaution to break up my partnership with Nicholson, putting him on the night shift. I immediately went into partnership with Private W.M. Masters, of Toronto, and we planned to make our getaway by an entirely new method.

The building at the mine where we changed clothes before and after work was equipped with a bathroom in one corner. It boasted a window with one iron bar intersecting. Outside the window was

49

a bush and beyond that open country. A sentry was always posted outside the building, but he had three sides to watch and we knew that, if we could only move that bar, we could manage to elude the sentry. So we started to work on the bar.

I had found a bit of wire which I kept secreted about me and every night, after washing up, we would dig for a few minutes at the brickwork around the bar. It was slow, tedious and disappointing work. Gradually, however, we scooped the brick out around the bar and after nearly four months' steady application we had it so loosened that a sharp tug would pull it out.

The next day Masters and I went into the bathroom last and delayed our ablutions until the sentry's round had taken him to the other side of the building. Then we wrenched the bar out, raised the window and wriggled through head first, breaking our fall in the bush outside. We got through without attracting attention and struck off at a rapid clip across country. Close ahead was a stretch of swampy country and we very soon lost our way and wallowed around the better part of the night, sometimes up to our knees in the bog and suffering very severely from the cold and damp. Early in our flight the report of a gun from the camp warned us that our absence had been discovered. Perhaps our adventure in the swamp was what saved us from capture, for the roads unquestionably were patrolled by cavalry that night. The Kommandant was keen to make good his boast that no prisoner would get away from him.

We found our way out of the swamp near morning, emerging on the western side. By the sale of more soap to miners we had acquired another map and a compass, so we had little difficulty in determining our whereabouts and setting our course for the border. For food we had each brought along ten biscuits, the result of several weeks' hoarding. A biscuit is a hard and almost tasteless substance, but containing certain nutritious qualities. We had half a pound of food apiece and eighty-five miles to go! That day we stayed on the edge of the swamp, never stirring for a moment from the shelter of a clump of bushes. One slept while the other watched. No one came near us and we heard no signs of our pursuers. Night came on most mercifully dark and we struck out along the roads at a smart clip.

We travelled all night, making probably twenty-five miles. It was necessary, we knew, to make the most of our strength in the earlier stages of the dash. As our food gave out we would be less capable of covering the ground. So we spurred ourselves on to renewed efforts and ate the miles up in a sort of frenzy.

"Got to keep it up," we said to each other by way of encouragement. "It's now or never."

When we saw or heard anything ahead of us we immediately made for cover at the side of the road. Perhaps three persons passed us that night.

We took cover next day in a bit of wood, with a couple of farm houses within sight. No person came near us, however. We slept pretty much all day by turns and again struck out at night.

This kept up for four days and nights. We kept going as hard as our waning strength would permit and we were cautious in the extreme. Even at that we had several close shaves. One night we passed what looked like a potato patch, and the thought of a raw potato to break the monotony, and the inadequacy of dry biscuit, lured us off the road and into the patch. We had been told in the mine that a law had been passed permitting the owners of potato patches to fire on thieves and that in case the intruders were shot the owner would not be responsible. This eloquent bit of testimony to the scarcity of food in beleaguered Germany we had not altogether believed. It had hardly seemed possible that such a law could stand even in Germany. But we had convincing proof that such a law did exist. Masters had found a potato and was showing it to me with almost childish delight when the report of a rifle broke the silence. It came from the far side of the field. We turned and ran, Masters clutching his precious potato as though it were a lump of gold. Another shot followed us but we got to the road again in safety and hastily resumed our westward jaunt. There was no attempt at pursuit. The owner of the potato patch probably thought we were hungry neighbors.

We ate that potato between us and it tasted like everything good to us—porterhouse steak and mushrooms and apple pie! It was the only change we had during the whole journey from our meagre supply of biscuit. We were extremely unfortunate in our

51

foragings. Potatoes were guarded like the mint and turnips simply hid themselves away when we went looking for them. Water was all we were able to obtain. A few mouthfuls of dry biscuit washed down with water was a meal to us.

Another time we were hiding in a bush when four women came along and passed within a few feet of us. They were looking for mushrooms and we could hear everything they said as they passed. One night a dog brought a man with a rifle on our tracks and he gave us a merry chase.

Our greatest difficulty was when we struck the Lippe River. Our first plan was to swim across, but we found that we had not the strength left for this feat. We lost a day as a result. The second night we found a scow tied up along the bank and got across that way.

Figure for yourself the plight we were in. We were slowly starving on our feet, we were wet through and such sleep as we got was broken and fitful. Before we had been four days out we were reduced to gaunt, tattered, dirty scarecrows. We staggered as we walked and sometimes one of us would drop on the road through sheer weakness. Through it all we kept up our frenzy for speed and it was surprising how much ground we forced ourselves to cover in a night. And, no matter how much the pangs of hunger gnawed at us we conserved our fast dwindling supply of biscuit. Less than two biscuits a day was our limit!

Finally we reached a point that I recognized from my previous jaunt. It was about four miles from the border. This was in the latter part of the night and we had come quite a long distance. We were tired out.

"Will we go on and finish it tonight?" I asked Masters. "Perhaps it would be better to get a day's rest and make the break tomorrow night."

"Let's toss," suggested my companion.

I nodded and he drew a coin from a pocket of his ragged prison garb.

"Heads we go, tails we stay over," I said.

It fell tails, so we hunted out a well-wooded spot and settled down for a rest. We had two biscuits left between us. The next day we feasted royally and extravagantly on those two biscuits. We did not leave a crumb. No longer did we need to hoard our supplies, for the next night would tell the tale.

By the greatest good fortune night came on dark and cloudy. Not a star showed in the sky. We started out early and crept cautiously on toward the border. We came to the same mile post in time and I pointed it out to Masters.

"Here was where poor Nick and I went wrong," I whispered. "We'll give it a wide berth this time."

So we crawled away off to the right, literally crawled on our hands and knees for over a quarter of a mile. At every sound we stopped and flattened out. Twice we saw sentries close at hand, but both times we got by safely. Finally we reached what we judged must be the last line of sentries. We had crawled across a ploughed field and had come to a road lined with trees on both sides. Sentries were pacing up and down the road. We could hear and, at intervals, see them.

"It's the border," said Masters, in a hoarse whisper. "Once across there and—God! we're free again!"

We waited until the nearest sentry had reached the far end of his beat and then we broke across. Doubled up like jack-knives we went over that road as fast as we could make it and plunged through the trees on the other side. We were not detected; at any rate not a sound came from the sentries. We struck across fields with delirious speed and nothing cropped up to stop us. We reeled along like drunken men, laughing and gasping and sometimes reaching out for a mutual handshake.

"Free! Free! Free!" was about all we could say. "No more work in the mines! No more German bosses! Real food!"

"Are you sure we're over?" asked Masters at last, voicing a fear that still persisted in both our minds.

"Of course we are," I said. "The sentries would have us by this time if we weren't."

Just then we struck a road and at once we got quite a scare. Marching up the road toward us was what looked like a white sheet. I guess our nerves were badly shattered with what we had been through. At any rate that moving splash of white looked uncanny and awesome. I confess that stories of ghosts and banshees began to run through my mind and Masters owned up to the same feeling.

It was a scare of brief duration. The sheet soon resolved itself into two girls in white dresses walking up the road with a man. We scurried to the side of the road as soon as we made them out. Then I decided to test the matter of our whereabouts, and stepped out to accost them.

"Have you a match?" I asked in German.

The man did not understand me. Thoroughly convinced now, I cried out to Masters to come out. We were free!

BURIED ALIVE!

—September 1918—
Lieutenant C.W. Tillbrook

"Zim!" I bobbed down quickly for a sniper was at work. I was more than ever envious of the man who measured five feet six. I was, and am, six feet and one-half inch.

I proceeded on my way to C sap. [A sap was a trench or tunnel made in order to get closer to an enemy; a sapper was a soldier, especially a private, of the Royal Engineers.] Arriving there, I took off my boots preparatory to descending into the works. This step was absolutely necessary for all mining operations must be carried on in silence, and one of the easiest sounds to detect is a man walking in the gallery.

I lit my candle and walked along about two hundred yards through the narrow gallery. My candle grew dimmer till it seemed on the point of going out owing to the bad air. I reached the "T" where the galleries turned right and left and met the shift sergeant again.

"Air very bad, sir."

"Yes, get the bellows installed right away."

"Yes, sir. Shall I come with you, too?"

"No."

That word saved his life as will be shown by what follows. I only wish that I could have said the same to the brave fellows working in the above-mentioned sap.

"Now get that done right away, sergeant."

"Very good, sir."

"Oh! by the way, how much have we to do to get to B sap?"

"About eighty feet, sir."

"Well we should be through in two days and I shall be very glad when it is all over. I don't like that place. The Hun is somewhere around. Well, carry on."

He turned sideways to let me pass and we both proceeded in opposite directions: I to what was to be a living tomb; he to get the means of ultimate salvation.

I walked about one hundred and fifty feet when my candle went out so I lit my electric torch. The air was fetid, smelling of sandbags and decaying wood, and can only be described as smelling like a sap. On reaching C 2 right, I found the men working with a will for they wanted to get through to the sweet air which was awaiting them less than one hundred feet away, but there was a deadly enemy but a few feet away who in ten minutes was to put an end to their desire for air or anything else, namely, the Westphalian Pioneers with about two hundred pounds of westphalite, the very powerful explosive used by the German miners.

I called the men's attention to the fact that they were making too much noise and had better stop work for a while as I wanted to listen.

I put on my G phone and proceeded to the listening pocket which was about eighty feet from the men, and at right angles to the main gallery about thirty feet in depth. For five minutes I could hear nothing but the tut-tut-tut of a machine gun away in the distance. Twice I heard the sound of a shell bursting: then silence. What was that? I was immediately tuned up. Somebody walking, several people quite hurriedly, then a dull thudding noise, which I diagnosed as tamping, the most deadly sound a mining engineer can ever wish to hear for it indicates that the enemy is loaded and is preparing to fire his mine. I stepped out of the pocket and went down to the men and said: "Get your things together and get out at once. Don't make any noise, but hurry."

I went back into the pocket and commenced listening again for sounds. I could feel my pulse beating in my wrists, neck and temples. It was the first time that I had ever heard the enemy tamp, so any acceleration in my heart's beat was excusable.

I could hear my men coming up the gallery. Then I heard a crack followed instantly by a muffled roar. I experienced a feeling as if I were being spun round on a roulette table: then I was hurled up in the air, and then as though a large door had fallen on me there came a complete blank.

My first sensations on regaining consciousness were not very clear. There was a ringing in my ears and a stinging numbness all over my body, especially in my face. Gradually it dawned on me that there had been an explosion. I was lying face down. I tried to rise but found I could not move for I was pinned down by some fallen timbers which were on my left side. I fumbled for my watch. It was still going and pointed to eight-sixteen.

I put my hand out and encountered something hard, wet and sticky, but could not imagine what it was. I tried to move, but my efforts were rewarded by a shower of dirt which fell from the unsupported roof. In feeling around my hand came in contact with my torch. I pressed the catch and it lit up the remains of our gallery and the sappers.

I never want to experience anything like it again—death, desolation and doom all around. The sticky something was the top of a man's skull. I screamed out. Nothing answered me but a shower of dirt. I was alone with darkness and the dead. The dead could not hurt me but the darkness I did fear. I soon realized that, if I were going to do anything, I would have to do it at once, so I commenced a rolling motion with my body. After about twenty minutes of this painful activity I was able to wriggle free.

I explored carefully and slowly and found I was in the main gallery which was very much "crumped." In the course of my search I came on a few arms and legs, all that remained of what had been probably as fine a sample of men as were ever on the Western battle front.

I then felt hopeless and I must confess that I cried as if I were an infant. Finally, however, I collected my wits and groped my way in the opposite direction, only to be abruptly stopped by a wall of loose dirt—I was buried alive! My next few moments were spent in a condition bordering on insanity. I shrieked and yelled and beat on the walls of earth in a frenzy. I clawed frantically at the damp bounds of my prison and in time my efforts served the necessary purpose of quieting me down. And then I started to crawl back to where I had been in the first place.

My head suddenly came in contact with a timber which had fallen down diagonally. I swore vigorously. That broke the spell, I realized that I had got a hold on myself again. So I sat down and began to think over my position more or less calmly. I reasoned out that our other work parties would know of the explosion and would try to find out if there were any person alive. I crawled into the listening pocket and found that it was intact. It was at right angles to the force of the explosion—a fact which accounted for my escape from the fate of my comrades. On the sills, or floor, was my G phone. I put it on and listened: I could detect a crackling sound, due to disintegration of the soil after the explosion: then, joy of joys, I heard two knocks followed by three sharper ones—the miner's knock, sometimes known as Kentish fire. I replied and listened again; and got the signal back "Coming through."

I started to claw with my hands at the face of the pocket and I very soon had a pile of dirt that was going to cut me off from the main gallery. I went back and got some sandbags. Then I noticed a change coming over me; my head was aching and I felt very big about the hands and feet. This was due to carbon monoxide poisoning from the explosion. If the relief party did not break through soon I knew it would be too late.

I started to fill the bags, but my hands and fingers seemed like bunches of bananas. I could hear by this time the other party with my ear; they were evidently boring. Would they be quick enough? It got very warm and comfortable and I did not seem to mind how long they were as long as they would let me sleep. I knew I was going off in a sleep which would be fatal, and the thought of death, when life was so close at hand, stimulated me to make another effort. I crawled to the face of the listening pocket and started to scratch at the soil. Then I tried filling more sandbags. How long this went on, I do not know, but I suddenly felt another shower of dirt and something hit me in the face. There was a clank of metal, and then a rush of cold air; the rescue party had got a bore-hole through to me. I heard the eight-inch auger being withdrawn, then a voice said:

"Who's there?"

I shouted back: "Me. For God's sake get me out!"

Then down the hole came something. I reached out feebly and felt a hose. Then came a piff-paff of air and I knew that the bellows, which I had formerly instructed the sergeant to get, were playing their part in keeping me alive.

In about one hour I crawled out to the rescue party. The officer of the previous shift greeted me with the anxious query:

"Did he get any of you?"

"All but me."

"Good God! Seven of the best gone."

The sergeant standing by said: "Oh, well, sir, it's all in the day's work—could the men have a tot of rum?" I do not remember if the answer was in the affirmative—doubtless it was—for the gallery began to tilt and everything went dark and once more I relapsed into unconsciousness.

The next thing I remember was opening my eyes to the glorious sunlight and my batman, my brother officer and the sergeant were looking at me.

"How are you feeling, Old Top?"

"As if I were going to die. Thank you very much."

"Are you past rum?"

"Try me." They did—with success.

I was still feeling shaky after the effects of being buried and was decidedly blue for some of my best men were gone. I felt like reporting sick. I could at least get back to a casualty station for a couple of weeks and possibly to Blighty. I tried a cigarette. It tasted like nothing on earth that I knew of—absolutely vile. So I threw it away in disgust. I heard someone entering my quarters and then a light appeared. I looked and saw that it was Major Henry—the O.C.

He lit a couple of candles and coming over to the side of my bunk, took hold of my wrist.

"When did you have something to eat last?"

"This morning, sir, before it happened."

"Now, old man, get hold of yourself, I'll call your batman."

In a few minutes I could hear the thrum thrum of the Primus stove at work. The O.C. looked at me sharply.

"Tilly, you have had a bad time but you have no bones broken. I can have you evacuated if you like but I would rather have you stay on. Those boys have to be avenged, and I don't think it will be long before we can get back at the Boche. We have lost some men but remember that this is war, and you can't make omelettes without breaking eggs. If every little setback we have is going to take the heart out of us, we may as well quit. Just remember that at present not one hundred yards away there are some Huns laughing up their sleeves because they 'got us.' The boys that are gone have to be paid for. Will you collect?"

I felt so mean that I was ashamed of myself and nearly forgot about my headache.

"I'll be ready next shift, sir."

"Good! Remember, don't get windy, get the Hun. After we have eaten we will go and look at the damage done."

Then my batman arrived with two plates of beef steak, fried potatoes and canned peas. I started picking at mine, but soon I was wondering what was going to follow. It is quite true that eating and fighting only want a beginning. The "afterwards" consisted of some canned apricots, canned cream and coffee. The war wasn't so bad after all.

I got back to my dugout and threw myself down on my bunk. The signallers were busy in the next dugout, tuning up their buzzers and with this music in my ears I gradually faded away into the land of nod. I awakened at 5:20 a.m. by my watch, and got up. A messenger came in from the signallers, and handed in a slip—"O.C. Blighty. Ajax condor fly A A A Able Fred Apple. O.C. Stone." It was a code message from Henry. I deciphered it and read the result out to my fellow officers.

"Something doing, Old Top."

"And soon too."

We picked out a party of six men, collected two torpedoes, three cans of ammonal, an eight-inch auger and ten rods—and then started for B sap.

About twenty-five feet up the gallery a candle light showed two forms crouching over in the listening posts. As we approached, the two listeners looked up towards us, their foreheads wrinkled and eyes opened, not so much in surprise, but more as if in protest at our having disturbed them in their vigils. The smaller of the two men, Angus by name, got up on his knees as we approached and, when I got beside, he handed me the ear piece of his G phone and whispered:

"We'll be shaking hands with him in a few hours, sir."

I put on the ear clips. Clomp! Clomp! Clomp, clomp, clomp! I took the G phone off and listened. I could hear the sound ever so slightly with my ear, but still it was there, just as if I were inside a brick building with very thick walls and someone was hitting the outside with a hard wooden mallet. The Boche was working on the face with great speed, and, as far as I could judge, he was about the same level and to the right. Was he coming towards, parallel with, or past us? Time would show. But that time had not to be wasted.

The boring party arrived and it was but the space of ten minutes before they had the auger at work and the first sandbag filled. The auger is practically the same thing as a post digger but instead of being used vertically it is used horizontally.

"Bingy"—my fellow officer—was arranging the ammonal containers placing them ready for use. I beckoned him to me.

"Send a wire in code to the O.C., tell him 'Enemy working to the right of B sap. Heard with the naked ear. Am getting ready to load, will not fire till absolutely necessary—wire approval, O.C. Blighty.'

"All right. How about the front line?"

"I was coming to that. Go to the O.C. Trenches and tell him enough to get his 'wind up.' Make him hustle. Tell him you are going to blow the Hun and he must hold his line very light for three hundred feet on either side of B sap. Tell him to have bombers ready in case the Hun gets by us. Pile it on good and thick. I don't want a lot of them hanging around the sap head, for if the observer at Hill 60 spots a crowd he will immediately start a 'strafe'—you know."

"All right, Old Bean, I'll pile the agony on." And he disappeared.

By this time the boring party had got their hole in ten feet. I stopped them and decided that they had gone far enough. The Hun could be heard much plainer now. About this time a new arrival appeared in the form of Captain Barker. He was a typical miner, a short and thick-set man with an eye like a hawk. He had a very determined mouth, but it was a good natured one when he smiled—which was only on rare occasions.

"Good morning."

"Is it?"

"Something doing, eh?"

"Quite."

"Where is he?"

"To the right, coming this way."

He listened for about a minute, then asked: "How far do you estimate him?"

"About twelve feet."

"He was—but now?"

I listened intently—I could hear the Boche talking plainly. Then there was a tapping of wood on wood, they were putting in a set or framework of timber with which the galleries are lined. Then work was continued by them. Clomp! Clomp! Clomp! Then patter, patter, as of the snow sliding off a roof and falling—it was the loosened dirt dropping. Then we could hear their shovels scraping on the timbers, as they lifted up the dirt to bag it. This was followed by a few dull thuds. They were bumping the nearly full sandbags to compress the material. They started work again.

Buried Alive!

"Put all lights out," I whispered.

The Boche was within two feet of us. Only a thin wall of sand separated us and this might be broken at any moment. We had the advantage if there was going to be a scrap in that we were expecting him and he was in blissful ignorance of our immediate presence.

Captain Barker and myself were lying with our faces towards the bore hole. He whispered back to the men: "Get back to the steps till you are signalled—three flashes—then one of you crawl quietly up."

With the slight noise of their clothing brushing against the timbers they left us.

The noise of the enemy's workers grew much louder. Suddenly there was a splatter and a scrunching, then a rush of cold air—he had broken through into our bore hole!

We heard his exclamation of surprise, and then silence for possibly half a minute, but it seemed ages before there was another movement. It came at last. A light flickered. He had got an electric torch at work.

Our bore hole was only eight inches in diameter, not big enough for him to investigate our gallery thoroughly. The torch came through the bore hole. We dared not move. I looked over at Barker, and he grinned. I put my hand down gently to draw my revolver, but when he frowned, I kept still. The light was withdrawn. There was silence again. Then something started to move and by the slight light filtering through the bore hole I saw a hand, a forearm. I watched it with fascination. It was grimy with dirt. It wandered around, clawing at the empty air, then it moved towards Barker, stopped, and came back towards me, closer and closer. I flattened down still more—it passed over my face but did not touch me, but it came so close that I could feel its warmth. I made up my mind that if the hand did touch me, the owner would rue it, for I would lay hold with my teeth. I bared them ready for it. Then there was a sudden disturbance in the enemy's gallery, a voice commanding and the hand was withdrawn. More guttural talking. I heard plainly: "Ja, Herr Leutnant Hartzenberg."

Then I got a glimpse of a face. It was that of a typical "square-

63

Captured German dugout, Aug. 1918.

head," fair and pale, but the one thing I noticed particularly in that brief glance was the animal-like eyes, cruel, cunning and close together. I don't know if either of us made any movement or not, but the next instant there was a flash and report. Herr Leutnant had fired his Luger pistol through the bore hole. My ears sang and my eyes refused to see anything but a dull green mist. Barker caught hold of my hand and squeezed it and I returned his pressure, indicating that each was all right.

The enemy started to move away up his gallery, presumably to hold a confab. Barker whispered: "Come on, Tilly, now's our chance."

We crawled down the gallery, and Barker flashed his lamp three times. He had given the signal, we were going to fight.

The chances now were equal. I saw Sergeant Evans starting to come. "Bring all your men," Barker ordered. He came on followed by Angus, Smith and Bingy.

I took hold of a torpedo and rammed it home into the bore

hole, which had reached to nine inches in depth before it was broken by the enemy's work. Barker came with two fifty-pound cans of ammonal, and placed this alongside the bore hole, then two more on top of them—the first part was done.

Crouching, we started to pile the sandbags. Two rows had been placed when we heard the enemy party returning. There was a clanking of metal—cans of westphalite! He was going to blow too. It was to be a case of Canadians and ammonal against Huns and westphalite.

We threw discretion to the winds as far as being silent was concerned, and started to heave in bags as they had never been heaved before. I looked at my watch and timed the work. In seven minutes we had six feet tamped; a hundred and eight sandbags in place— approximately five thousand five hundred pounds.

The enemy was working with great vigor. We could hear directions being shouted and the bump bump of his bags being driven home. Angus was beside me and said with a grin, "Heinie'll lose his rum ration if he's not careful, sir."

I told him to shut up and get back ten feet. Here we started tamping again. This air chamber between was to act as a pneumatic cushion, for the charge was fairly big, and there would be a considerable backfire. As the enemy was tamping as well, it was going to be necessary for us to have the line of greatest resistance in our gallery.

On we worked, sandbag after sandbag. Our arms ached, the sweat pouring down our faces, necks and bodies; sand and grime settled on us and formed a paste. It got into our eyes, into our mouths. Tasting salt, our mouths became dry but still we didn't have time to remedy it. I saw that the fuse leads were not displaced. Barker from time to time tested them and found that the circuits were intact. If they were destroyed we had still one more chance— that was the time fuse from the torpedo, a little white cord about one quarter of an inch in diameter. I watched that as a mother does her sick child. Another six feet was completed but we kept on. Every sandbag meant another degree of safety.

Smith growled out, "What a job at a dollar ten a day!"

Angus smiled sweetly and murmured through his parched lips, "But think of the rum."

Neither of them said any more. Bingy panted out a few lines of a popular mining song—

> I asked him how much he paid,
> He said a dollar a ton,
> I said to hell with the man who works,
> I'd rather be a bum.

And then he grinned his awful grin. It irritated me; would the job never cease? Then we all seemed to get our second wind. We redoubled our efforts and at last we were finished. Another ten feet had been tamped; Barker tested the leads again. They were all right.

"Clear out all now."

Nobody seemed to want to go, but they turned and walked towards the steps, their breath coming in pants and sobs. At the foot of the steps, Angus turned and said: "When do we get our rum, sir?"

"After we've blown. Now get on out."

I believe on Judgment Day he will ask for an issue of the above-mentioned fluid before he answers for his sins, and I'm certain that after the interrogation is over he'll ask for another.

Bingy inquired if there was anything for him to do.

"Yes. Go up to the front line and see if it craters."

The reason for this was that by this means we would be able to see if the enemy got the full charge in his gallery. If there was any waste it would blow out of the ground and it would be classified as a mine, if not it would be a camouflet.

"All right, Old Top."

Captain Barker and myself were left alone. I put on the G phone for a minute, and I could distinctly hear the thud of the enemy still tamping. We had won!

All that remained was to connect up and explode.

I told Barker what I heard and he said: "We'll give them the time fuse. That'll take thirty seconds."

I put the fuse slantways so as to get a good surface and thereby give it a good start. Then I applied the match and the fuse began to hiss.

We ran along the gallery and up the steps. Just as we got up to the trench there was a rumble and shaking. The earth seemed to go up and down like an angry sea, then quivered, and came to rest.

We waited for an instant. Then Bingy shouted out: "Not a spoonful, old dear. We got him cold. By the way, here's a runner asking for you. He says his message is important."

Barker turned to me and smiled. He started to whistle, "Now the day is over." Then he said, "I think we broke an army record. How long, Tilly?"

"Twenty-seven minutes."

We had placed approximately three hundred sandbags or ten thousand pounds in twenty-seven minutes—six men for five tons. We did not have to fill these sandbags, for that was already done. We always had one side of the gallery lined with filled bags so as to save time.

I suddenly remembered the important message and turning round my eyes fell on the runner. He looked very much done up and evidently fagged. He had been pretty near "it" as a sear across his right cheek denoted. The blood had coagulated and dried on the wound except at the corner from which a thin red stream trickled down his face. As he handed me an envelope I remembered. "You are wounded."

"Only slightly, sir. An M.G. bullet."

"Pretty close."

I opened the envelope fully expecting to find the O.C.'s sanction for our blow, which Bingy had previously wired for. I leaned against the parapet and read the following amazing message:—

> From G.H.Q.
> To O.C. Blighty.
> You have been referring to the enemy in your report as the Hun.
> This must cease. In future refer to him as the enemy.
> C.R.E.

Speechless, I handed the message to Barker, who in turn gasped and handed it to Bingy. He broke the silence with:

"Heavens!!! The things that matter!"

AN UNDERGROUND TANK

—October 1918—
Lieutenant C.W. Tillbrook

Bingy walked into the dugout, soaking wet. "Dirty night in the trenches," he growled.

I knew something must be wrong with him. He was not smiling.

"What's the matter?" I inquired.

"That d—d sniper's got five men in the last hour. You can't get by in Canada Street without crawling on your stomach—and it's such a beastly undignified way to go around!"

I nodded in sympathy. This sniper was an absolute mystery. Somewhere in No Man's Land he had his nest. We had

Open living quarters under dugout, Jan. 1917.

been unable to locate him owing to the fact that his rifle was fitted with a silencer. We had heard the "chug" of it and we knew that he was not far away. He had, however, located us "good and plenty"— in one week he had accounted for eleven men and now five more in an hour.

It was the wet season, January, and it rained all the time as it can only rain in Flanders. Our trenches were no longer trenches but just a series of mounds connected by sink holes. The only places that were at all inhabitable were our saps. We had carefully built small dams with sandbags round our sap entrances and these kept the water out. Also we kept our gas curtains down. These curtains were blankets on rollers, and could be pulled up or down at will. They were saturated with the vermal solution to neutralize the gas if it came our way and prevent our galleries filling up with the dreaded invisible death. The result of these precautions was that underground we were dry and warm and the envy of the infantry (only for our comfort, not for our jobs).

Bingy and I sat around and discussed ways and means of "getting" the mysterious sniper. We finished a meal in the meantime and were waiting for the shift to come off when we received a visitor in the form of one Lieut. Gills, commonly known as the Fish. He was a cadaverous individual with a continuous smile that revealed protuberant teeth, half-soled in gold. Incidentally he was the inveterate gossip monger of that section of the front.

The Fish greeted us with his customary form of salutation, "God's rotten night, you chaps!" and sat down on a bully beef box. Then he elevated his muddy boots on my bed and helped himself to a cigarette from a package on the table, absent-mindedly dropping the package into his pocket. That had to be stopped of course and, after the affair of the dirty boots and the bed had been settled, we demanded to know what had brought him over.

"Well, Old Top, you see I'm shy on timbers. Some rotter stole all my 2 ft. 3 x 4 ft. off the dump and I didn't discover it till tonight. So I want you to let me have some."

Bingy glared. "Somebody stole our 2 ft. 3 x 4 ft. last night. The dump corporal said it was one of your sergeants came up with a party and took it. Are you trying to rub it in?"

The Fish grinned. "Fact is," he said, "I'm short of rum and I promised the fatigue party I'd get some. Could you let me have a jar?"

I saw it was time for me to join in the conversation.

"Nothing doing!" I said, "abso-bally-lutely! You swipe our sills and then come to us for rum to reward your bank. Go home, Ali Baba, go home to your cave and your forty thieves."

"Well, what'll I do?" moaned the Fish, his hand stealing over towards my cigarettes again.

"Smoke your own," I suggested.

So he gave up his felonious efforts and came around to the real object of his visit. "I'm coming on duty here tomorrow," he announced.

Bingy squirmed and breathed an audible "Hell!" The Fish ignored the frank ejaculation and proceeded to enlighten us with the latest news which he had discovered in the bowels of the earth. "The tunneling companies are going to move out of the salient. Didn't you hear? Well. Just nursing parties to be left here. I suppose most of the officers will transfer into something else. Me, I'll go into the tanks. Ripping idea, tanks, what?"

We agreed and the Fish, having passed on his news, rose to depart. "Am I to get that rum?" he asked in a placating tone.

"No."

"Shylock!" he snapped.

Bingy called after him. "Beware sniper!" Then we looked at each other with mutual commiseration for the presence of the Fish was not going to add anything much to the pleasantness of our lot. We turned in. A few hours later I was awakened by a sapper shaking my shoulder.

"A sergeant hit, sir."

"Where?"

"Canada Street, sir. Sergeant Wicks."

I was out of my bunk in a minute.

After pulling on my trench boots, I rushed up the steps into the front line, the sapper just ahead of me. We reached a group barely discernible in the darkness, gathered around Wicks and another outstretched form. I was very much agitated, for there had been a close bond between us.

"How did it happen?" I asked. "He shouldn't have been here. All our men have orders to travel underground."

"That sniper got them both."

We carried the two inanimate forms down to my dugout. I attended to Wicks. It was pretty evident that his time was short. He was bleeding copiously from several wounds, the worst being in the neck. Wicks remained unconscious while I bound up his wounds. In the meantime one of the others related how it had occurred:

"Three scouts went out to see if they could locate that sniper, sir. But instead he got 'em all. Two were killed outright and the third one, this man here, got shot in the stomach. It was horrible, sir. He was paralyzed from the waist down and he kept calling out to us for help for he couldn't crawl a yard. We called for volunteers to go out and get him and as Sergeant Wicks was above ground for a breather he said he'd go. He said he knew this 'ere salient better than any other bloke and he couldn't stick hearing the poor beggar howl like that. So he was out of the trench before anyone could stop him and he got over to the other one and was starting to bring him back. The wounded man was delirious I guess, sir, because he kept calling out and the sniper was able to follow each change of position and pepper them all the way back. He got Wicks but not until they were within a few feet of the trench. Wicks got up to his feet and lifted his man up and lowered him over the parapet and the sniper got him in the neck."

As the man finished his story, Wicks opened his eyes and, seeing me, attempted a salute. It was a feeble effort, falling off half way. It was a full minute before I could speak. Then I asked:

"Comfortable?"

He smiled. "No, sir. I shan't be till I'm gone West. I won't be long. That bloody sniper, sir, he's just opposite O'Grady's walk— sixty feet out. Can I 'ave a fag, sir?"

I lit one for him and stuck it between his lips. He pulled at it with evident gratification. The other wounded man here moaned loudly and Wicks, with the sense of authority of his stripes, rolled his head slightly in his direction and upbraided him. "Now then, me man, stop makin' that noise. Don't forget ye're in officers' quarters."

Soon after this the cigarette fell from his lips and he looked at me wistfully. "I'm goin' now, sir. I'd like to 'ave—stopped with yer—'elped yer to finish the job—with the bloody 'Uns. I 'opes yer get that b—— of a sniper." He gasped for breath. "Write my missus—."

"We'll get that sniper!" was all I could say as they carried poor Wicks out.

For the rest of the night I could not sleep. At daybreak I got up and made my way to the sap head for some of God's good air. It was a beautiful morning but there was nothing of beauty in what I saw. In front of me stretched the Armagh Woods, just a few blackened posts, mockeries of trees. In the valley below nothing could be seen but a slate colored mass of mud mounds and shell holes—various sized circular puddles of stinking water. All around was nothing but a deathly stillness, broken occasionally by the squeaking of rats. It was so depressing that I felt like the last man alive in a dead world. Here was an old, crumped dugout with its buried inmates—how long would it be before they would be churned up by a shell? To my right were innumerable sandbags—our spoil dump, under which were buried hundreds, friend and foe alike. I watched a rat come out from underneath a tin can, so diseased that it could hardly walk. It crept to a brownish, green heap that stuck out between some sandbags and began to nibble. Was it a human thigh? I turned away in disgust only to be faced by many such sights.

Overhead a solitary shell pursued its way on to Valley Cottages (our advance dressing station), whining as if in protest at its inhuman work.

I re-entered our saps, relieved at the darkness and the poor air. This, at least, did not smell of putrification. We kept the place sprayed with a creosote and chloride of lime solution.

I made my rounds of the works. All was well—no sounds. We had big workings now and it took me two hours to go over the whole system. It was more than satisfactory to know that we had beaten the Hun at this game and were monarchs of all we surveyed. Then I decided to go up to the front line and do a little observing; I wanted to get a line on the sniper. So I proceeded to Canada St.

opposite O'Grady's Walk. I got a periscope from one of the infantry men and put it up. Zimmer! It was out of action in a trice. Our friend in No Man's Land had put a bullet right through the centre of it. So that was no good. But Wicks's information was correct with regard to his location.

That night we built up the parapet at this point and strange to say the Hun did not fire a shot. We built a cunning little O.P. (observation post) and watched. But it was no use; we could not locate the sniper. And still men were being hit.

In due course the Fish arrived on the scene, full of his schemes and inventions. In spite of them, he wasn't such a bad fellow. He hailed from the Yukon and we had that one-time famous land served up to us continuously from that time on. But he was very handy and useful in some ways. If we wanted any supplies very badly, the Fish would go out with a fatigue party and bring back what we wanted—and several things, always, that we did not want and could not possibly use. Trench mortar ammunition, guns, anything he could lay his hands on, he would bring along. He was like the Jack-daw of Rheims. He just had to steal.

I went out on rest several days after his arrival and had a talk with Major Henry. Since the death of Sergeant Wicks I had been turning over in my mind a scheme for catching the mysterious sniper. If we could not locate him from above, why not from underneath? This plan I outlined to the O.C. and he was impressed with it. "Good scheme," he said. "When you go back, carry on with it."

Before proceeding to put the plan into effect, however, we were destined to have a still more exalted sanction placed on the plan. Word came up that Major Henry would be along with the C.R.E. (Commander of the Royal Engineers) and that a general clean-up would be advisable. We got everything shipshape, even to the extent of preparing to serve tea in the dugout and opening a box of very special biscuits that a lady friend had sent us and that we had reluctantly held in reserve for just such an occasion. The arrival of our distinguished visitor was heralded by a most unusual commotion and a storm of blasphemous language.

"That was awful, Major, awful!" we heard. "I don't mind being strafed by the Huns but I object strongly to taking a liqueur of mud.

I must have swallowed a quart of the beastly stuff!"

The sniper had nearly reached the C.R.E. as soon as that distinguished officer had reached Canada St. A shot had taken away one star and crown off his shoulder strap, thereby reducing him from a full colonel to a subaltern, and brought him down still lower in the mud through which he had groveled to our dugout. He was red in the face and covered with mud from head to foot and pretty well mad all through.

So I unfolded my plan to his Brasshatship, and he was violently enthusiastic. He authorized the immediate construction of a gallery to a point close enough below that sniper to "blow" him.

But now it was a case of work. I unfolded my scheme in detail, which was to start a gallery at right angles to our first defensive and push it forward on an upgrade. By careful listening from this gallery we could detect the chug of the sniper's rifle and "tease a rabbit's hole" right under him.

We started in that night and were soon working away merrily. Our system was thirty feet in depth and from the map the sniper was approximately sixty-six feet out from us. Allowing the sniper's nest to be six feet in depth and deducting two feet for foundations this made a grade in proportion of 22 to 66 or 1 in 3. We put in a track so that we could evacuate our bags quickly on the gravity run.

The Fish was in charge of the supplies and materials and on the third night he returned with a goodly stock of timbers and sandbags, not all strictly belonging to us, but very useful nevertheless. After his last trip he came into the dugout with something that clanged when he dropped it.

"What have you got there?" I enquired.

"Only a sniper's shield, old dear, I thought it might be useful."

"So it will—in the right place. Now take the damn thing out of here!" was my rejoinder.

"Oh, but be reasonable. I thought—"

Here I interrupted him by summoning the orderly. "Take that shield outside and throw it on the spoil dump."

"Yes, sir." The orderly left with it and the Fish mournfully watched the exit. I did not know then that the said shield was going to prove a gift from the gods. But of that more later.

An Underground Tank

In three days we had fifty-five feet done and I put the listeners in. They reported no sounds. I listened myself for five hours during which time the sniper was reported to have fired eight shots, and all that time I heard absolutely nothing. Here was a poser. Was Wicks's information wrong or had the sniper moved away? I held a conference with the O.C. Trenches with the result that we made two dummies with sandbags and put them up at the extremities of a measured base line. The bait took. The sniper fired two shots which were effective and we noted the path of each bullet by the angles they made on our decoys. On triangulating these directions I found Wicks's information to be practically correct. The sniper was firing from the exact spot he had indicated. I decided that there was nothing for it but to carry on.

Two shifts after I was making out my reports preparatory to resting when the Fish rushed in to the dugout, and cried:

"Come at once, Tilly! They've broken in on us!"

I jumped off my seat as if I had been shot. "Where, man?" I asked.

"In the new gallery," he replied.

I snatched up my revolver and belt and made my way up to the spot. I soon found out that the Hun apparently had sensed this move of ours and had run a protective gallery in front of the sniper. From this they had broken in on ours. Why had they not blown us? I discovered the reason later. They had a greater scheme on hand and that was for the destruction of all our systems, the ingenuity of which I will show later.

"Why didn't you rush him?" I demanded.

"We had no rifles, sir, and he had. He got two of the face men. The rest of us got away, sir," was the reply. I walked up to the entrance and lay down. I peered intently into the darkness but could see nothing. I put my hand around and flashed on my torch. There was a deafening clamor and rattle, my hand felt as though paralyzed and the light went out. A bullet had hit my torch, but luckily my hand had escaped injury. Still the rattle kept on. The timbers started to splinter and little showers of wood flew around. Fritz had wasted no time for he had a machine gun installed, and had divided our system in two. Now we were really "up against it."

We could not bomb him, for the gallery was sixty feet in depth and only four feet high. Every move we made brought up a hail of bullets. We were blocked out of our own gallery.

But this was not the worst of it. About midnight I was called down to find that we had another element to fight—water. The wily Hun had installed pumps and was draining his system into ours. Remember, our new gallery ran at a sharp angle up to within eight feet of the surface—and the water poured down in fetid streams. Certainly they had turned the tables on us.

The only thing to do was to build a dam of sandbags, caulked with blue clay, at the sap head and then get our pumps at work. The pumps were only small affairs, excellent enough for light work, but hardly equal to the additional strain. They started to break down. It was then that the Fish loomed up as a real asset. "Don't worry. I'll fix it," he declared. And he went out and got another system of pumps! Where we did not ask. We installed the double system and managed to keep the flow of water down.

All this time the Hun was keeping up intermittent strafes with his machine gun. In spite of our work the water was slowly gaining on us. And such water! Evidently he was draining off all his sewage. The stench was abominable.

The idea that enabled us to extricate ourselves finally came to us more or less by accident. Let us depict the conditions under which it was born. A dugout, six foot high with two foot six inches of water; the lower bunk under water; three very miserable officers, without any cigarettes, sitting on the upper bunk watching a lighted candle float around in a block of wood. When the wood got into a current and floated away, candle and all, Bingy tried to cheer us up with something about submarines.

"I wish," I said, as I shivered in my soaked clothing, "there was such a thing as an underground tank."

The Fish let a shout out of him. "That's it, Old Top. The very idea!" He jumped off the bunk into the water and we could hear him splash his way out to the gallery. In a few minutes he came back with an electric mine lamp and the sniper's shield that I had ordered to be thrown on the dump.

"I'm going to make a tank," he explained. "We'll get a trolley and put this shield on the front of it. Then we can push it up the gallery and blow that machine gun and the whole crew."

The much abused Fish had struck a real idea. We jumped at it.

A sniper's shield is made to resist bullets, and it took us two hours to punch six holes through the base of the half inch chrome steel of which it was constructed. The holes were made at intervals of two inches. We carried the shield up to the entrance of the new gallery which was by now a regular mill race. Our trolley was there, badly battered but still serviceable. The shield was soon attached to the front and reinforced with sandbags. Then we pushed the trolley on to the track. The Huns heard us and began to work the machine gun at once. The bullets rattled on the shield like hail on a tin roof.

"Get a 50-lb can of ammonal and another trolley," I whispered.

They were brought. The final detail that I attended to was the securing of two small blocks of wood that I put into my pocket. Then I crawled on to the second trolley and ensconced myself there with the can of ammonal. The Fish, crouching low, pushed our underground tank ahead of him into the new gallery and the full range of the enemy machine gun.

It was a strange journey that we made. Our progress necessarily was slow for the grade was rather heavy and the Fish found the weight of the two trolleys to be almost an overtax. The water rushed down and past us and swished around the ankles of the laboring Fish.

After we had pushed up about fifteen feet the enemy, although he could not see us, concluded that something was up and opened on us again with the machine gun. Bullets whizzed above us and around us and played a regular devil's tattoo on the shield. I crouched as flat as nature would permit and behind me the Fish doubled up like a jackknife. Through the dim he yelled into my ear: "He's trying to break the world's record on that typewriter of his." At this point he incautiously raised his head and immediately ducked down. "They've got the range—an outer high up and to the left."

I flashed on my lamp and saw that the tip of his ear had been shaved off. It was only bleeding slightly, however, for the heat of the bullet had burnt the wound. He pushed valiantly on.

The vibrations of the bullets on the shield were tremendous. By this time we were within about ten feet of the gun and I carefully lowered the can of ammonal and pushed it under the tank. Then I signalled the Fish to back up five feet. We were going to use our "tank" as partial "tamping." I now used the two wooden wedges that I had put in my pocket before starting to block the wheels of the tank. The water from the Huns' works was racing down and surging round us, so I got out my watertight match box and lit the fuse. The Fish was already seated on the second trolley and, as I gave the trolley a shove off he yelled: "Strike two! I'm hit in the ankle. Now for the home run."

The trolley started back. Remember we had no shield to cover us this time. We raced down our one in three grade, the rushing water adding to our speed, and the bullets spitting out of the darkness all around us and miraculously not hitting us. In less time than it takes to write we had reached the junction of our main gallery. The trolley left the rails and tipped up. The Fish disappeared into the torrent, I on top of him. I dragged him out and pushed him about six feet down the gallery on to the trolley which I righted.

There was a muffled chug followed instantly by the angry umph of the exploding ammonal. I felt as if I were torn out of myself—then a blank. The next thing I remember was the flavor of rum and someone rubbing my wrists and feet. I looked up and recognized Bingy who was feeding me. I felt very sore all over; in fact as if I had been passed through a separator. I began to get rid of my haziness and sensed that the water had stopped rushing. I could hear the sucking of our pumps. Beside me was the Fish, profanely rejoicing and babbling something about getting out a patent on our underground tank. He had always wanted to transfer to the tanks, he said.

"Can you understand what I'm saying?" asked Bingy. "Well, O.C. Trenches reported that the pestiferous sniper was blown hell west and crooked. It seems he was right above where we left off our digging after all and of course that meant right above the machine gun. You got gun, crew, sniper and all—and now the waters dammed up—and everything fine."

THE CANADIANS
IN SIBERIA

—May 1919—
Captain W.E. Dunham

"Look at that, will you?"

A Canadian soldier, standing at the rail of the troopship, pointed a finger across the ice-choked bay to where a huge galvanized iron warehouse with a rounded roof stood out against the grey sky of the early January morning. It was a peculiarly shaped building, what we learned later to speak of as a "godown." The outstanding feature about this particular "godown," however, was the fact that painted across it in huge black letters were the words Canadian Ordnance.

"Look at that, Old Top. Musta been expecting us!"

"I'm too blank cold to talk," grumbled his companion, getting further back from the rail. "This place is Siberia all right. Whew! I'm frozen clean to the marrow of my bones. Remember that fellow that Service wrote a poem about, that Sam McGee who got froze up? Well, I'm going to be Sam McGee the second."

It was unquestionably cold. It had been a pretty frigid trip across, in fact, right from the time that we came within hailing distance of Japan. The men—we had one thousand Canadian troops on board—were luckily a picked lot and in the very finest of condition. So they had been able to stand the rigors of the trip without real difficulty. The night before, however, when the word got round that we would dock in the morning, a high wind had sprung up as though to confirm the news that we had reached Siberia, the land of snow and ice. The morning showed a temperature of 27 below and a high wind from off shore that cut like a knife. It was none too comfortable along the rail and even the discovery that

79

Canada had already made her mark on Vladivostok to the extent of having a dock warehouse labelled as our own, failed to create much interest. For myself I was chiefly interested in the work of the icebreakers.

The harbor of Vladivostok, or "Vlady" as we soon got to calling the place, is kept open the whole winter by these energetic and sturdy little boats.

All day and all night long they weave back and forth across the harbor, cutting swaths through the ice which forms so rapidly in that climate. I understand that they never let the ice get thicker than six inches and they steam through that thickness like a keen knife through cheese. As a result the harbor is churned up and kept in navigable condition, although our ships steamed in through masses of floating ice. I found that we had been navigating a sea of ice from a distance of forty miles out. Our bows were covered with it.

As we drew in toward the dock, I found myself beside a staff officer who had come out to meet us with the pilot. He had been in the country some little time so I seized the opportunity of finding what was doing ashore.

"What's ahead of us?" I asked. "Any chance of the Bolsheviks sending armed forces to drive us out?"

He shook his head. "No," he declared, "they fight with a new kind of weapon. You'll have your hands full, I'm afraid. The Bolsheviks have sent another Battalion of Death to stay our advance, an army of women—only the members of this battalion have blonde hair and rouged cheeks and they're scattered all along the line from Vlady to Omsk."

He proceeded to give me the details of what clearly is one of the most diabolical phases of the whole war. Hordes of the most attractive women of questionable character in European Russia were gathered up and sent out to Siberia. They were promised abundance of money and their instructions were to create havoc among the Allied forces. "Which," my informant proceeded, "they succeeded in doing during the early stages of the Allied occupation. Luckily, we found out what was in the wind early and all the Canadian troops have been kept strictly within bounds."

The men were lined up along the dock after disembarkation.

The Canadians in Siberia

By this time the sun had come out but it made little difference in the temperature. It seemed to be light without warmth, a hazy glow that turned the sombre grey of the Siberian sky into a dull yellow and touched the edges of the gloomy buildings with the same almost unhealthy tint. The men had to stamp their leather "kitcheners" most vigorously and even swing their arms to keep warm.

They were wearing the full Siberian kit, which is a most sufficient and superior outfit indeed. "Yukon caps" were worn—cloth tops with a fur band which, when turned down, covered the ears and part of the face, leaving only eyes, nose and mouth visible. This was enough, more than enough for some, however. Most noses appeared too long that day and continual rubbing was required to keep them from freezing.

The cold did not seem to bother the coolie laborers, who swarmed about the landing like ants. They were muffled up in rags and were indescribably dirty. A European, as scantily clothed as these lean Mongolians, would soon have succumbed. The coolies did not seem to be even inconvenienced and they went about their task of unloading the cargo with the chatter of a thousand tongues. They worked under Russian supervisors, who kept them on the rush with sharp commands that pierced through the hubbub.

I found my staff acquaintance at my elbow with another interesting piece of information.

"Look at those poor brutes of horses," he said, pointing at the patient rows. "All that are a decent size are blind."

"How's that?" I asked.

"The owners put their eyes out to prevent them being commandeered by the authorities. Used quicklime, I understand."

It was a fact. The callous cruelty of the men who made their living out of the labor of their faithful four-footed slaves had not stopped at this infamous practice.

Vladivostok has been accumulating supplies ever since the war started. Munitions of all kinds, and civil supplies as well, billed for Russia, were sent by the Pacific route when war blocked the European frontiers of Czardom and bottled up the Dardanelles. Vlady became the neck of the Russian bottle and a serious effort was made to pour through it four times as much as its capacity allowed.

The Trans-Siberian railway, which connects Vlady with European Russia, is a single-tracked road. It could not begin to carry the freight that came in by boat. As a result the goods stocked in Vlady, awaiting shipment by rail, grew and increased and multiplied. Every available bit of space around the harbor front was utilized and huge tarpaulin-covered mounds arose on all sides.

The Canadian troops swung off through streets that were literally jammed with humanity. We took more interest in the crowds, however, than they took in us. The arrival of more foreign troops meant little to the people of Vlady. The streets were thronged but the crowds were scurrying along about their own business—the Canadians were a mere incident of their kaleidoscopic life. There were Russians and Chinese and Japanese and Czechs. There were United States troops and Jap policemen and German tradesmen. I soon learned that Vlady is at present one of the most cosmopolitan cities of the world and that every nation under the sun is represented in the street throngs. The strange feature of it was the prevalence of uniforms. My first glimpse of the streets was a little bewildering on that account. Nearly everyone seemed to be in a uniform of some kind and some of the combinations were indeed fearful and wonderful!

There were two reasons for this as I learned later. When the citizens of Vlady found that Allied armies of occupation were being poured into their city, they concluded that safety for them would be in some pretention to military status. Every man who could get a uniform, or any part thereof, promptly donned it. Sometimes only military boots were worn or a long military coat, no matter what the color or cut. Military medals glittered on breasts that had never been exposed to the foeman's steel.

Another reason given—and perhaps the main one—was that the people had nothing else to wear. Refugees had flooded across Siberia when the Red Terror began in Russia and many thousands had reached Vlady in almost destitute condition. In order to clothe them military stores were requisitioned. Perhaps some of the almost ludicrous nondescripts that we saw on the streets once ruffled it among the aristocrats of Russia. Perhaps the man we saw with canvas sacking for shoes and a ragged tunic on his back had once driven in his fine linen and furs along the Nevski Prospekt!

Here indeed does East meet West. The customs, the products, the people themselves of two different worlds converge here, making Vladivostok one of the strangest and most cosmopolitan corners of the earth.

One of the buildings we passed was the British Mission, so named because of the present use it was being put to. It was chiefly interesting to us as the scene of the last stand of the Bolsheviks in Vlady. A story is told of their characteristic treachery. When the Czechs had driven the Bolsheviki forces to take refuge in this building a white flag was shown and when a couple of Czech officers went forward to investigate, they were shot dead as they approached. In a frenzy the Czechs attacked and immediately captured the building, out of which eighteen dead Bolsheviks were taken.

There were still some signs of the engagement quite noticeable in the shattered masonry where the bullets of the attackers had struck.

The railway station was another point of interest. I visited it often later and always found throngs of refugees in the waiting rooms, both day and night. It was one of the few buildings to which the homeless could go for warmth. A companion remarked to me as we left the building one evening: "I do not know which it is hardest to stand, that atmosphere in there or the cold without. Personally I'll take my chances with the cold." Within the building the air was almost unbreathable, a sweaty human stench. Without it was bitterly cold; but I agreed with my friend.

The troops were glad indeed when they finally reached their quarters, for the cold had become so intense that not even the exertion of marching had served to keep them warm. The first sight of our quarters was very cheering—huge stone barracks that had been erected after the Russo-Japanese war. They were roomy, clean and well lighted. What was more important than all, they were splendidly heated. There were huge furnaces in each barracks, reaching clear to the ceiling and capable of heating the buildings in any weather. As the supply of coal was ample, we were always able to keep comfortably warm when inside.

There were groups of these well-built barracks around the city and vicinity with a total accommodation of 120,000.

The activities of the Siberian Expeditionary Force have been very limited. There has, in fact, been very little to do. The Bolshevik forces had been driven nearly four thousand miles back when we arrived and, as far as I know, our forces have seen little or no actual fighting. A unit of artillery was sent up to support the British force at the "front" before Omsk. Some Canadians were left in Vlady and attached to General Elmsley's headquarters staff there. The bulk of our forces, however, were stationed at East Barracks, four miles outside the city, and at Garvastai Barracks, eight miles out, which are situated on the hills surrounding a bay of the same name. It was from this bay that a Japanese fleet of cruisers shelled Vladivostok during the Russo-Japanese war. The hills are very heavily fortified to prevent any such occurrence again in the future.

At Second River, about ten miles from the city, another large Canadian detachment was quartered. Small units are stationed elsewhere along the line between the base at Vlady and the "front" at Omsk, four thousand miles away.

At best the expedition has little more activity than garrison duty. The monotony of the life is, to say the least, irksome and to these high-spirited Canadian lads after their splendid work in France it is proving very dreary and drab. They recognize that they are being well cared for and their boast is that no force in Siberia can equal the Canadians in point of equipment, organization and personnel; but that is not enough to keep them up.

"A soldier with nothing to do becomes a devil," said one of the senior officers, as soon as it became apparent that active service was out of the question. It was recognized that something would have to be done to keep them occupied. Drill and training exercises were ordered to be rigidly maintained. Steps were taken at once also to provide healthy amusements. Hockey rinks were laid out. The Y.M.C.A. had sent over a consignment of hockey equipment—enough for an eight-team league. These were supplied gratuitously to the troops and the league was organized at once. Hockey has been one of the main amusements right through the winter.

But nothing we could do served in any adequate way to mitigate the homesickness that permeates the force. If the war were still on the troops would accept their monotonous lot as part of the game. But they know that the guns are silent on the Western front, that their comrades are pouring home across the Atlantic and they long for Canada and civil life again. It is the same in all ranks.

"If I could get back home by reverting to the ranks, I'd do it in a minute," said an officer to me just before I sailed for Canada.

"If I could get out of here now," said a husky young private to me, a wistful look in his eyes, "I wouldn't stay if they offered to make me a colonel!"

They both meant it. The hunger for home is in every heart. The homesickness is quite as prevalent as the sea-sickness on the voyage out, and that is saying a great deal, for most of the men learned by experience what Irwin Cobb meant when he, in writing of sea-sickness, said: "You can't eat your chicken and keep it too."

Of course, this condition makes the menace from the harpies still more intense. This was, we found, the great problem to be solved—to keep our men out of their clutches. I want to allay at once the anxiety that must be felt in Canada on this score. The difficulty has been solved and the men have been protected; but the menace is always there.

Too much praise cannot be given the authorities, military and medical, for the network of restriction and education they have thrown about the troops. The medical men from the first did not give any encouragement to the idea of cure or prevention or treatment of any kind. Their primal warning was "stay in barracks." The military authorities placed the men in areas far removed from centres where the Bolsheviks were carrying on their diabolical attack. Places known to be frequented by the emissaries were placed out of bounds by most of the Allied armies.

Realizing the value of the social work of the Y.M.C.A., General Elmsley requested the increase of its establishment to three times its present strength. In doing so, he remarked: "I consider this increase in establishment necessary owing to the fact that the force is scattered, which makes it most important that a larger number of

85

recreation rooms, canteens, etc., be established. I also consider that, by increasing the opportunities for entertainment, the men will be kept out of town to a greater extent and this fact will reduce the number of venereal cases. This necessary personnel should be recruited and be dispatched from Canada at the earliest possible date."

People in Canada, I find, are asking what have we got to do with Siberia? Why should our troops be there? In the first place they are there at the request of Great Britain. They are not necessarily a punitive force but they are to hold Siberia from becoming the bloody ruin that European Russia is today. There are huge military stores on the docks and in the "godowns" of Vladivostok. Should these fall into the hands of any particular political faction they would be used to exterminate their opponents, for the first thing the Russian thinks of when opposed is force, brute force. He believes implicitly in the now exploded German philosophy that the end justifies the means. Moreover since the military occupation of Siberia by the Allies, and particularly the arrival of the British including the Canadians, the political factions have not dared to resort to force. They are proceeding in a more peaceful manner to sift their theories and change their leaders until they obtain what they want. They know they want a new form of Government but they are far from one mind as to the form it should take.

The people of Siberia resent the presence of the Allied troops there, despite the fact that the occupation is the only thing that prevents carnage and anarchy. They regarded us as intruders. They probably still do. Some of them, who were opposed to the Bolshevists, were anxious that our forces should be employed to attack the Reds in Russia. Our Allies, the Czecho-Slovaks, had grown impatient with the inactivity and were threatening to fight their way through Russia to their own home land again, just as they fought their way out. The Czechs are splendid fighting men and deserve a great deal of credit. They will withdraw almost certainly from Siberia this spring.

The people of Siberia, as I said before, are striving to get a better form of Government but they do not know yet what form it is to take. They are all Bolshevists in the meaning of the word as it is

86

used here. A Bolshevist, with them, is one who wants a change.

If the Allies should withdraw before a stable Government is established it would mean that that vast land, so long a land of sorrow and suffering, would become a bloody riot from end to end. If they stay until the people have settled upon the most workable method of Government there is no reason why it should not become in the very near future a bright and prosperous country, similar in life as it is similar in topography and climate to our own Northwest.

And so, the Canadian Expeditionary Force has the consolation of knowing that its enforced stay in this now dreary and uninteresting country is serving a tremendously valuable purpose.

SECOND WORLD WAR

—Europe—

WHAT WE LEARNED AT DIEPPE

—October 1, 1942—
Wallace Reyburn

London (by cable)—Was or was not Dieppe a success? Was it worth the high sacrifice in men? What were the lessons learned about our own tactics and those of the enemy?

At this writing Combined Operations Headquarters is working hard at sifting detailed reports of the operations of August 19 and the final findings are not yet ascertained. As General McNaughton told me when I talked to him a few days after the raid, it would be unwise to draw conclusions until the full evidence has been accumulated, because the lesson

Allied dead on the beach.

learned from one service might give a completely wrong picture of the whole.

Even when the Combined Operations assessment is finalized, the full story of Dieppe will be unpublished until after the war. However, there are certain things we can say and certain conclusions we can draw.

In choosing Dieppe for this first large-scale raid, Combined Operations, who planned it, selected what is possibly one of the most strongly defended points on the French coast. We could have landed a force as large as this in many other parts of France with relative ease, but it is doubtful that we would have learned very much from doing so.

In attacking such a strong point as Dieppe, both Combined Operations and the Canadians knew that casualties would be heavy, but this fact in no way detracted from the eagerness of the latter to be the first chosen for a large-scale raid.

If we had gone into France cold with our full force but without the experience of Dieppe, we would have been like a boxer who runs out of his corner, takes a wild slug at his opponent without first sizing him up through some sparring.

That is the first thing Dieppe taught us.

Another lesson driven home to every last man in the raid was the necessity for the most meticulously detailed plan of operations of this kind. The plan for this attack was a honey. I remember the day when Major Cliff Wallace, Army Public Relations Officer, got us correspondents together in the summerhouse of an orchard near a town somewhere in England. There was a sentry posted outside the door. Wallace outlined what was going to take place. We could feel the mounting surge of excitement and we thrilled at the brilliance of the audacious plan. I am not allowed to tell anything about the detail of the plan but I can tell you something of how it was formulated.

Broadly speaking, six main factors were taken into consideration. First, weather, tide, moon, etc. Second, how long it would take the Germans to bring up reinforcements. Third, air coverage. Four, sea patrols. Five, composition of attacking forces. Six, security.

I know that countless times during the raid the great need of careful planning was brought home to me. So many things had to be brought into consideration, from patrolling the sky to having brandy on destroyers ready for the wounded. Timing was the vital factor. Everything worked out to the minute.

Our troops had to know the area where they were going to fight thoroughly. They learned about it from aerial photographs taken by reconnaissance planes, from holiday postcards, from interviews with people familiar with the district, from models of the coastline and the town built by Combined Operations. Our troops were versed so thoroughly in their subject that when they got ashore they could remark with truth that they knew the place as well as their home town.

While in the thick of it, an officer from Weyburn, Saskatchewan, who had never been out of Canada before, told me how to find my way to the British Hotel and the Grand Hotel. He sounded as if he had spent every summer vacation at Dieppe.

I was six-and-a-half hours ashore, going in with the South Saskatchewan Regiment [at Pourville, just west of Dieppe], and another thing that was fully proven in those six-and-a-half hours was the Canadian Army's policy of having young commanding officers. The average age of the lieutenant-colonels in the Dieppe show was thirty-two. Their leadership was an inspiration.

The way Lieut.-Col. Cecil Merritt, of Vancouver, conducted himself is typical of what the young leaders did on the raid. He is only thirty-three. A former football star, he is of an athletic build with big broad shoulders and square-cut features. A lawyer before he went to Royal Military College, he joined the Army in 1935.

Across a 200-yard bridge, upon which the enemy concentrated everything from snipers' bullets to artillery fire, he led his men back and forth no fewer than six times. He showed how cool he was about the whole thing by carrying his tin hat in his hand. I watched him doing this. I watched him, too, as he stood with the signalers at the Command Post, controlling operations, calm, collected and unflurried. He was a perfect example to his men.

When the last men were leaving the beach, Colonel Merritt was down there with them. He told them to take cover behind the breakwater while awaiting the barges that came in to take them off. Standing erect on the rocks, he organized their getting to the boats.

When he was satisfied this job was done, armed with a weapon in each hand, he returned to the town where German reinforcements were penetrating and endangering our men on the beach. He said as he started off, "I am going to get even for what they have done to my regiment."

Another lesson we learned is that battle drill training, criticized in many quarters, is the perfect way of training soldiers for modern war. For instance, after the South Saskatchewan Regiment had stormed the beach, got through the wire and into town, we discovered that the housecleaning methods our men had been taught in battle drill were perfect.

I got a thrill seeing our troops keep a house covered with Bren guns and Tommy guns, and other men battering doors in with the butts of rifles and still others clambering into windows, exactly as we had watched them hundreds of times in England during training.

It was a joy to see the Saskatchewan lads bringing in at the bayonet point fourteen sullen German soldiers with their hands raised. If there were ever any doubts about battle drill being the right type of training, they should be dispelled now. Our boys cleared those houses with the same speed and thoroughness as if they had been clearing away houses ever since they joined the Army.

Something else proven at Dieppe was the fact that we have air superiority in the West. Recently the RAF had been undertaking countless sweeps trying to entice the Luftwaffe out to fight, but without success. At Dieppe we brought them out—which was one objective of the raid—and the biggest aerial battle since the Battle of Britain resulted.

In the Battle of Britain the Germans sent hundreds of planes over as a possible prelude to the invasion of this Island, and these our Air Force smashed. At Dieppe the RAF proved that it can now furnish a successful air umbrella for our invading troops.

Nevertheless, there is criticism current that our bombers were not used as effectively as they could have been. One of the main things which held up the landing of troops on the main beaches of Dieppe was heavy fire from strongly fortified pillboxes. The

What We Learned at Dieppe

Commandos on the extreme right flank were able to spike half-a-dozen six-inch guns, but when the Germans knew of our presence on the main beaches and were on the alert, the only way to have put their forts out of action would seem to have been by bombing.

What bombing was done at Dieppe was on a small scale and was not effective against the tremendously heavily concreted forts. One feels that what were needed there were dive bombers or heavy bombers carrying big loads, going in immediately before our troops landed.

Another criticism is that the land forces consisted entirely of infantry, tanks and Bren gun carriers plus engineers and other ancillaries. Apart from the Navy and the tank guns there was no artillery. Moreover the naval guns were not heavy enough and in some cases their trajectory was too low so that their missiles flew ineffectively over the town.

It is probable that the reason artillery was not landed was because the planners wanted to have a lightly equipped and speedily mobile fighting force along Commando lines.

Practically every minute of the six-and-a-half hours we were ashore, we learned things about German defenses and realized improvements that we could make in our own methods of attack. This was the main objective of the raid.

For instance, when we were once up on the beach and tackling the barbed wire, we found out just how Jerry goes about building barbed wire entanglements. It is extremely heavy wire, packed very tightly together in ugly masses of barbs.

One thing that impressed me about German defenses was the deadliness of their mortar fire. Whether they were using three- or four-inch mortars I cannot say, but I do know that their range was long and their accuracy of fire amazing.

When the Germans started pounding our first shore headquarters with mortar shells, we decided to move across a grass patch behind the house. Established there, we were interrogating prisoners when a mortar shell landed bang in the middle of the grass square.

I luckily was lying down. The blast sent me flying and I felt what seemed to be pebbles hitting my back like little stones thrown up from an automobile wheel. I didn't think anything more about it until later, when my trousers and shirt began to feel damp. It was blood and the "pebbles" had been shrapnel.

My ears were ringing from the blast of mortar shell explosions and, in fact, my ears were ringing throughout the six-and-a-half hours I spent amid the street fighting in Dieppe. Fortunately few of our men suffered casualties from this particular explosion, but four German prisoners were killed and I saw their bodies lying there stiff and pallid when I departed from the town hours later.

As the battle developed it became obvious that the Germans were able to follow Battalion Headquarters wherever it went.

They were able to do this by one of three methods as far as I can gather. Naturally, the defenders would have the ranges fixed beforehand on all places likely to be used as our headquarters. Secondly, Focke-Wulfs were flying over us constantly and whenever they appeared over our headquarters mortar fire seemed to follow almost immediately. Thirdly, the Germans may have been able to get the range from our wireless sets.

The Nazis' Runstedt Plan of Defenses, as publicized widely in the British Press, was definitely in action at Dieppe.

This plan is to have few troops in the coast areas, but to have the beaches and shoreline heavily covered from strong pillboxes and batteries. The aim is to suck invaders in, pound them while they are there and then bring up heavy reinforcement of land troops to mop them up. I had a front seat viewing the enemy's system of defense in action though; fortunately, through our excellent planning we were too quick for them and after our job was done, reinforcements were unable to find many of us there to mop up. We were out and on our way as scheduled.

At Dieppe, Jerry didn't have strong concentrations of troops in the forward area and it was not until we got farther back, behind the town, that we encountered them in any numbers.

The Germans are formidable soldiers but going purely on evidence seen with my own eyes, when it comes to a man-to-man struggle they just haven't got the guts.

It is popular to say that Germans can't stand cold steel. I had heard that many times and I wondered if it were true. Like the man from Missouri, I wanted to see for myself. Well, at Dieppe I did.

Germans are like a certain type of underworld gangsters who are brave men when behind a Tommy gun, but deprive them of their weapons and they are yellow rats. When in strongly fortified pillboxes with machine guns and heavier guns pouring venom on approaching Canadians, the Germans were in their element, but time and time again when the prospect of hand encounters loomed, they ran out of their pillboxes with upraised arms.

Remember that they had everything on their side. They were in strongly fortified positions. The Canadians were the attacking force and had to expose themselves when advancing. The Germans had heavy reinforcements coming up behind them to give support. They were fighting on their own terrain and they knew it perfectly. Yet, on one occasion, I saw a group of Canadians approaching a machine gun nest atop a small hill. Before they were halfway up, two Jerries ran out from cover, weapons still in their raised hands, shouting "Kamerad!"

We learned much at Dieppe. So did the Germans. They know now that when they are up against Canadians, they are up against Fighting Men.

One question much asked is did the Germans know we were coming? The chance encounter with our left flank of approaching ships by German E-boats must surely have placed shore batteries on the alert, but there seems no evidence that the Germans were specially preparing for us before this.

As anyone knows who has studied the tactics of invading from the sea, there are only certain times governed by the moon, tides and weather that a landing can effectively be made, and it is natural to suppose the Germans have their shorelines most heavily garrisoned at these times.

At the beginning of this article I mentioned security as one of the six main factors taken into consideration in planning a raid. I can relate a personal experience to show how closely security was guarded. When an Army officer first invited me to go on a "trip" he told me I would need, among other things, a water bottle—which I didn't have.

I was told by the officer to buy that water bottle—not in a

downtown store—but in an isolated suburban shop. The reason was because a friend might see me doing so and put two and two together.

The success of the Dieppe raid was borne out by the fact that since their initial derision, the Germans have not minimized it.

The Germans are making small beer out of the significance of the raid because they know, as we know, that the United Nations can land troops and tanks in France and that we have air superiority to do it. But if there should be any Nazis who feel that the Canadians who returned are sitting in camps feeling they have had their fingers burnt, I'd like to take them down among the men.

What the Nazis would see there would not please them. To give an idea of how I feel about it, I might mention that when I talked to the men and heard them say they were ready to do it again tomorrow, I came away feeling so thrilled and inspired that there were little quivers going up and down my spine.

I wanted to shout from the rooftops.

Wallace Reyburn was a correspondent for the Montreal Standard.

"BUZZ" BEURLING

—January 15, 1943—
Webb Waldron

"We went up to intercept a mixed raid of bombers and fighters," said Beurling. "We got over them, went through the fighters to get at the bombers. Then the bombers turned and beat it for Sicily. So we were left with just the fighters."

"Where was this, George?" asked Beurling's father. "Right over Malta?"

"No, just off the island. The odds were about eight to one against us—"

"Eight to one!" I exclaimed.

"Oh, that's not uncommon," said young George Beurling, DSO, DFC, DFM and Bar, Canadian ace of the RAF,

---

Flying Officer "Buzz" Beurling posing at his cockpit.

lifting his lanky six-foot-one up in his Montreal hospital bed and shoving back his mop of yellow hair, "I've been up when the odds were twenty to one. But in this case it was only eight to one."

"Briefly, what happened?" I asked.

"I went after a group of four—two Jerries and two Eyeties. I hit one—blew pieces off him. He made a couple of spins, went down, and crashed just off shore. Then I attacked another and blew him up. Then two Messerschmitt 109s passed under me, but I half rolled onto them and went under them and gave one a burst in his belly. Just as he went down, another 109 attacked me and I damaged him, but didn't bring him down. That was three, and one damaged. I came down to refuel. Then another raid came over, and I went up and we attacked six 109s. A couple of our fellows got hit and had to bail out, but I sailed in and destroyed another Jerry— he fell into the sea. That made four. Then I attacked another and he streamed black smoke, but I didn't see him hit the deck. Well, that made four in the bag that morning—and one probable. So," said Beurling, with a grin, "they thought I ought to take the afternoon off. They thought I looked kind of tired."

"Were you?"

"No, not much."

Beurling's father looked across at me, his blue eyes sparkling with satisfaction.

One, two, three, four enemy planes brought down in a forenoon—many a fighter would consider that a good bag for a season—and Beurling ticked them off as casually as if they had been four partridges.

This lad George Beurling, now only twenty-one years old, is a phenomenon worth study. Not alone because his total bag up to date of twenty-nine enemy planes brought down, plus three probables and nine damaged, is very close to the top RAF record and the best by far any Canadian or American can show in this war, but chiefly for two other reasons.

One: he is man-in-the-air incarnate, completely a creature of the air, more completely than I dreamed any human being could be. Since he was six, this lad has been fascinated by the air, scheming every hour of every day how to get into the air and stay there, up in the air constantly since he was fifteen, a pilot at seventeen, and now at twenty-one a master of the air, unhappy on the ground, happy in the air, thinking of his life and his future only in terms of the air. Thus Beurling is a sharp clear-cut symbol of the future.

Two: he is the war killer incarnate—hard, cold, ruthless when engaged in airfighting. Beurling will tell you that his superb record is partly due to luck, but actually it is due to the fact that he has studied his job of killing the enemy, and keeps constantly studying it, and pursues the job with relentless precision. He is, in fact, what every man of the armed forces of the United Nations must be if we are to win this war.

Beurling puts it this way: "There is no room for stupid soft-heartedness in this war. The enemy is trying to get you, it is up to you to get him first—hard and plenty."

George Beurling has been putting this conviction into practice with calculated scientific skill.

When he says, "I blew him up," "I gave him a burst," it doesn't mean he simply cut loose at an enemy plane, hoping to bring it down. It means that—whenever possible—he has fired at the enemy plane from a certain intended distance, at an intended moment and an intended angle, and often at an intended spot in the enemy plane.

His first bag is an example. It was in April 1942. For months, at training camps in England, he had been itching to get into action, and then suddenly his squadron was assigned as part of a daylight sweep of Spitfires into France, escorting bombers in a raid on Lille. Beurling asked to be put last in the squadron—the most dangerous spot. "There wasn't much action over France at that time," he said, "and I thought if I was last man I might see some fun."

A squadron leader doesn't like to ask a man to take last position, Beurling explained. If the man happens to get knocked off, then the leader will feel responsible. But if a man volunteers, it's fine. No one's to blame but himself. The trip to the objective was comparatively uneventful, but on the way back to England a swarm of Focke-Wulf 190s attacked the sweep. Five of them attacked Beurling.

"One after another tried to get on my tail," said Beurling, "and I kept whipping around to get them off." Then by a trick of his own Beurling almost stopped his plane in midair. The Focke-Wulf which was behind him at that moment shot past and crossed in front of him. "By the speed he passed me, I judged he was going at 450 miles an hour," said Beurling. "So at about 300 yards I allowed him four and a half rings and gave him a two and a half second burst."

The six guns of the Spitfire—two 20 millimetre cannon and four .303 machine guns—are arranged so that their fire converges at about 300 yards. That is the ideal distance. If a plane is travelling 100 miles an hour across your sights, you aim the diameter of your ring sight ahead of it. This Focke-Wulf was going 450 miles an hour across Beurling's sights, so he aimed a distance of four and a half rings ahead. In other words, he fired so that the enemy plane and his bullets and shells met in the air at the same spot and the same moment. It all happened in seconds, but it was done with expert precision. "The Jerry exploded," said Beurling, "—went down in a trail of black smoke."

When George was a kid of six, in Verdun, a Montreal suburb, he came home on the run one day sobbing: "They're chasing me!" His father said: "George, I'm going to teach you how to defend yourself." He took the boy downtown and finally found a pair of little boxing gloves that fitted him. "I used to get down on the floor and teach him how to box," said his father. "Soon he was good enough to give me a good fight. I said 'George, I don't want you to look for a fight, but I don't want you to run away.' "

Since then George has never run away. He has let the other fellow do the running. When I asked him whether he was ever afraid, as for instance when once he was alone over Malta against twenty enemy planes, he said, wrinkling his brow: "Why, mister, in a fight I don't have time to be afraid."

Incidentally, George doesn't smoke or drink. His family brought him up that way and he thinks abstinence is a good thing for his airfighting.

At the same age of six his father made him a model airplane and from that moment George began to watch the skies and dream

"Buzz" Beurling

Beurling meets Prime Minister Mackenzie King
in Ottawa, Nov. 1942.

of flying. When he was eleven he began to hang around the nearest airdrome, the Curtiss-Reid Flying School at Cartierville. He said to his father: "How can I get over that fence?" "Well," his father said, "get one leg over, and when they get used to seeing one leg over, get the other leg over, and then jump down inside." So George did, and presently he was a pet of the pilots and mechanics. They let him hang around and ask questions because they saw he was no idler but really interested and intelligent. Pilots took him up on flights. His passion for planes and flying got him the nickname "Buzz," which has always stuck to him. By the time he

103

was fourteen, he was taking flying lessons. He paid for them by selling newspapers and doing odd jobs around the airdrome, washing off planes, helping roll them in and out of the hangar, running errands for pilots. His greatest pal and mentor, a bush pilot named Ted Hogan, used to take George along on trips into the bush country north of Montreal, delivering freight and passengers to mining camps, and on these trips George often handled the stick.

"When George was fourteen or fifteen," said his father, "I remember when we'd be walking along the street he would suddenly burst out, 'Pop, do you know what Rickenbacker did when he had four Jerries on his tail?' Or 'Remember Richthofen, that big German ace? Do you know what he did when he was outnumbered three to one?' George studied the air battles in the other war and he could describe and argue about the tactics of all the leading fliers. He ate, drank and slept airplanes and especially airfighting."

To test George, his father tried to interest him in his own profession, that of a commercial artist, but George couldn't see it. The air was for him. An uncle, a doctor, offered to put George through medical school. His parents favored that; his mother, especially, thought George had the makings of a surgeon. But George couldn't see it. The air, the sky and its freedom, was for him.

In 1939, when he was 17, just about the time he got a flying permit, he lit off for Vancouver, riding the rods, and tried to enlist in the Chinese Air Force. "I thought I'd see some good fighting out there," he said with a grin. Balked in his attempt at Vancouver, he tried to get to San Francisco, planning to hop a ship to China. "I knew if I got out to China, I could get into the Air Force," he said. But U.S. officials stopped him at the border—he had no papers and no money—and sent him home.

He tried to enlist with the Finland Air Force. His dad, who is of Scandinavian ancestry, blocked that. He tried to enlist in the Royal Canadian Air Force. They advised him to go back and finish high school—he had another year.

"So," he said, "I thought I'd try the RAF."

A friend told him that there was a munitions ship down at the docks needing deckhands. He rushed down, signed on and sailed. This was the summer of '40. It was an exciting trip. The convoy was attacked several times. George's ship narrowly missed being torpedoed. Landing in Glasgow, George tried to enlist in the RAF, but in his hurry he had come away without his certificated logbook giving his flying time. RAF men advised him to hop home and get it. So he signed on for the return voyage, got home, grabbed his papers, signed on again with the same ship, said good-bye again to his family who by this time were reconciled to his ambition, and was off again for Britain.

During his RAF training in England, George paid special attention to two things. He trained his eyesight. "I would pick out a hill in the distance," he said, "then a tree on that hill, then a branch of that tree, and bring my eyes to focus on it and try to make out the details as quickly as possible. By doing that again and again, I found I could spot aircraft in the sky and distinguish what they were quicker than other fellows could."

At Malta, it was said that he could always spot a squadron of approaching enemy planes before anybody else. Also he constantly trained his eyes to take in the whole heavens in one searching and regularly repeated glance. "You've got to do that constantly when there may be enemy planes about," he said. "Especially you've got to watch the sky above you—that's the dangerous place—and when you look, make sure there's nothing there, or if there is, *what* it is."

He paid special attention to shooting. In Canada, knowing he was going to be an air fighter, he and a friend had practiced with an old Vicker machine gun. Especially he studied "deflection shooting," believing from his study of air combats that it was a vital factor—possibly the most vital—in success in the air. Deflection shooting means shooting which takes into account the angle of your plane to the enemy plane, their respective speeds and the distance from each other. If you were always dead on the tail of the other fellow and always got him dead in the bull's eye when you fired, you wouldn't need to know anything about deflection shooting. "But," asks George Beurling, "how often does that happen? Most times you are coming at him on an angle and he has one speed, and you another, so there are several factors to take into account. Without knowing deflection shooting, I'd have a bag of five or six today instead of twenty-nine."

Beurling has become such a master of deflection shooting that the British Air Ministry has now a book he has written on the subject, for the use of RAF pilots.

In getting his second bag, Beurling had a narrow squeak. Determination, quick wit and skill brought him out of it. His squadron was on a fighter sweep over the French coast near Calais. Attacked by a swarm of FW 190s, they were outnumbered five or six to one. Beurling, again in the rear by his own request, got all the fun he wanted. "I got it from both sides," he said, "cannon shells and machine-gun bullets. The plane bucked and shuddered with the impact. I thought it was going out of control. Shrapnel pierced the cockpit and got me in the ribs. My port cannon and machine guns were knocked out of action, my starboard cannon was knocked loose so it was pointing down and flapping in the breeze, my only effective guns were my two starboard machine guns. A shell burst inside one wing, blowing it up to three times its size, so the whole lift of the wing was thrown off—the wing was actually wobbling. And I was out over the middle of the Channel. I thought for a minute I'd have to bail out. Then the Jerries who were on my tail turned and flew after me, but the sun must have blinded them as I thought it would. They flew right on over me without seeing me. I gave the middle one a burst with my two machine guns. He was only fifty yards ahead of me. I couldn't hear the guns, as only two were firing, and thought I'd run out of ammunition, but he blew up, and the other Jerries beat it for France."

And George staggered home toward England…his plane riddled, the engine shot through and through and leaking, one wing almost falling off…but he got home.

A month or so later, he went to Malta. A fellow he knew had been detailed there, but didn't want to go because he had a wife in England, so Beurling volunteered in his place. "I understood Malta was a hot spot, so I thought I might get some good fighting."

At that time, last summer, and indeed all through early fall, Malta was the hottest spot on earth. Raids of German and Italian bombers and fighters would come over from Sicily sixty miles distant, seven or more times a day, beginning at four in the morning, day after day. Then there would be a few days' lull, and it would begin again. There would be perhaps fifteen bombers and from fifty to one hundred and fifty fighters, and against this the island's defenders often had only eight, ten or twelve planes. Once there were only four Spitfires on hand to protect the island.

The purpose of the attacks was to destroy the airdrome and the shipping, and make Malta ineffective as a base from which air attacks could be launched in aid of the armies in Libya. But due to the brilliant defense by the RAF, the enemy signally failed to destroy Malta. In this defense, Buzz Beurling played a star role. He destroyed twenty-seven enemy aircraft and helped boost the total of his squadron to over three hundred planes brought down—the best record of any fighting squadron in the world.

On account of the nearness of the airdromes from which the enemy took off, the advance warning was very short. Even if the RAF felt sure a raid would be coming at a certain hour, they couldn't send fighters up ahead of time to meet it, because of the shortage of petrol. The Spitfires had to remain on the ground till the raid was actually reported. Then they took off.

"It would take us about ten minutes to get up to twenty thousand feet, maybe fifteen to get to thirty thousand," said Beurling. "After we got in the air, the airdrome would let us know what was coming. It might be radio, 'Boys, there's some Jerries coming,' and in that case we would look alive, but they might say, 'Boys, there's some Ice-cream Merchants coming over, take it easy.' Then we could relax. The Eyeties are comparatively easy to shoot down. Oh, they're brave enough. In fact, I think they have more courage than the Germans, but their tactics aren't so good. They are very good fliers, but they try to do clever acrobatics and looping. But the Eyeties will stick it even if things are going against them, whereas the Jerries will run."

Beurling would watch the flying of an enemy squadron and pick out the really good ones and go for them. "After a pilot has made one or two turns you can tell if he is really good and worthy of a fight," said Beurling. The really good ones, he explained, are the boys to get rid of first, because they will wait outside and at the right moment come in, *whish*, and knock you out.

On one occasion he engaged a number of enemy fighters that were escorting Junkers 88 bombers and shot down two. In the evening of the same day he went up to help repel another raid and shot down another fighter at 800 yards. "I elevated my guns to get him at that range. I wasn't sure I had him at first but he was seen to fly ten miles out to sea and explode.

"I had a wonderful ground crew," he went on. "They deserved as much credit as I did. They always kept my plane in perfect shape. Sometimes when I came down riddled full of holes, they spent half the night patching up my ship so I could go up again in the morning."

Of course it is more valuable to bring down a bomber than a fighter, Beurling said, but a fighter is more fun, because it can give you a better scrap. He learned just where to hit a bomber to knock it out.

"Suppose you hit one in the bomb rack?" I said.

Beurling's face lighted up. "Then it's really good, the whole thing goes up with a bang!"

As Beurling developed his tactics and his system of deflection shooting, he began to knock them off with a sureness and regularity that astonished and delighted his pals. It was said at Malta that if there was anything in the sky when Beurling went up, he would get it.

Once last August he was up with another fighter and the other man's engine developed trouble and he had to go down, leaving Beurling alone facing twenty enemy fighters. They poured a hail of bullets into him. One got under him and put a cannon shot in the belly of his ship, wounding Beurling with shrapnel in the heel. The tail of his plane was riddled, the top of his cockpit shot away, but his guns kept firing. "I got one of them," he said, "then the others kind of faded away. I think they were running out of gas."

Not long after that, he and another pilot were mixed up with fifteen. Beurling shot down one Messerschmitt, then all the rest of the enemy came for him riddling him with bullets. Suddenly his engine conked out. He would have bailed out, but he found that he had picked up somebody else's parachute—the harness was very loose and Beurling was afraid that, if he jumped, he would be brought up with such a jolt that he might rupture himself. So he put his ship's nose down and glided precipitously to the island, a twenty-five thousand foot drop. Malta is a very difficult place on which to make a crash landing, for the island is all divided up into small fields separated by high stone walls. To hit one of those walls would be fatal. Beurling picked out the biggest field he could see, one that looked little bigger than a big backyard, and dove for that.

"I had seen a couple of crash landings in the movies here in Canada, and I noticed that they always took the force of the crash on one wing. So I stuck one wing down and when we hit, I hardly felt the shock," he said. "My plane was smashed, but all the damage I got was my arm ripped open and a few scratches."

He caught a truck ride back to the airdrome, had his arm sewed up, and in half an hour he was up again in the thick of another raid. "We were short of pilots that day," he said.

Beurling's mother, who happened to be in the hospital room as he was telling this part of the story, looked at her son and sighed with relief. Then she said: "What about night fighting on Malta, George? Did you have much of that?"

Beurling rose up in bed excitedly. "It's a wonderful show! Best on earth! Lights, red, green and yellow from the shells, red strings of flame, 'onions,' they call them, like great yellow fingers—aircraft caught in the searchlights—aircraft falling in flames, flaming pieces falling off and being caught by the wind! Oh, Mom, it's really great! When they drop their incendiaries they just cover the whole island, it's like liquid hot metal, one big solid mass. You see high explosives hit the aircraft and explode in a deep red glow! And you're up there too—"

Now Beurling was standing up beside his bed, his face glowing, his blue eyes shining, a tall blond Viking of the air.

"—sometimes your own anti-aircraft guns pick you up and cut loose. Once I was up at night looking for Junkers bombers and I saw shells curving up and then turning and coming toward me. I thought they were firing at a Junker, but then I realized they were firing at me! They thought I was a Jerry! I radioed down to quit it and they radioed back, 'Okay.' Oh, it's terrific, and wonderful! I wish I was back there this minute!"

He sank back in bed.

As Beurling's score rose at Malta, he got citation after citation. First, the Distinguished Flying Medal, then a bar to that medal. He was offered a commission, but for a time refused it, saying frankly that he wanted to remain a sergeant. But later he was persuaded to accept a commission as Pilot Officer, equivalent to Second Lieutenant. Then he was awarded the Flying Cross. "A relentless fighter whose determination has won the admiration of his colleagues," said this last citation.

Because of the strain of constant air raids day and night, other fighter pilots on Malta worked on alternate days, one day on, one day off, but "Buzz" Beurling worked straight through, "because," he says, "I loved it." Other pilots could stand only two months or so of it at a stretch, then had to get away on leave. Beurling was there almost five months straight and probably would be there yet if he hadn't been shot down, wounded.

On a day in October, Beurling went up in a squadron of eight fighters to meet a raid of bombers and fighters.

"I spotted them coming from the east," he said, "and we climbed to get above them. My leader destroyed one fighter, No. 2 damaged another, and I half rolled onto a bomber, hit him and set him afire; his wing fell off and he spun down. But just as he fell, the gunner got a shot at me from below—wounded me in the arm and fingers. Then I saw a Messerschmitt attacking my leader. I gave him a couple of seconds' burst; he spun into the sea. Then I heard two Spitfires calling for help down below. I went down in a power dive at about 600 miles an hour, got under the whole formation of enemy planes, came up under one Jerry and blew off one of his wings. But another had followed down; I didn't think anybody could be as fast, but he was, and he gave me a burst, shot my controls away and put cannon shells into the belly of my plane. Shrapnel got me in the foot. There I was at eighteen thousand feet, my engines out of control, doing a power dive in spirals down toward the sea. My engine was on fire, flames coming over toward me. I tried to climb out of the cockpit, but the way I was spinning, centrifugal force pressed me into my seat. I fought to get out and at the last minute I did get out and jump. Another split second and it would have been too late."

The power dive had taken him from eighteen thousand feet to one thousand feet above the sea in an unimaginably brief tick of time. His parachute opened. He floated gently down into the Mediterranean. A power launch rushed out from shore and picked him up. His foot was bleeding badly; shrapnel had cut an artery. He went right to the operating room. While he lay in hospital, he was awarded the DSO, an honor usually reserved for senior officers.

Shortly afterward the RCAF asked that Beurling, Canada's greatest air hero of this war, be granted leave to come home. He came—narrowly missing death in a plane crash at Gibraltar which killed fifteen of his fellow passengers—and I found him chafing in a hospital bed, crazy to get back into action. When he gets on his pins, he will make a tour of Canada talking to young air recruits, telling them what airfighting is like, what to look out for in a fight, how to train for fighting. "But I want to get back to Malta," he said.

By the end of the war "Buzz" Beurling, named one of the top ten Allied pilots in the war, had shot down 31 enemy aircraft. But he died in mysterious circumstances in 1948, in his tenth crash. It happened while piloting a transport plane before landing in Rome, en route eventually for Israel where he planned to fight for the fledgling state. His grave is in Israel.

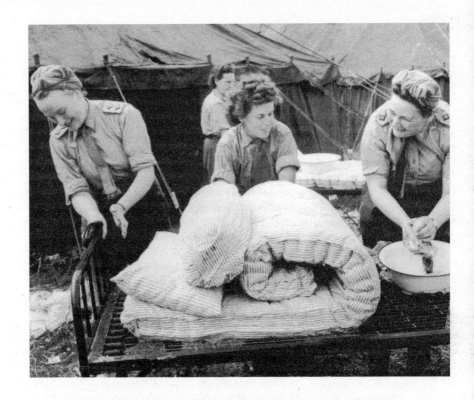

FRONT LINE HOSPITAL

—September 15, 1943—
Peter Stursberg

Nurses washing beds at Canadian General Hospital.

Algiers (by cable)—Cicadas crackled among the olive trees. Underfoot the earth was grey and spent-looking as though all its life had been sapped by the heat. It was the hottest time of the day and the Canadian nurse looked like a cool wraith in her light-blue uniform as she stepped across the grove. One moment she was in blazing light and the next in dappled shadow.

I can't remember what I said to Nursing Sister Elizabeth Lawson, Saint John, N.B., or what she said when we first met. I think I must have stood there under the

olive trees with my mouth open like a stage-struck yokel. I was gaping at her fresh appearance as she had a look about her as though she
had just come out of a beauty parlor to be met by a nippy fall breeze.
It just could not happen in Sicily.

Paul Johnson, CBC engineer, and I had just landed on the
island. I was returning to the front after making a number of broadcasts from North Africa. It was a triumph getting to Sicily with
portable recording equipment but we still had to reach the Canadian front which was some 100 miles away.

An ambulance drove across the field to a transport plane
parked directly in front of the hut and began unloading wounded
soldiers. I walked over and saw the red patches on the sleeves of the
men. They lay smoking and chatting under one of the plane's
wings where they had been placed before being loaded into the
plane. The ambulance was returning empty and we asked the
British medical captain if we could hop a ride to the Canadian
front. He said yes but pointed out that the ambulance was not
going far. However, we could keep changing ambulances, he said,
and eventually get up to the front line.

"You see," he said, "we run a sort of bus service from the front
and there are all kinds of stops—such as advance surgical centres,
casualty clearing stations and field hospitals where the wounded
get attention and change buses. This airfield is the last stop."

We lugged our portable equipment to the empty ambulance
and shoved it in between two cots. We clambered in the back of
the vehicle and it started down the dirt road but there was so much
dust we couldn't see where we were going. When the ambulance
turned onto a paved road we saw limestone walls and olive groves
unfolding behind us. But the vehicle had not far to go and in a
short while we stopped at an air evacuation centre.

There I met Nursing Sister Lawson. I should not have been surprised at seeing Canadian nurses in Sicily as we knew that this
Canadian General Hospital unit had landed. At the front we
always talked about going down to see the girls but there was
always another advance, another captured town, or another battle
to write about and we never did get back to see them.

I must have blurted something inane such as, "Well, what are

113

you doing here?" She told me that she and five other nurses had been sent to help the British at this air evacuation centre for the time being.

"If you are riding ambulances to the front," she said, "you will see the rest of the girls from the General Hospital. They're not far from here."

The Canadian nurses were living under canvas—three to a tent. They were sleeping in camp beds and washing in canvas basins set under trees whose branches served as towel racks. Their quarters were just like the men's in Sicily except that in each tent there was a table covered with a bright-colored cloth on which were bottles of scent and silver-mounted portraits. There were even vases full of flowers. The nurses also had their own mess tent with wicker chairs which the British had scrounged somewhere.

"We have lots of air raids here because we are close to the airfield," Sister Anna Cran, Winnipeg, told me. "Sometimes the raids last nearly all night."

Sister Lawson said she was playing bridge in their mess when anti-aircraft guns opened fire. She said, "We all dived under the table. When it was all over we were as mad as anything because our hands were mixed up."

I remembered the first nights on the Pachino Peninsula when enemy planes attacked the ships and the flak was like a devil's fireworks in the sky and shrapnel came hissing down all around and you wished you were small enough to fit under your helmet.

We lunched at the air evacuation centre before going on. There were flowers on the bare wooden table—the girls had seen to that. We sat on benches and ate stew and hardtack from mess tins. The British doctors talked about Africa for they had taken part in the Tunisian campaign. The Canadian nurses talked about Rome and what they would do when they got there. Afterward we had coffee which the girls had brought with them from England.

As Sister Lawson said, it was not far to the hospital. This General Hospital unit was housed in a building formerly used by the Italians for the same purpose. We drove through an imposing gateway to a row of low two-story buildings. A blue-uniformed nurse was walking across the grounds and she entered what must have been the former hospital kitchen. The walls were white tile and the water faucets were shining bright. There was a scrubbed table in the centre of the room and it was altogether the cleanest place I had seen in Sicily.

A number of nurses off duty were sitting there drinking tea with sliced lemon. They gave me a cup while they told me they were the first nurses to arrive in Sicily. They disembarked at Augusta on July 19—just nine days after the troops leaped ashore on the beaches. The Canadian girls arrived almost a week before the first British nurses.

"And weren't they mad when they found us here first!" Sister Isobel Gervin, Winnipeg, said. "You see they had been told they would be the first to arrive."

The first Allied women to step ashore in Sicily got a tremendous hand from the troops. Sister Jessie Blair, Perth, Ont., said: "We sure got a thrill over the great cheers we received."

However, the Canadian nurses were not expected that soon and their arrival caused consternation among the authorities. They were hurried away from the port which was being bombed. During the first days they helped at a casualty clearing station until their own hospital was set up.

While we were talking, the bark of anti-aircraft guns sounded outside. The girls crowded the doorway. High in the hard blue sky a thin white exhaust trail looked like a chalk mark on a blackboard. At the end the exhaust faded as though the chalk had been lifted from the board and pin-point puffs like cotton wool appeared.

The firing did not last long but while it was going on the nurses talked about other air raids they had experienced in Sicily— one last night and one the day before. They were old campaigners now and used to this sort of thing.

"We've been bitten by fleas and bugs," Sister Beville Compston, Winnipeg, said. "Nearly everyone has."

"You're telling me!" I said.

The Canadian girls quickly got used to conditions in Sicily which were so different from what they had known in England. They were just as much at home in the dusty Italian institution as they had been at the beautiful Cliveden Estate where they were formerly established. They kidded and joked but they were enjoying roughing it.

"You ought to see my bedroom," Sister Trennie Hunter, Winnipeg, said. "It's so nice and it would be so quiet if there weren't 49 others in it."

"Yes, there are 50 of us upstairs in the building next door," Sister Margaret Stanley, Brandon, Man., said. "We all go to sleep at the same time as otherwise we would be stepping all over each other." Another nurse in the group was Sister Hunter, wife of Louis Hunter, Canadian Press War Correspondent. I had seen Louis at Tunis the day before and he was a forlorn figure waiting to come to the front.

There is one thing our nurses have not got used to and that is the dirt. Matron Agnes Mcleod, Edmonton, said, "The place was filthy when we arrived. We just got one building cleaned when they moved us to another one. I'm afraid it's not fully clean yet."

The matron showed me through one low two-story building which was part of the main hospital. Men were scrubbing and sweeping while the nurses were attending wounded lying on stretchers and cots.

The Canadians were the first to set up a hospital in Sicily. The hospital I was visiting was the last link in the medical chain on the island.

When a soldier is wounded at the front he is brought by stretcher to the regimental aid post. Sometimes he is given sulfa drugs and opiates by the stretcher-bearers but usually he receives these at the regimental aid post. Each man gets a number of sulfa tablets whatever the nature of his wound. These build resistance to infection. After he has received first aid he is put into a stretcher-carrying jeep and taken to a reception depot. There he is transferred to an ambulance and rushed to the advance surgical centre.

The advance surgical centre is really a mobile hospital. It includes headquarters, a field ambulance unit, two field surgical units, a field dressing station and a field transfusion unit. The centre brings surgery almost to the front line.

I was at one of these centres at Agira and it was only one mile

116

from the front. Major Don Young, Ottawa, former McGill football star, who was one of the doctors there, told me that only badly wounded soldiers and those requiring resuscitation were treated at the advance surgical centre. If a wounded man could travel he was sent to a casualty clearing station and from there to the Canadian General Hospital.

However, quite a few sickness cases are kept at these advance surgical centres and there have been a fair number of these cases. The main sicknesses suffered by Canadians have been dysentery, sand-fly fever and "gyppy stomach." This latter is a hangover from the Middle East and should be called "Sicilian stomach" instead, but I suppose everyone is afraid it might be shortened to "sissy stomach." It is known as gastroenteritis by the Canadian Medical Corps. At any rate most of these cases are cured in three or four days and they are kept at the advance surgical centre as they are not serious enough to move farther down. There has been little or no malaria as yet.

The First Canadian Division has several of these advance surgical centres and they keep close to the front by leapfrogging each other. Usually they occupy buildings but if none are suitable the doctors work under canvas. The advance surgical centre at Agira was in a school.

This Canadian General Hospital is the last link in the medical chain in Sicily but it is also the first link in the further chain which stretches to Africa. The fifteenth Canadian General Hospital is established there. Prolonged cases such as broken bones are sent back to Africa.

And so here is the medical chain and all its links: stretcher-bearer—regimental aid post—stretcher-bearing jeeps—reception depot—ambulance—advance surgical centre—ambulance—casualty clearing station—ambulance—field hospital; and another smaller chain—ambulance—air evacuation centre—ambulance—hospital plane—base hospital.

Matron Mcleod told me the hospital had two operating theatres and would eventually have 200 beds. The hospital unit lost most of its medical equipment and was operating with captured equipment. Strangely enough this captured equipment was of

British manufacture which the Italians took at Tobruk and we recaptured in Sicily.

Sister Evelyn Gregory, Winnipeg, was working in the wards I visited. She said to me, "We all think the Eighth Army boys are wonderful. They are the best patients we have ever had." This hospital was looking after British as well as Canadian wounded when I was there. Eventually it may handle only Canadians.

There is no doubt at all that the soldier in this war has a better chance for survival and speedy recovery than the fighting man of the last war. And from what I saw the Canadian soldier has the best chance of all. This is due to the efficient organization of our Medical Corps with its advance surgical centres and field hospitals. Bringing surgery to the front line saved many Canadian lives.

But I think many of them must be getting well fast because of the Canadian nurses. The troops must have been as surprised as I was that noon in the olive grove at the way the girls looked. Their appearance was a tonic which no medicine could equal. I hope their powder keeps dry—and lasts.

Peter Stursberg was a regular Maclean's *contributor during the war. He now lives in Vancouver.*

I BOMBED BERLIN

—October 1, 1943—
Flying Officer Walter Scott Sherk, DFC and Bar (as told to Gordon Sinclair)

It was my thirty-fifth raid over enemy territory and our plane was one of the target finders—those planes that go in front on a raid and drop marker bombs to light up the objective. This requires expert navigation and split-second timing. Most pilots insist that their aircraft is navigated by the best man in the business. Our navigator was Flight-Lieutenant R.G. "Mouthpiece" Morrison, a former lawyer from Vancouver—hence the nickname Mouthpiece. No tribute I can pay Mouthpiece is adequate. His navigation was always wonderful and in this particular

Handley Page Halifax bomber in flight.

raid he put us at the very front of the target finders that night over Stettin.

One moment of danger on such a raid is the take-off. Both the bomb and fuel loads are at their maximum and there is not much lifting strength in reserve. However, I have never had—nor even seen—a take-off crash on an operational flight, and this time, once we were airborne, we were seven confident men, confident because we knew our jobs and knew each other.

We hummed through the night in routine flight until we neared the target area when I reported to the navigator, "Someone shooting at us, Mouthpiece."

"So what?" came his reply over the intercom.

"Gunner here," a voice came in. "Let's go down and take a crack at them."

"Some other time," I told him. "We're getting near target area."

There was silence for a time while Morrison worked over his charts.

Then Flight-Sergeant Stan Keon, the bomb aimer, a chap from Saskatoon, spoke up, "Stan here...Flak bursting dead ahead. Better turn port a bit."

"Pilot to navigator...Target ahead."

"Pilot to bomb aimer...Get ready. Getting close. Aircraft on either side of us coned (trapped) in the searchlights. That gives us a clear run. Here we go through the middle."

"Bomber to pilot...Thirty seconds. Steady as you go. Left a bit. Left. Right...Right...Steady. Bombs gone. Turn off."

I started to swing off the target area and set the course for home but at that second there was a crash and a burst of blue-white flame which slowly turned to orange. We spun downward.

The chance of a bomber being struck by explosives from other aircraft in its own attack group is about a million to one. But we had suffered that millionth chance. A plane, 2,000 feet above, dropped its bombs without seeing us below.

I assumed we'd suffered a direct anti-aircraft hit and so did the other boys. The roof had been blown off. One bomb had crashed through my compartment. The back of my flying suit was on fire and the cockpit ablaze. I struggled with the jammed controls. The idea of a prison camp kept flashing through my mind. "A prisoner ...I'll be a prisoner..."

We lost 5,000 feet in a minute or so and we were still diving with the flames growing hotter when I gave the order to bail out. All the controls, so far as I could feel, were useless but I had figured without Sergeant Doug Bebensee, Bothwell, Ont., the engineer, who could do more with a screw driver and loop of wire than many a man with a tool kit. With the pilot compartment filled with smoke, the plane still diving and lit up like a Christmas tree, he worked quietly over the controls.

As the captain gives the order to bail out the crew is supposed to report back over the intercom as they take to their chutes. The pilot jumps last. I was still pulling on the stick, and the back of my suit was still on fire, when word came over the intercom, "Bomb aimer bailing out," and away went Stan Keon. Then came "Rear gunner bailing out," and Harry Woonton (Fort Saskatchewan, Alta.) dropped toward the fires below.

I turned toward the right in my seat, swung my legs out and was standing up getting ready to leap through the emergency exit when "Scrammy" McGladery (Flying Officer G.C. McGladery, Chemainus, B.C., wireless officer) came twisting his way through the flames to shout, "Wait ... wait! I can't bail out. I haven't got a chute."

"What have you done with it?" I shouted.

"I've been beating those flames out with the chute. Look! I've got this fire licked."

The fire did seem to have diminished. Most of it was confined to the rear of the plane although there were occasional spurts of flame toward the cockpit and some still blazing under my seat. I gave another pull at the controls and when they failed to respond I ordered McGladery to hook onto the navigator's parachute. "Link up with Mouthpiece. You men are light. Those chutes will carry two of you down safely. You're next to go. Good luck."

McGladery went over and stood beside Morrison. It was difficult for them to remain erect because of the pitch of the plane. Then Bebensee, who was still working to free the controls, looked up and said, "Try her again, Skipper. Try her gently."

We were down to about 9,000 feet now. I pulled back gently and could feel the aircraft take hold, then stall. She did not right herself all of a sudden but there was an encouraging tug of air. I shouted, "Stand by. Stand by."

The crew stood watching me. I pulled again and as she answered I kept repeating, "Stand by. Don't bail out. Stand by." Now the plane swung on an even keel and another attempt was made to put out the fire. I remember McGladery trying to squirt liquid from an extinguisher on the blaze but nothing happened so he took a flashlight from his tunic and with flame dancing around him read the instructions. It was bright enough to take photographs but McGladery used his torch. When the extinguisher still failed to work he tossed it out of the open roof.

As the flames died I found we were not losing further altitude but I couldn't steer and I didn't know if we were travelling in circles or not. However, after we'd beaten out the flames from my seat and tunic I found that by throttling back on the two port motors I could steer a straight course.

The others in the crew were standing beside me by now so I turned to Morrison and said, "Okay, Mouthpiece, the rest is up to you. Where do we go from here?"

All the navigation equipment, maps, charts and instruments had gone, but Morrison had already been examining the stars through the shattered roof and said, "Sweden." He estimated we were somewhere north of Stettin, with the Baltic on our right, and it was worth a trial to reach Sweden, although in addition to the lost charts we learned now that the wireless was dead. It was navigate by the stars, or not at all.

On we flew toward Sweden. After 15 minutes McGladery had put the fires entirely out while Bebensee had the controls free. We had gasoline to spare and I began to feel hopeful about reaching or almost reaching England if night fighters didn't find us. I had never been chased by a night fighter, so on past performances we had a good chance.

The intercom was not working reliably so I shouted to the crew that everything was okay and told them that we were now flying evenly and suggested we might try for England. "England it is. Keep her flying," they said.

Mouthpiece Morrison gave me a course for Denmark, which was on our way. We'd been led to believe the citizens there were helpful and friendly, in case we were forced down. Along the German Baltic coast flak came up toward us but no searchlights picked us out and we weren't pursued. It began to look more and more like a routine home-coming except for the wind whistling where the roof had been and the absence of two crew members.

We got over Denmark, crossed the North Sea and landed at base in England an hour late.

None of us knew until grounded at base that two incendiary four-pounders from one of our own aircraft in the raid had hit us. One tore out the roof and exploded in Sergeant Bebensee's compartment below me, but fortunately he was standing beside me at the time. The other landed in the largest petrol tank, broke the main spar holding the wing, but failed to explode. It is easy to imagine what would have happened if that four-pound bomb hadn't been a dud.

Out of that assault I got a bar to the DFC, Mouthpiece Morrison and Scrammy McGladery each got the DFC while Bebensee got the DFM.

During my 36 trips, my aircraft, either a Wellington or a Halifax, dropped 1,860,000 pounds of explosives. I lost two crews, limped home with a dead motor five times, saw 12 aircraft shot down, all of them in flames.

Of my 36 raids, five really stand out in my mind. Most others were like delivering the milk. But these five that stand out were my first raid, a tense occasion with any bomber pilot no matter how experienced or blasé he might later become; the raid on Cologne when I picked up the DFC; the raid on Berlin when we really accomplished what all of us had come into the Air Force to try; my first raid on Italy, and the Stettin attack when we were struck by bombs from the plane above us.

I got into the RCAF after two tries at enlistment and two rejects. I was accepted as an AC2 at Hamilton on May 5, 1941. At first they said I was too old at 28 and that I lacked sufficient education for a pilot. But after training at Toronto and Goderich I got my wings at Number Five Service Flying Training School at Brant-ford and landed in England, Jan. 20, 1942, hopeful of getting into action quickly. I used to be a hoistman in a northern Quebec mine so they tagged me "Rocky" when, as a sergeant, I went to Number 25 Operational Training Unit in England to learn how to handle a Wimpie (Wellington). This is the heaviest two-engined bomber in the RAF and a magnificent aircraft to fly. Of the 60 men in my class at OTU some have since taken administrative jobs on the ground, some have been killed, some are missing and some are prisoners. None are flying today although I expect to be back on operations shortly.

I made my first operational flight in a Wellington on June 1, 1942, and I will never forget it as long as I live although nothing spectacular happened. This was one of the first imposing raids of the war—1,000 aircraft in a raid on the Krupp armament works in central Essen. I was first pilot with a four-man English crew in a new plane. It was "first ops" for all of us and we were excited as schoolboys.

We were airborne with precision but when we got 30 to 40 miles from the target the flak started coming up and I thought we must be there. I had never seen anti-aircraft fire before and neither had the others so I called all the men up to the cockpit, one by one, for a look. Anti-aircraft fire seems to drift upward ever so slowly. It blossoms out, then curves in an arc or twists like a hog's tail. The noticeable feature is its drifting tempo until all of a sudden it comes at you at what seems like a mile-a-minute and sweeps past like a comet.

I was a little frightened and quite convinced that we had already come over the target so I kept demanding on the intercom, "Hello navigator...Are we there yet?"

"Not on target yet. We've got a long way to go."

"Are you sure? Check again. This looks like it."

"Twenty minutes to go. We're on course and on time."

As we neared the target area the navigator gave me a play-by-play account of our location. The first planes had already fired on the target area when we got over and I could see flak coming up, bombs going down and aircraft all around. When we came to make our run over the target area—a dangerous time because of the need to hold true to course—I missed our aiming point and had to go back.

I Bombed Berlin

I made the second run over the target area and now it was brighter than day but the flak was widely dispersed and I felt the aircraft leap forward and upward as the word came through the intercom "Bombs gone." I let out a shout of delight. We had at last done the thing training and costly equipment had been leading us toward. We had bombed Germany! I was jolted out of these reflections by the voice of the aimer repeating, "Bombs gone. Turn off target."

Our instructions now were to come home low. But how low is low? I should have remembered that it meant 7,000 feet in this case but I went down to 5,000 and set a fast course for home. Soon the gunner reported, "Searchlights feeling for us." A moment later we were trapped by two, then by four, and soon by a dozen searchlights.

"Stand by for dive," I said.

I cut down to 1,000 feet but still the lights held us. I checked speed, then throttled full out, made 90-degree evasive turns and steep climbs but could not throw the lights off. The flak was getting close.

"Keep close lookout. Going lower."

I cut down to rooftop level and flew wide open at 75 feet. Occasionally someone would drone out, "Lights below." In most cases this was someone in Holland giving us the V for Victory signal.

We crossed the sea at 1,000 feet and then—my fault—we got lost.

We were briefed to approach England over the Humber River then set course to base from there; so when we crossed a river I breathed a premature sigh of satisfaction and declared, "Navigator …Humber below. Give me a course, please."

He set me a course but we got lost as thoroughly as any babes in the wood. What I'd seen was the Wash, not the Humber. When we got straightened away, we were last home and had already been posted missing. We didn't care. We were happy as any five larks but base probably decided I needed more schooling, because on the next three operations I went as second pilot. We attacked Lorient, Wilhelmshaven and Duisburg and I made life weary for the pilot by pestering him with questions. You never know it all and don't learn unless you ask. One thing I understood was that when they give you your wings you may be a pilot, but you're not yet a flier. That

125

only comes from experience.

We first learned that flak stings as much but looks less pretty by daylight when we did a leaflet raid between Dunkirk and Ostend. The leaflets were quotes from five Nazi leaders whereby they showed themselves unskilled liars. Flak put a few holes in us. We returned soon afterward with instructions to bomb the docks at Le Havre, but only if we could see the target area clearly. When we got over the target area thick cloud engulfed us. We circled but finding no opening streaked for home, intending to drop our three 1,000-pounders into the sea.

These bombs cost the price of a house, and much time, and it seemed a pity to lose them but that was the order. But we all forgot about it. Arriving at base I set her down, gently enough, but the aircraft rolled and pitched and was difficult to control. I was puzzled until one of the boys shouted, "The bombs, the bombs! We've still got 'em." Nothing happened, however.

The raid on Cologne when I got the DFC was my third raid on Cologne. Going in for the third time is neither easier nor more difficult than the first. The pilot is in the hands of his navigator and Canadian planes have the best navigators in the skies. About 70 miles from the target area a motor cut out. I didn't think we'd been hit although some flak had been buzzing about. The motor just grunted and died so I said on the intercom, "Pilot to crew...One motor dead. Approximate position 70 miles from aiming point. How do you fellows feel about going in anyhow?"

They all spoke at once. "Go in by all means," they said. "All right, chaps," I said. "But remember we're carrying 8,000 pounds of bombs and can't hold height with that load and one motor is gone."

"Take her in," they said. "Keep flying."

That decision brought me the DFC and the citation said it was for "pressing on with great determination to his target" but I didn't make the decision. The crew made it.

As we neared Cologne, Morrison cut in on the intercom to tell me, "Four minutes off target. How are we for height?"

"We're low. But check that timing, Mouthpiece. Four minutes makes us nearly over the target and how can we have got here early with a motor gone?"

"Can't tell about motors. I do the navigation. We're zero minus three fifteen right now."

That meant I had to fly in circles waiting for the correct timing because in these saturation raids precision timing is vital. In flying around I lost 3,000 feet which put us down to 6,000. Lights caught us several times but bounced off.

The searchlight crews were not looking for anyone as low as 6,000 feet that night. The flak was intense and by now its beauty had become old stuff and flak was just a menace. If those searchlights had coned us I think we'd have been shot down. When zero hour came I had a fear we might get hit by bombs from our own planes because we were well down from our proper position but I was too busy trying to control the aircraft to worry seriously.

We got directly over our target with some of the most accurate bombing we have done. Reading about it afterward I remembered the Germans admitted their cathedral had not been hurt but rail yards next door were flattened. I could tell there would be a good deal of flattening as my kite leaped 200 feet when a blockbuster dropped. Had we wanted we could have wiped that cathedral off the earth but we only sought military objectives.

Back at base after that raid there were dozens of holes, big and small, in the aircraft but nobody aboard had been hit. I have never had a man hit.

On our raid on Berlin we let go a shout of delight when we got our orders. This was what we'd been looking forward to since the first hour of our training. I had developed a healthy hatred for Berlin and what it stood for and what trouble it has cost us all. The flight to the capital was what we'd call a piece of cake—an easy flight. Either we took them by surprise that night or the outer defenses of Berlin are a lot weaker than Hitler will admit. We approached from the north and as we neared the target area I went on the intercom, "All right, chaps. This is it. This is Berlin. This is where they run their war from. We've got a 4,000-pound bomb. Everybody steady now and we'll put that 4,000 pounds right where Churchill wants it."

But Berlin's inner defense ring was powerful. As we were making our target run, aircraft on either side of me suffered direct hits and went down in flames. I could see the crew bail out of one ship. Our target was the centre of the city and in the brightness of the fires started by the pathfinders we could pick it out easily. I remember the many domes on the bigger buildings and my determination that we'd get directly over our target even if I had to make the run 10 times. We dropped the big bomb on the first run, then swung sharply to watch it hit.

People have asked me how it is that anti-aircraft fire doesn't detonate those enormous bombs. We did a little unwilling research on that subject during a raid on the Ruhr. Flak in that industrialized area starts 30 miles from any target and the valley is studded with searchlights sweeping beams over the skies. The flak and the lights both seemed to have us bracketed that night.

As we made the target run they trapped me in lights, and the bomb aimer said I was off course and he couldn't drop his explosive. We circled to come down from the other side. Flak hit us, tearing holes in the kite in several places. The concussion of the flak bounced us this way and that like a cork. I had trouble controlling the aircraft and my back was sore for a week afterward from the pounding I took.

The flak tossed us far off course a second time and McGladery from his wireless compartment came on the intercom with, "I'm afraid this bomb might explode." He was sitting right over the big 4,000-pound bomb.

"How about it, bomb aimer?" I asked. "Are we over the target?"

Stan Keon, the bomb aimer, was one of the coolest men I ever knew and his voice was as calm as a radio announcer's. He spoke now in the flat voice. "Better make another run."

I turned onto the target and he let the bomb go this time.

On the way home we got coned. There were 30 or 40 guns on us with more swinging our way each minute. We felt like a rabbit in the middle of a pack of hounds. I pushed forward on the stick at 14,000 feet and gunned downward at 340 miles an hour. The vibration was so severe I couldn't read the instruments. The plan was to level off at 7,000 feet but the weight of the aircraft dropped us another 2,000. If the lights could still find us we'd catch it sure. They were sweeping inquisitively high above us. Our chances looked good for getting clear. In a minute or two we did and we headed for home.

There are numerous superstitions among fliers, as everyone has heard, and when I came to flight 13 I wrote it down as that but many pilots decide to call it 12a. In our crew nobody else was on their 13th flight except myself so I decided not to give it a thought. We were briefed for Kiel that night and it turned out to be the only occasion that Mouthpiece Morrison ever let us down with his navigation.

About 100 miles south of the target area Morrison came on the intercom to say, "Sorry to tell you we're off course. Far off. My fault."

"Well, what do we do now besides beat your brains out when we get down?"

"We can pull back on course and reach target area well after the rest of the raid if you've got fuel."

Morrison gave me a course. It was a hard flight. We discovered our course took us up the Kiel Canal, which is heavily guarded with flak and searchlights. They have some scientific novelties for downing planes up there. They did not seem too effective but I had to change speed, height and course constantly to throw their predictors off. It was a regular forest of lights and guns but no burst came closer than 100 yards.

We ran into a comparatively dull period after that raid but even the dull spots have their moments. On one raid, for example, I had Sergeant Bill Gray along as second pilot for an instruction flight when I suddenly noticed his face go chalk white and his mouth sag open. He couldn't speak or move. Then roaring by us, so close I could have touched her with my hand, went a four-engined aircraft. We had missed a mid-air crash by three feet.

We did some gardening (mine laying) which calls for accuracy of a high order and on one trip flew low over a flak ship we hadn't known about. The flak crew were crafty and waited until they could see the whites of our eyes before firing but even at such range they didn't hit us.

Then we undertook a daylight raid over Crefeld in Germany. There were only 15 of us that day and our instructions were to bomb from height through clouds—that is, we were not to expose ourselves to fighter or flak attack. When we got near the enemy coast the skies cleared and there were no clouds so we headed for base, dropping our bombs in the sea. This was the only time I failed to complete a mission.

The longest distance we ever travelled on a raid was the nine-hour, 35-minute assault to bomb the Italian navy at Spezia, near Genoa. It was my first raid on Italy. Intelligence had learned that the Italian Fleet, previously widely dispersed, was concentrating in the Gulf of Genoa. The Italians may have expected an attack from north Africa but squadrons based in England went after them and it must have given them quite a shock.

Soon after we were airborne with extra petrol and a heavy bomb load, the navigation equipment went dead. We decided to push on anyway and we got over the target with the rest of the attackers, met weak opposition and attacked almost at will. Photographic confirmation of results was good. On the way home we ran into strong headwinds with some icing and it looked as if it might be impossible for us to get back to base. This unpleasant impression struck me as we were flying over Switzerland.

Soon we'd be flying over France with the chance of night fighters trying to ambush us. Then the gunner tried his guns and found they wouldn't work. He went at them busily, got them firing, but later one failed us again. No attack was made on us, but wondering about the guns stopped us from worrying about our fuel supply.

When we were over the sea, near home, all petrol tanks showed empty so I said over the intercom, "Pilot to crew…All tanks show empty. Looks like a crash landing on the sea. Stand by."

Just then the first grey glimpses of dawn showed us the English coast. I thought now we'd get there, but not to base, and I told the crew.

We had no wireless to ask permission for a landing at a strange field but I flashed my recognition lights and was preparing to set her down when the landing gear stuck. I told the men it would be a pancake landing after all, but before I screwed up enough courage to really drop her without wheels we had overshot the runway and were again over the sea. I kept wondering when those motors would cough out but we were circling around, still under full power, when Bebensee spoke up, "Landing gear cleared. All set to land, and I could do with a cup of coffee." That Bebensee could almost build a bomber with a piece of wire and pliers.

We soon did a second raid on Italy, met even weaker opposition than before, but ran into bad icing conditions over the Alps when coming home. The gunners kept telling me on the intercom how bad the ice was around them. We dropped from 14,000 to 5,000 feet, which is dangerous in those areas because of the mountain peaks. Two motors cut out from time to time. An over-enthusiastic newspaper reporter, describing that homecoming, said we crossed the Alps on one motor. That's impossible. No Halifax could get home on one engine. Two motors were out for brief periods but all four were ticking when we reached base.

Thirty operational flights are a "tour" for a bomber crew and are followed by six months instructing, but when I passed my thirtieth—a raid on the Ruhr—I decided to sign on for another tour and so did the others of my crew. We were a good crew. We worked well together and understood each other's abilities.

In all my flights I was never shot down or forced down, never seriously hit by flak, never chased—let alone attacked—by night fighters, intruders or any other type of aircraft. I never had a member of my crew wounded or killed while I was a pilot. The pair who bailed out over Stettin are safe in prison camps. Yet I'm now at home in Canada on convalescent leave. I broke my neck when the steering gear of a car I was riding in cracked up in Cambridge in England.

My only injury came midst the cloisters of a University city. While I was learning how it feels to live inside a plaster cast with my broken neck, the good chaps who made up my crew kept flying—but their luck ran out. I'm the last survivor of two crews. I think my luck will hold. Soon I'll be flying again to test it.

Sherk never did return to active duty, but was allowed to continue his service as a flight instructor in Canada. After the war, he worked for the Niagara Parks Commission near his home town of Ridgeway, Ont. He died of a heart attack at age 63 in 1976.

Gordon Sinclair, who wrote for the Toronto Star *for many years, had a distinguished journalism and broadcast career before dying at age 83 in 1984.*

A PRISONER IS LONELY

—February 15, 1944—
Flight-Lieutenant Don Morrison, DFC, DFM
(as told to Scott Young)

I don't suppose I'll ever know exactly what happened after the cannon shells started crashing into my cockpit. I was surprised, at first, because I had just shot down an FW 190 and wasn't expecting an attack. I must have passed out because all I remember is something hitting my leg an awful wallop and then I woke up in a hospital bed and found out it was 10 days later.

I don't like thinking about that crash very much, but I can pretty well figure what happened. I got out of the aircraft somehow and came down by parachute.

Unidentified German camp, April 1945.

But I don't know how far I was off the ground when I bailed out, although possibly it was 25,000 feet. I would have had a lot of things to do around the cockpit, like shaking loose from my oxygen connections and safety belt, and in my condition it might have taken me quite a while. I guess nobody really knows the details. I thought the chaps who were with me might have seen what happened, but I'm told now that they didn't know until weeks later that I had come out of it fine. So I guess if anybody knows what happened, it would be Germans or Frenchmen who picked me up and took me to the hospital. And I never got a chance to talk about it to any one of them because I was moved so fast.

Maybe I'm getting a little ahead of my story, but the only part I really like talking about in the year beginning on Nov. 8, 1942, is the part about coming home. We were lucky, I guess, because the Allies never had been able to arrange an exchange of prisoners with the Germans until ours was fixed up for last fall, just about one year after I had been shot down. I'd like to make this story all about the trip home, but I know there must be a lot of people who have friends or relatives in German camps and are wondering how they live, and how they are getting along. So I'll tell you what I remember of how I lived, and what happened to me, and maybe you can judge from that.

So we'll start at the beginning, with when I was shot down. When I came to again there were doctors and nurses around me, and they were speaking a language I recognized as German because I had studied it in school. And where my left leg should have been, there was none. It had been amputated just above the knee.

That was a bit of a shock, I guess, but it didn't seem to take me long to get over it. I was in a Luftwaffe hospital at St. Omer, France. They couldn't tell me much there about what had happened, except that I came down by parachute. I spent five weeks there, and I can't really tell you much about it because I wasn't in very good shape. In fact it was about five weeks before I was well enough to be moved, and about all I remember about that first hospital is that it was just like any other hospital—quite a few beds in every ward, and some people in really bad shape, and some not so bad. I guess I was one of the ones in bad shape.

133

From there I was moved to an interrogation centre near Frankfurt, Germany. This was the place where they used to take all the boys to see if they could find out anything of value. There was a hospital attached to it because, I guess, they often had cases like me—chaps who wouldn't be really well for quite a while, but had to be questioned anyway. They questioned me twice, for about half an hour each time. I didn't say much, naturally. They asked me what kind of a plane I was flying when I was shot down, what squadron I was flying with, and a lot of details about equipment. But they really didn't bother me much.

I was 25 days in that interrogation place, and then they moved me again. The next hospital was the best one I'd been in. It was run by captured British medical personnel, and we were well-fed and well-treated. We got the regular Red Cross prisoners' parcels and then we also got some special ones made up for invalids. They have a lot more fancy stuff in them. Anyone who has ever been in a prison camp will tell you, too, that it is practically impossible to get along on German rations. I certainly would hate to have to try. They could give us stuff like bread and potatoes and some staples like that, but the Red Cross parcels made up all the rest. Those parcels really made life worth living.

This hospital was in a typical little village in central Germany, not close to any city that I can think of. It was a very old place, and we got out once a week and took a walk through it. We would have one guard come along with about 12 or 15 of us, and we would go pretty slow. We used to stay out an hour and a half or two hours, and some of the chaps used to get pretty tired. But when anybody did, we would all just stop and let him rest a while.

The people in the village didn't pay much attention to us. They were used to prisoners by that time I guess. Of course, that walk was the high spot of every week. We didn't have much space to walk in the hospital grounds, and it was nicer being outside of those walls.

Most of the patients in the hospital were Canadians captured at Dieppe. There were also a couple of Canadian doctors on the staff.

We were fairly well-treated. We used to be wakened at about eight o'clock for our first meal. We had three meals a day—no tea in the afternoon, something we did have at some of the other places. The German guards didn't bother us very much, just came in about three times a day to count us.

I was getting quite a bit better by this time, and in May they moved me to a convalescent home near Kassel. I had been hopping around on crutches for months—not the same ones I've got now, but something the same. This convalescent home was manned by British personnel, too, and was quite comfortable. It had been a monastery. The grounds were lightly wooded and the scenery was pretty good. The daily routine was just about what you'd expect. Monotony was one of the problems we all had to contend with and there was the inevitable knowledge every morning that this day would be just like the last. The boys played quite a bit of poker and bridge. We used to go sun-bathing in the grounds because the weather was quite warm by then, and twice we were allowed out of the grounds to a river, just a little piece away, to have swims. That was a great thing. I hope I haven't been painting this picture like a holiday resort, though. It was far from it. But life under those conditions, even in the hands of the Germans, isn't as bad as a lot of people seem to think.

I'm not going to go into any great detail about some of those places because I imagine most people are interested in the prison camp and how we lived there. Well, I went to my first and last— thank God—in July.

Most people can't possibly imagine just what a lonely place a prison camp is, and if they do understand that they probably have trouble understanding how our morale was as good as it was. I can't really understand that myself. It was surprisingly high, even among men who had been there for years. We had some funny characters in there. There was one, for instance, who must have been almost 65. He had been a ground officer back in Britain, and had talked the authorities into giving him a flight to see what real operations were like. So he had gone into an operation as a passenger, and the aircraft had been shot down. And there he was in a German prison camp, with only himself to blame because he had talked himself into the flight, but it didn't worry him a bit. He said it wasn't as tough as living with his wife.

Anybody who ever has been in a prison camp will tell you this:
I don't think we could have got along at all without the Red Cross
parcels. We got our meat from them—bully beef and that canned
chopped pork you see so much in England. There was sometimes
some bacon in cans to break the monotony, but there weren't any
fresh eggs or milk.

Each room did its own cooking, and there was only one small
stove for each hut. The people in the 10 rooms in our hut had
drawn up a schedule. Each room could have the stove to itself for
15 minutes, or two rooms could pool their time and have 30 minutes between them. The only trouble was that with such a short
time at the stove we ate more fried food than was good for us. But
we made out all right. We used to toast the German bread, because
it was heavy and hard to eat any other way. It was black bread, of
course. We had the odd pie now and again. We didn't have the
stuff to make pastry but we used to crush up some biscuits and add
a little margarine. Most of the pies were raisin because we used to
get quite a few raisins in our parcels.

My little world was about 12 or 15 barrack huts enclosed by
barbed wire. The huts were one-story affairs, with a long corridor
down the middle and rooms branching off on each side. There
were 10 rooms to each hut besides the kitchen, and there were usually six officers in every room.

Our room had two windows. We had three of those double-
deck bunks, one on each of three sides of the room. We also had a
couple of tables and stools. It wasn't exactly like home, but it did
all right. We spent a lot of time in the rooms, of course, talking and
arguing. There sure were some weird and wonderful conversations.
We talked about literally everything under the sun. You probably
couldn't name a subject we didn't talk about. Politics, home, the
war—everything.

We had a phonograph and some records, which helped a lot.
We used to play the thing for hours every day. Needles were
awfully hard to get, though. Incidentally, things like that in parcels
are often just what the boys need.

To get back to the room, though. I slept in a lower bunk, of
course, because it would have been hard for me to get into an upper.

A Prisoner Is Lonely

We used to wake up about nine or so every morning, but there was nothing to make us get up in a hurry. There was really no incentive to be up and around until the camp's bugle sounded at nine-thirty or so, and after that we would have about 10 or 15 minutes before we would have to form up in a hollow square on the parade ground for the first roll-call and count of the day. There were two of these counts in this camp. The second one was about five o'clock in the afternoon.

After that we would go back and start getting breakfasts and clean up our rooms. The other men in my room were all Canadians—Flt.-Lieut. Gordon Clancy, an RAF man from Semans, Sask., who was shot down before Dunkirk; Flt.-Lieut. Harvey Fraser, Esquimalt, B.C.; Flying Officer Don McRae, Whitney, Ont.; Flying Officer Omer Levesque, Mont Joli, Que; and Flying Officer J.A.S. Ferguson, Glace Bay, N.S.

Washing and shaving were a little tough because there was no hot water except what you could heat on the little stove. But we got by all right and everyone kept himself in fairly good shape all the time. We had our clothes to keep clean and our dishes to do after breakfast, and things like that. We each had a knife, fork, spoon, cup, plate and bowl.

After breakfast and cleaning up, sometimes some of us would go out and walk around the compound. Our hut was over near one side of the enclosure, just about 50 or 75 yards from the wire. There wasn't much scenery—except a few trees, and the goon boxes, and the wire. We used to call the sentry posts goon boxes, and the Germans, naturally, were goons. These sentry posts were raised about 15 feet above the ground and had machine guns mounted on them.

We had lunch around noon, and incidentally, my appetite always was pretty good. There were cold showers, which were okay in the summertime, and hot ones were being installed as I left.

We had tea about four o'clock and dinner about seven. We could walk about the compound, or talk, or play cards, or play the phonograph during the other times. There were some books around, and we had a little money, but it wasn't of much use. There was a canteen where we were supposed to be able to buy stuff, but it seldom had anything to sell. You could usually get things like tooth powder, and every once in a while there were razor blades and other things. We used German marks.

When I first came to the camp, in July, we all had to be indoors by black-out time, but later they let us visit back and forth between the huts until 10 o'clock. There were some concerts in the evenings, and just before I left someone dug up an old English film some place and showed it. It was pretty ancient, but it sure was welcome.

Mail is one of the biggest things in prison camp life. It came into the camp in driblets all the time, and each hut had a man who went over to the post office every day to see if there was anything doing. If there was mail the chap would come hustling back and seek out the people it was for. Almost everybody got mail pretty regularly, but some fellows were luckier than others—and got more. The mail sure is important. Letters—and especially snap-shots—were just like a breath of home.

We had a football pitch and a baseball diamond and there were interhut leagues going on all the time. They had baseball divided into senior, junior and beginners' leagues because they were teach-ing the game to a lot of the Englishmen—and that was the funni-est thing you ever saw. I'll never forget some of those games—those correct Englishmen trying to keep up the kind of chatter our lads had, and doing everything wrong. Besides the interhut leagues there was a Canadian team, and an American team while the Americans were there. They moved the Americans to a camp of their own before I left.

We used to laugh at the Englishmen playing baseball, but they had their turn the day a Canadian outfit played them at cricket. They almost died when the Canadians started throwing the ball around the pitch after every inning, just like tossing it around the field in baseball. And they almost collapsed at the way our lads left the field at a sharp trot instead of the dignified gait they used. It was quite a stitch.

Life went on like that, dull and lonesome, but with its high-lights. There was always constant talk about home, and for me there was constant repetition of the rumor I'd heard first from a German guard in my first hospital, in France—the rumor that disabled men would be repatriated. But that was a stock rumor and got to be a joke.

Then, one Monday, it happened. The lieutenant came around and told me and some others we were going to be exchanged—we were going home!

Strangely enough we weren't very excited. We didn't like to put too much stock in it because we didn't want to be disappointed. I was just walking along the hall when the adjutant came up, pretty excited himself, and told me to be ready to leave anytime. We began to believe in it a little more a couple of days later when they came around and asked for any heavy baggage anyone wanted to take. That seemed to make it better. But the real business came the following Sunday. I was just getting ready to go for a walk as the adjutant came flying up and told me to be at the gate in 15 minutes, ready to go home! I can't describe how it felt, but I can tell you that nobody was late. I just went into my room, gathered up enough clothes to last me until I got to England, grabbed my shaving stuff, and moved out of there.

A little later we were taken to a train heading into northern Germany. Something happened on that trip that was sort of tough, even happening to an enemy. Our escort was a colonel, elderly, because the Germans can't spare any but elderly men for back-line duty. And as we rolled along toward the coast, the colonel started telling us about a town we were nearing. It was a beautiful town, he told us. He had spent his cadetship there, and would have liked to go back there to live. He talked on like that while the train steamed through northern Germany, and then we came to the town's outskirts.

"Here it is now," the colonel said, and waved out of the window.

We all crowded around to look.

The bombers had been there. The town was in ruins.

The colonel was heartbroken. He nearly cried. There was practically nothing left.

People have asked me if we had a chance to talk over the course of the war with the colonel while we were on this train ride.

Naturally, we didn't. We weren't worrying about the course of the war. We were going HOME!

We went across the Baltic to Sweden on the regular ferry, then took a train to Göteborg and were taken aboard the *Drottingholm*. In a few days we were in England; and then in another little time we were in Halifax, on a hospital train, and were starting on the last lap. A few days later the hospital train pulled into Toronto and I was really home.

After the war Don Morrison, who received both the Distinguished Flying Cross and the Distinguished Flying Medal from King George VI, opened a general store with his wife, Jean, in St. George, Ont. Later, he worked as a customer-relations manager for Air Canada in Toronto for 36 years. He died at 72 in January 1994.

Scott Young, an assistant editor of Maclean's *from 1945 to 1948, earlier served with the Royal Canadian Navy in Europe. A longtime columnist with the Toronto* Globe and Mail, *Young went on to write more than 40 books.*

PLANE VS. SUB

—March 15, 1944—
Warrant Officer W.F. Beals, DFC

Warrant Officer Beals, Vernon, B.C., was wireless operator air gunner of a Sunderland flying boat which engaged two U-boats in the North Atlantic. Before she was shot down, the Sunderland accounted for one of the submarines, and naval vessels, guided by a "position" which the flying boat's mortally wounded navigator provided, probably destroyed the other. The story of the engagement was told by Warrant Officer Beals to Flying Officer David Griffin, RCAF Public Relations Officer.   —The Editor, 1944

Sunderland flying boat at Tower Bridge, London.

I'm going to tell you a story about a Sunderland flying boat and two U-boats. [The Sunderland was a highly successful, long-range RAF float aircraft used for reconnaissance and anti-submarine activity.] All three are on the bottom of the Atlantic Ocean now, but we—the ones who came back—think we got better than an even trade in some respects, and took a big loss in others. It would take more than two German crews to make up for the four pals we lost.

Our crew was part of a Sunderland squadron on a Coastal Command station on the other side of the ocean. We'd been together for more than a year, had flown thousands of miles of patrol, and always lived in the hope that we'd spot a Jerry some day and let him have it. We liked our work; we liked each other and we liked our ship. You get attached to those big Sunderlands. They're a great aircraft and have done lots to clean up the ocean.

One morning not so long ago we were called and given a whopping big breakfast. We knew there was something in the wind, but we didn't know what it was.

It was cold and there was a suspicion of fog rolling around the corners of the buildings as we jogged over to an "ops" to get our briefing. There was Flt.-Lieut. Paul Sergeant, Toronto, our skipper, and one of the swellest guys in the world. Flying Officer "Art" Bellis, Victoria, was our copilot; Pilot Officer Chesley Steves, Elgin, N.B., was at the navigator's desk, and Flying Officer Bill Campbell, RAF, was third pilot. Our others were: Flt.-Lieut. Woodward; Flt.-Sgts. Needham, Georgie Rutherford and Douglas Mesney, RAF; Flt.-Sgt. J.D. Stafford, Calgary, on the waist guns, Pilot Officer J.D. Shand, Lethbridge, wireless air gunner, and myself, on the radio.

We'd figured on something pretty big, but when they told us that five aircraft would take off on a straight sweep, we had an idea we were going to get our wish—that this time we'd really tangle with the enemy.

Everything was fine. The skipper got her up and the engines were rolling over like a song. It was dark, good and dark, but there we were, the old gang, going out to do some work.

Daylight broke grey and down below the ocean was rolling. You see lots of ocean when you're on patrol, so nobody bothered to admire the beauties of nature. But we were watching.

Plane vs. Sub

I was up forward when we got to the place where we were supposed to turn back. We'd been flying straight out for nine hours. Then, around one o'clock in the afternoon, we got a sighting—two enemy submarines. I couldn't believe it at first. It's like when you're fishing and you're just about to give up when you get a walloping big strike.

I let out a yell and the skipper gave her the gun. At the same time he snapped, "Attacking immediately" over the intercoms.

The skipper was standing up trying to get more speed out of her and from the look on his face you could tell that he was as excited as a kid. Not any more excited than the rest of us. Bill Campbell, the RAF boy who was third pilot, was in the copilot's seat by this time and he was really working to get her around on the course indicated. Bellis and Shand were standing by in the waist with guns and camera; Stafford was in the mid-upper turret checking his guns and Georgie Rutherford was in the tail, all set to blast. Needham was on the job as engineer and I was banging away at the radio, sending out the first sighting report.

We'd been hunting a sub for months and here were two, surfaced, and running along about 10 or 11 knots on a 90-deg. course.

The skipper took her down, joggled her around a bit for evasive action and started his run. Then we saw the Jerries were staying on the surface to shoot it out with us. What a hope! We were laughing and yelling every time these puffs of the shellbursts would drift past us. They didn't look dangerous and neither did the U-boats as they washed along down there, cutting out their wakes.

But we took it differently when we really got within range. I don't know what kind of range finders they use on those subs, but they're good and the crews can really shoot.

Just as we were going in for the kill a shell exploded in the front of the Sunderland and blew everything there all to blazes. I don't know whether it was a 20 millimetre or an Oerlikon shell but it surely messed things up. The skipper kept right on. Tracers were coming up thick and fast but he shoved her down.

We must have taken 20 or 30 hits. The jolts were terrific. Every time we took one, the Sunderland would shake and shudder and then go on again, just like a man shaking his head when he's got a hard punch on the nose, and plowing back into the fight.

Meanwhile other shells were knocking out our radio, putting holes in the hull you could stick your head through, and generally raising Cain. They had us in a cross-fire, and if we wanted to get in on them we had to take it. The skipper could have turned back—he'd have been justified—but that wasn't like our skipper. He kept on. The big compass took a hit and was knocked clean through the side of the ship, leaving a hole you could crawl through. One second the compass was there and the next second it wasn't.

We were so busy we didn't notice the uproar. I can't remember anything about noise, but I know there must have been a lot of it. You don't think of what a spot you're in at a time like that. You're too intent on what you have to do. That's where training comes in, I suppose. Remember all this took place in a few seconds. We got that shooting up in a lot less time than it takes to tell about it.

We also did some work on our own. We went over that sub and the depth charges were away. But they were short. You could see them spout up in the sea just behind the sub, close, but not close enough. At the same time Shand and Stafford were pumping it into the gun crews with their guns. We were down to 75 feet and the tracers from our Sunderland were really pouring onto the deck of that first sub, and all the time we had to take the fire from the other one. The gun crews just wilted in a flash. We must have got them all. The one sub's guns stopped shooting.

We kept on taking hits ourselves, and this is where the business about Pilot Officer Shand losing his pants comes in. Our intercom had been knocked out and I had to run up and down stairs with instructions from the skipper to the men at the battle stations. A Sunderland is a big ship and there are two decks to it, so with the intercom gone you practically need a messenger boy.

When I got to Shand he was sitting on the floor, no pants, and holding up the broken plug from his intercom. He'd point at it and point at where his pants should be. He said afterward he was dead scared. Bellis and Stafford were standing over him, Bellis with his helmet blown clean off his head. He didn't get hurt. Those two started to laugh and they got me going, too, and in a couple of second Shand cracked a smile and then he started to laugh. We really roared.

Plane vs. Sub

I think we all must have been scared stiff, but it didn't seem to strike any of us at the time. When I got back on the top deck, Needham, the engineer, was singing at the top of his voice. On the U-boat it couldn't have been very good. Those depth charges we dropped must have rattled everything aboard and broken a few legs, and the machine guns with which Shand and Stafford hosed the decks didn't do anyone in sight any good.

But we were hurt. Our good old ship was loggy on the controls when we came about for the second attack. The skipper was putting her in again! The Jerries on the sub we'd attacked had manned their guns again and the other one joined it in sending up a regular curtain. It was cross-fire, down low, just where we'd have to go to get at them.

The skipper bulled in—ignored all evasive action to make sure of a kill. We wanted that Jerry. The skipper seemed to want him most. There he was, with everything shot away, his cabin full of holes, everything gone, going in again.

The old girl was down to 75 feet by now, and going straight for the Jerry through a regular storm of stuff. There was another shuddering wallop and Needham and Woodward were killed.

We went in over the sub, taking the cross-fire, and let go with more charges. Rutherford, in the tail gun, let out a yell you could hear all over the ship. I looked and the sub seemed to lift about four feet. When I looked again it was gone. That was no crash dive. It just disappeared. There were no cheers. We were all too busy.

It was just about this time that a shell hit near me. I was on a machine gun, strafing the decks of the remaining sub and not bothering about doing anything else, when I felt a jar against my hand. I looked down and found that the handle had been shot right out from between my fingers.

The second Jerry was still pounding away, registering the odd hit, but we were getting beyond range.

It was about this time I first remember hearing any sound I could identify. It was screaming, and you could hear it above the engines. They were banging as if they'd come apart, but this screaming rose above them.

Stafford and Shand went forward over the catwalk and the

skipper told them to get the two dead gunners into the wardroom. He was as cool as a cucumber. Everything below the catwalk had been shot away, leaving the whole front of the ship sort of hanging there. When they crossed the catwalk there was nothing under them but ocean. They got the gunners out and I rushed to where the screams were coming from.

It was Steves, the navigator. He was on the floor, beside his table. There was no hope of saving him. He was still alive, and he knew me. He made a motion and I bent down. He could hardly talk by this time. His good hand held his pencil—his navigator's pencil. As I bent close he said to me: "We're in 50, 40 and course to the convoy is 46. Tell the skipper."

Then he held up his right hand, still hanging onto his pencil, and gave me a thumbs up sign. I damn near cried. It was the last thing Steves ever did, making that sign.

There was no use moving him so I went to the skipper with the position, and then reported on damage. Our starboard outer engine was making 2,350 revolutions a minute; our starboard inner was doing 2,100, our port outer was making 700 and our port inner was making 300. They'd been nearly torn apart, but they were still on the job, doing the best they could. We were falling apart. All our dinghies except one had been shot off the wings, and that one might not be in the best of shape.

The skipper hauled her around and headed for the convoy, 20 miles away. He ordered us to get ready for ditching.

How we went that 20 miles none of us will ever know. Maybe the skipper put some of himself into the ship, because she managed to hang together. I was busy with the wireless, trying to make it run, and everyone went to the station the skipper had assigned. We didn't do it according to the book, because at a time like that there are things the book doesn't always take into account.

We spotted one of the escort ships and our flares went out. I had the Aldis lamp and was flashing signals by this time. Then the skipper let her down. It was the most perfect landing you could imagine, and the toughest piece of luck.

We hit 100 feet to the leeward of the escort, landed on the crest of a breaking wave, and bounced into the air again for perhaps 150 feet. Had we landed a split second sooner we'd have been all right. The breaking wave filled the lower half of our hull with water and the next second or so, when we went down again, it was a crash landing. The tail came off and we were knocked around. I came to underwater and must have gotten out through a hole in the aircraft. I don't remember.

Talking to the others afterward I found that Shand crawled out through the broken tail. Mesney, with a broken leg, went through a hole in the floor, and so did Stafford and Rutherford.

She was still floating when I came up, and the escort vessel was right alongside. Bellis lay on one of the wings, snarled up in loose wires. She'd sink any second. A sailor skinned down a ladder and got him free.

The skipper and Campbell, the third pilot, must have been thrown out through the glass in front, because I saw the skipper come up about 40 feet in front of the sinking Sunderland. I grabbed for the ship's ladder and looked down. By this time the escort ship had drifted up to where the skipper had been, and I saw him again. He was about a foot under water, and I don't think he was alive. Campbell, the RAF man, was on the ladder with me by this time and we made a grab for the skipper's jacket. We got him to the ladder, and tried to get him up, but we couldn't. He must have got caught on some of the loose wires from the old, battered Sunderland, which was just barely floating nearby. When she gave a lurch and went down, he was pulled out of our grip and went with her.

That's the way our skipper ended up. He had been just Paul to us—nobody in the crew ever called him sir. It would have made him sore.

I think that the few seconds that Campbell and I hung onto the ladder and looked down into the ocean, where the old Sunderland was drifting down with our skipper, were the worst either of us will ever put in. We would have been crying when we got on the deck of the escort if there'd been a tear left in us. But we'd gone through too much, too fast, so we just stood there until the doctor and the medical orderlies led us away, cut our clothes off, and put us to bed.

We were able to give the course taken by the second sub and the destroyer *Drury* went away in a hurry, and I heard it came back later licking its chops. They were sure they'd made a kill. That kind of squared things.

The *Drury* brought us in to Newfoundland and we were all right in two or three days.

I'd just like to note something before I wind up. A Sunderland is a good swap for two submarines, but two U-boat crews can't make up for our skipper and the pals we lost. We've got a big score to settle with the Jerries, and I hope to be in on some of the settling. That goes for everyone that's left of the crew.

After the war, Beals returned to his former job in Vernon, B.C., as a tinsmith for a heating and air-conditioning firm. He died at the age of 63 of a heart attack in January 1984.

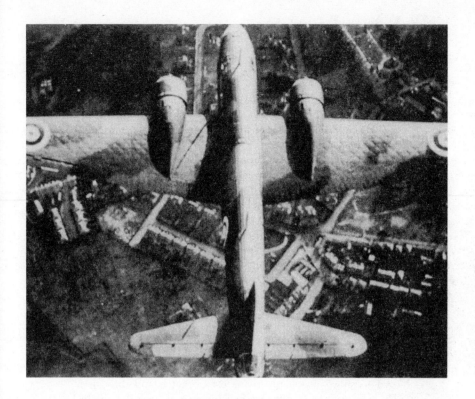

DITCHED!

—June 15, 1944—
The late Flying Officer John D. Shanahan
(as told to Geoffrey Hewelcke)

We regret to advise our readers that in the interval between the writing and the publication of this article its coauthor, Flying Officer Don Shanahan, RCAF, was killed in the crash of a Flying Fortress mail plane in Scotland.

—The Editor, 1944

"Stand by!" I shouted. "We're going to ditch her."

I reminded the second pilot not to release the dinghy until after we'd pranged [crashed]. Then I pulled the throttle back and cut the switches. I also pressed the button to full feather our one

Vickers Wellington bomber in flight.

remaining prop so's it would stop turning before we hit the water.

I had time to put on my landing light, pull the lever for the escape hatches overhead and then pull back on the wheel, trying to pancake her in.

But it just didn't work that way. We knifed into the water with one wing slightly low. The wing tore off and most of the boys were spilled out through the hole it made in the fuselage. But the navigator and I and the Wimpy kept on travelling straight down to Davy Jones.

The safety straps kept my face from bashing the remains of my instrument board, and then water rushed clean over my head.

How far down we went I didn't know but my ears were sore from the water pressure for a couple of days.

I managed to release the safety straps and get out of my seat. I made for the escape hatch above. But bobbing around between me and the hatch was a body. It was the navigator. The only way out for me was to shove him up first. I straightened him out and away he shot, his Mae West taking him up.

I needed a breath of air pretty badly at this time. Still I managed to shove myself up to the escape hatch and through it. Then—I was stuck! My foot had somehow jammed! I reached down, with my ears popping, and tore the laces off my boot. That freed my foot and I took off for the surface.

It seemed an awful long way up. I remember I had time to pull the release on my Mae West and the compressed air cartridge shot it full of air. I rose in a hurry then, but my lungs were bursting by this time and I breathed in a mixture of water and air as I shot up into the night like a porpoise.

For a while I coughed and spat and knew that I was, at any rate, still alive. Then a feeling of loneliness came over me.

"Lord, where are the rest of the guys?" I thought.

This is about as good a time as any to introduce my crew. I say my crew because although I was only a sergeant at the time, I was in charge of the Wellington bomber that we were ferrying from England, via Gibraltar, to Benghazi to help the Eighth Army push back Rommel.

But luck was against us and after we had knocked down one

Ditched!

Junkers 88 in a dogfight over the sea we ran into a swarm of 'em. Our machines were no match for their cannon. We took an awful beating and when the starboard motor caught fire I decided to hit the deck. The deck in this case was the cold, black Mediterranean.

We were a six-man crew. Me, I'm Don Shanahan from Toronto. The other Canadian was Lou Rymal from Leamington, Ont. He was front gunner. At the time both of us were serving with the RAF.

Now I run into a spot of difficulty. The other members of the crew were not Canadians. Three were members of the RAF and one belonged to the Royal Australian Air Force. Hence I don't know that I have the right to mention their family names.

This much I can do, I'm pretty sure. I can use their first names. There was George, the Australian. He was a pilot officer, superior to me in rank, but nonetheless serving as second pilot.

My navigator was another pilot officer. His first name was Jules, a dark heavy-set Jewish boy from somewhere in the south of England.

The wireless air gunner was the third pilot officer. His first name was Johnny. He was a Welshman.

The last man of the crew, quite literally, was Tim. He was a sergeant rear gunner. Tim was a young Cockney.

Now, as I said before, we were all floundering around in the dark waters of the Mediterranean. I had no idea where the others were. Then I heard the most welcome sound in the world. It was a steady hissing—the dinghy filling with air from its cylinders. If I'd seen George just then I could have kissed him for doing such a good job of releasing it.

The moon popped out of the clouds again and there, not two feet from me, was Jules. I looked at him and saw trickles of blood running down from his ears and spreading on the wetness of his cheeks.

My own ears felt funny, too, and for a moment I wondered if I was kidding myself about that hissing noise from the dinghy. Then I spoke to Jules. I told him that I'd get the dinghy because I was a good swimmer.

And so I set out for the rubber boat, which was beginning to drift away before a 20-mile wind. I kicked off my other shoe and within 50 yards I'd caught the dinghy, hauled myself in and unlashed the paddles.

I'd started paddling toward Jules when I suddenly realized that the other boys would be unable to see me if the moon dodged behind the clouds again. So I tossed a flare into the sea. It was one of those automatic things. You strip off some surgical tape and as soon as the flare touches water it burns with a bright white light.

Within that circle of light I saw a Mae West with somebody's arms waving around helplessly. I paddled up and found it was Tim. He hadn't ditched his parachute harness, which was extra weight, and had forgotten to tie his Mae West properly down. The result was that the life jacket had got up over his ears and he was shipping water.

I managed to unbuckle his parachute harness and grab his arms. I lifted his arms over his head and then shoved him under water and pulled up. Up he popped like a cork—and I grabbed him and had him over the side of the dinghy.

Then I saw George. He seemed to be hurt. He wasn't unconscious—simply dopey. He was floating there in his Mae West and apparently didn't know what was going on and couldn't help himself. Later we discovered he had been seriously hurt internally when the Wimpy pranged into the sea. I pulled him in next.

That flare was good. It burned for five minutes or more and lit up at least 100 yards around the dinghy.

Next I saw Lou Rymal. He was bobbing along in a swell as calm and placid as could be.

"You all right, Lou?" I called.

"Sure," he said. "What's all the excitement about?"

So I pulled him in and he took another paddle—things like huge web-fingered gloves that you had to use while bending way over the inflated side of the dinghy.

We paddled against the wind, looking for Jules. Presently the flare burned out and we used our little signalling flashlights and called his name. But we didn't have any luck. We never found him. He was a good guy...

But we did find Johnny, the wireless op. He was bleeding like a stuck pig. Tim fixed him up with the first-aid kit in the dinghy. We'd all got roughed up considerably in the crash. Lou developed a couple of the nicest black eyes I've ever seen. George, of course, was the one who'd got it worst.

We bailed the dinghy dry and took stock of the situation. Right away we could see it was a rum go. For instance, we had no provisions. The leather boxes which were supposed to contain a week's grub for each man had been torn away. We had four rubber hot-water bottles that were supposed to hold drinking water. But they had been punctured and the water had leaked out.

Lou had a pint flask half full of water in his pocket. That was the only water we had.

We tried to figure our position and decided we were about 300 miles east of Gibraltar and about 60 miles off the Spanish coast.

That first night we spent in misery. It was cold. There was a nasty swell and the wind freshened to nearly gale force. We were all wet and chilled. Also we were crowded. There were five of us in the dinghy and we had to sit with our legs drawn up.

At daylight we had another confab. Chances of being rescued by any aircraft looking for us were pretty thin. Still there always was a possibility. So we tossed overboard two of the water markers that would leave a yellow trail behind the raft for rescue aircraft to follow. We also put on the yellow hats they keep in the Mae Wests so that we'd be more easily seen. Then we unshipped the air pump and used it until the dinghy walls were firm and hard again.

The first day we had a look at Lou Rymal's flask. We decided we'd better not touch it until we absolutely had to. So that day we didn't drink. Nor the day after—not until the third day.

Prevailing winds in that part of the Mediterranean were usually east and west. But by a break we had a wind that blew us due north, toward Spain. Our Mae Wests had yard long wide collars that were bright yellow. They were supposed to float on the water if you were in the drink and so make you more conspicuous. We sat with our backs to the wind and held these collars up like sails until our arms ached.

But before long we got a rough awakening about the nature of the Mediterranean. The wind was getting stronger all the time and now the seas were getting wicked—it's a lot of baloney about the Med being lovely and blue and tranquil. It can be dirty—very, very dirty.

During the first two days we were capsized six times and it was a shaky do each time because the lightened craft would drift away in the high wind so fast that we had a tough time catching it.

This is what used to happen. We would be riding along all nicely and then the first of a series of great seas would overtake us. We found they always came in threes. It would tower up over us, maybe 30 or 40 feet high, and the dinghy would start riding the wall of water. We'd ship a lot of water and usually the third wave would tip our waterlogged craft right over.

Lou and I had both played around with sailboats on the Great Lakes before the war and we decided we'd better do something. We took apart a short rope ladder in the dinghy. We tied the four corners of my leather flying jacket to it and made a sea anchor, which we let drag about 10 feet behind the dinghy. That slowed down our speed before the wind a lot—but it kept us right side up.

That storm kept up the whole nine days we were at sea. Sometimes the wind velocity must have got up to 50 or 60 miles an hour. You couldn't hear yourself speak. The words would be torn right from your lips and hurled away and smothered in the crashing roar of the breaking seas. Never once was the sun out for more than an hour in a single day. Clouds tore along low in the sky and we wished they'd give—we wanted water so much. But they never did.

On the other hand we never were dry. Constantly soaked in salt water our skins bagged and shrivelled like a scrub woman's hands.

The storm blew us north for the first three days and we tried to help the dinghy along with the paddles, figuring it was best to keep busy. All of us took turns at the paddles except poor George, who was hurt badly inside and could move only with great pain.

About 6 p.m. of the third day Lou and I sighted cliffs ahead. We knew it was the coast of Spain. We got within a mile and a half of the shore. Then the wind died down and promptly switched to offshore. We started paddling like mad then. At first we made a little gain. Then Lou and I jumped overboard and tried to tow the

154

dinghy with the rope from the sea anchor. But we were a lot weaker than we thought and had to give up after half an hour.

By this time we had forced our way within a mile of the shore. We could see movement on the cliffs, but couldn't be certain whether we saw people or cattle. There weren't any fishing craft in sight. Nor was there any house or village.

Four hours had passed since we had first sighted the coast and the wind was getting so strong that we gave up battling against it. So we decided to set off a marine distress rocket. It shot up stars like a Roman candle—13 of them, red, yellow and green. Then the rocket itself glowed red for 15 minutes. We got out our little signalling torches and flashed SOS at the dark cliffs. Nothing happened.

The whole of that night the wind blew strongly, carrying us in a south-easterly direction, away from Gibraltar and away from the Spanish coast toward the centre of the Mediterranean.

Then the dinghy started to leak air. This was due to the jerking of the sea anchor and we finally posted a man, kneeling, in the stern, facing the storm, with the rope twisted about his hands. We all took turns playing shock absorber for the sea anchor while the rest of us took spells at the pump. Also, we had to contribute more clothes to the sea anchor because they kept on tearing loose.

Each time a dangerously big sea came along the man at the stern would jerk the sea anchor toward him to allow some slack. Then he'd grab the gunwale rope at the stern and bend the rear of the dinghy up so that the top of the sea would not surge over it.

At the same time the rest of us would lean well toward the bow to help him raise the stern as much as possible and when he yelled we'd scramble aft just as the crest of the sea passed under the dinghy.

During the worst weather we had to do this every two minutes for hours at a stretch—and then grab the pump and try to keep the dinghy walls inflated between seas. It was grim work.

None of us had had any sleep from the time we pranged into the deck and we were getting so tired we were dopey. It took every ounce of will power to stay awake. Actually, during the entire nine days there were only about six hours when we could relax—and four of these we spent in paddling furiously while trying to reach the coast of Spain.

Finally the boys would drop asleep for a few seconds at a time, waking up when their heads jerked down. Then they'd ask me what time it was. My watch kept on going and I must have given the time thousands of times during those nine days.

Johnny was not doing too badly. Either the first-aid bandages or the salt water had stopped the bleeding. George, however, was in really bad shape. Also he suffered more from the cold than the rest of us because he couldn't keep himself warm by working.

On the third day we'd given the injured men a mouthful of water each from Lou's flask. Lou and I stuck it out until the fourth day and then took a mouthful each. Then we gave the rest of the water to the lads who had been hurt.

The evening of the fourth day, however, Lou and I were pretty thirsty. We'd read that if you soaked yourself in sea water you wouldn't die of thirst and we also wanted to see whether we could fix up some of the dinghy. The wind dropped for about an hour just before sunset and nearly all of us went overboard to float in the sea. We fixed the worst leak in the dinghy. One of the boys had chewed gum from his escape kit until it was all tacky. He used this with some Cellophane from a packet of cigarettes to make something like a blowout patch, which we crammed into the crack at the joint. It made a pretty good repair job.

Being in the water relieved our thirst to some extent, but it seemed to leave us awfully weak. At sunset we climbed back into the dinghy and wrung out our wet clothes, trying to get them moderately dry for the night, working in a dopey daze because we were so exhausted.

Suddenly Johnny lifted a hand over his eyes and stared at the horizon.

"I'm beginning to see things," he said. "That ship's duff gen, isn't it?" Lou glanced up.

"Holy smoke, no!" he said. "That's pukka gen!"

A small freighter was poking across the horizon. It would come fairly close to us, we thought.

Immediately our exhaustion vanished. We started paddling on

a course that we thought would intercept it. But presently we could see that the freighter would pass at least a mile off.

We built a human pyramid on the raft, with two of us below and one man on top waving a shirt. But the sun was setting directly behind us and we must have been hard to see. Next we lit a red flare—but that was also killed by the sunset. We really ran into tough luck with that ship. We had helio mirrors to flash, but with the sun sinking directly behind us we couldn't bring the reflection to bear on the freighter.

One or two of the boys absolutely refused to believe that the lookouts had not spotted us. They thought that the ship's skipper wasn't having any part of us because German submarines have used lifeboats and all kinds of other traps to lure ships within gun or torpedo range.

Finally the freighter crossed the horizon and night fell. With darkness the wind came again. Along came the big seas once more.

A couple of the boys lost heart now. George was the most affected. He'd been badly hurt and had a concussion besides. Johnny didn't feel any too good either. Both of them started to talk about their mothers and how they were going to pull through for their sakes. But they'd lost their fighting spirit.

The next morning we prayed to God for rescue. Before that we'd only cursed our luck. Prayer helped. We were all of different denominations, but we'd all join in the Lord's Prayer. It got to be a regular thing to pray in the morning and again at nightfall. We'd recite the Lord's Prayer and then each of us would add a prayer of his own.

On the fifth day George wouldn't brighten up at all. He was in terrible pain and despondent as well. Lou Rymal's flask of fresh water was empty by now and we saw George sneaking little drinks of sea water.

Suddenly he handed me his escape kit with money and maps in it. Up to that time he'd had it in his tunic pocket.

"This bothers me," he said. "Look after it, will you?"

Then he said that he hoped the boys would get through all right.

I threw the kit back at him and told him not to be stupid. We'd

CANADA AT WAR

all get through together.

He seemed to quieten down after that but some hours later methodically took off his Mae West and his leather flying jacket. He said he wanted to dry off. After a while he put his jacket on again and said he wanted to sit on the stern gunwale and stretch his legs a bit. Suddenly he heaved himself overboard.

We made a wild grab for him but he kicked himself free. I threw him my Mae West but he just waved to us and inside 30 seconds we lost sight of him.

This was a bad day. Now Johnny started getting delirious. We tried to keep an eye on him to prevent him following George but it was terribly difficult because we were so played out.

There were only three of us strong enough to do any work now: Lou and Tim and I. We tried to fix a schedule. One of us would pump for 10 minutes. Another would hold the sea anchor and the third would try to get a 10 minute nap.

In one of these I was dreaming of Niagara Falls—all beautiful fresh water. Suddenly I wakened with my mouth full of something. It was wet! It was salt water! I spat. I looked. Tim had gone to sleep at the pump and Lou, holding the sea anchor rope, with his back to him, hadn't noticed it. The dinghy had leaked so much air in less than 10 minutes that it was barely afloat.

Lou and I started bailing like mad until the gunwales rounded out again. Tim was apologetic. We knew that he was pretty far gone and suspected he had been drinking sea water.

The night was really terrible. It seemed so long and cold and dark. Johnny mumbled and moaned to himself all night long. He talked baby talk and became delirious. He flung himself about wildly. The dinghy by now was braced together with a harness of ropes and neckties and was in a really precarious condition. But Johnny kicked at the ropes and lashings in his delirium and we couldn't stop him.

The sixth day dawned. We held our prayers and then looked at the compasses. The wind had turned again and now was sweeping us toward the African coast. We thought we could keep afloat for quite a while yet and had a good chance of making a landing if the wind kept up. So we started talking about what we might run into.

158

Ditched!

Our chief worry was that we'd be washed up against a rocky cliff coast because North Africa is pretty mountainous. But mostly our talk was wishful thinking; trying to encourage ourselves to live; trying to give our minds something to chew on to take them off our thirst and hunger.

The seventh day was wicked. It was still storming and we were being pitched up and down. I felt very low that day. I kept thinking of home and of mother and of everything that was swell back in Toronto. Then I realized that I was going the way Johnny and George had gone and that I'd better snap out of it.

By this time all the clothing I had left consisted of my underpants, vest and my service shirt. But despite the bitter temperatures, despite the wind and spray I never caught cold, never once sneezed or coughed or had a sniffle. I shivered often. Lordy, how I shivered! I'd shake all over and my teeth would chatter like castanets—and then I'd get over my shivering and be almost comfortable for a little while. Later on doctors told me that I probably shivered so much and so hard that I warmed myself up as if I'd run half a mile.

On the eighth day neither Lou nor I could swallow the hard black chocolate left in our escape kit. We could grind it to powder between our molars but couldn't get it down. The inside of my mouth was as dry as an old shoe. In desperation, I dropped a chlorine water-disinfecting tablet into some of my urine, let it dissolve and then took a sip of it to wash the chocolate dust down my throat.

Tim and Johnny were barely alive—nothing more. We did our best to keep their heads out of the water washing about in the half-filled dinghy. We were too weak now to do any bailing.

On the ninth night Lou and I decided that we were too weak to paddle. We were too weak, also, to take spells acting as shock absorbers for the sea anchor. Besides our wrists were torn to ribbons from the rope. So we tried a new system. We tied the rope around our ankles and lay down in the water in the dinghy. Our leg muscles were still strong enough to take the drag from the sea anchor, even if our arms and wrists were not.

Gradually, that evening, the waves changed in nature. They

became a huge rolling swell. Then we saw sea gulls. Soon after that Lou made a grab overboard at something floating in the water and came up with a handful of seaweed. We knew then we were near-ing shore.

Around 10 that night I saw a light on the horizon. For a while I looked at it steadily and kept on pumping, thinking that it was a planet just coming over the horizon. Then I saw another light. This was too good to keep to myself. So I shook Lou and pointed.

"Lights," I said.

Lou was still half-asleep. He'd been dreaming that he was com-ing back from a raid on Germany. He looked up dopily, first at me and then at the lights.

"You're a lousy navigator if that's the best airport you can find," he grumbled. Then he dropped off to sleep. I shook Lou again and again. I got real mad at him. Finally he snapped out of his sleep and looked at the lights with intelligence in his eyes.

"Land," I shouted.

"Well, I'll be…," said Lou slowly. "You're right!"

We set to work then. We blew up all the Mae Wests and lashed them low on ourselves and the invalids in case we had to swim for it. We pulled up the sea anchor and scudded as fast as we could before the wind.

It was getting on to 11 p.m. now. We kept staring at the lights, wondering what they were. Later we found they were markers for the port of Mostaganem, a bit east of Oran in Algeria, and later used by the Americans as one of the landing ports for the invasion of North Africa.

But at the time the lights put the wind up us. We figured, rightly enough, that where there were lighthouses there must be a bad coast. Actually the coast was dangerous—huge rocks and cliffs. But for once our luck held. We hit a spot that was not too foul.

At the time we didn't know our luck. All we knew was that surf was breaking all around us. The white water started to break over into the dinghy. We had to bail like mad and pump at the same time. We tried to rouse Tim and Johnny to help us or at least to keep their heads out of the water by themselves. But Tim was cold and stiff—and so was Johnny. We couldn't get a movement out of either of them.

That was about the worst part of the trip. The suspense was terrific because we were certain the dinghy would be bashed into the rocks or against a cliff. We bailed and pumped and just when we thought we had things under control a big comber suddenly flipped the dinghy up and almost over. Lou was thrown overboard. I grabbed him and caught a handful of hair. When the next wave lifted his side of the dinghy I jerked forward and brought him into the boat. Lou splashed face down into the water and rolled over till his face was clear.

In about 10 minutes more we were on shore. By a miracle the dinghy made a crash landing on a bit of sandy beach. Lou and I got out and tried to stand. We fell flat on our faces. We crawled to the dinghy and the next wave helped us to push it farther up the beach. Then we collapsed in the sand.

Presently I looked at my watch again. It was four o'clock in the morning. Over to the east there was a faint greyness in the sky.

Then Lou and I tried to haul Tim and Johnny out of the dinghy. But we soon gave up that effort. They were stiff. In the uncertain light their faces and hands looked bluish. We knew then that they were dead; that they had probably been dead for hours.

About this time a crazy delusion overpowered me. I was certain, somehow, that we were in the Bay of Fundy, where there are the highest tides in the world. Above us there was a 300-foot cliff. I had the feeling that we had to get to the top of this cliff before the tide came in and trapped us. It was all a lot of nonsense, actually, because at that point in the Mediterranean the tide is only about a foot.

But I suddenly started hounding Lou to climb that cliff. I felt the tide was lapping right at our heels. Lou, I guess, climbed just to humor me. But we were woefully weak, and it wasn't until six hours later that we stood on the top of the cliff.

It was broad daylight now and out of the shelter of the cliff we noticed that there was a strong wind blowing. Lou turned to face it.

"It's changed," he croaked. "It's blowing *offshore* now!"

Editor's note: The two Canadian survivors stumbled into a nearby settlement where they were befriended by a priest. A doctor called in to attend them turned the airmen over to the Vichy French authorities. Shanahan and Rymal were interned in a desert prisoner-of-war camp and were not released until some months later when the Allied invasion of French North Africa took place. Eventually they returned to Canada.

After the war, Lou Rymal moved to Winnipeg where he worked as a parts manager for a car dealership before dying at 59 of leukemia in 1974.

Geoffrey Hewelcke was an assistant editor of Maclean's.

STAND BY TO BEACH

—July 15, 1944—
Commander Peter MacRitchie, RCNVR

London (by cable)—Along the runnels that carve the Seine Bay from Ouistreham to Grandcamp, landing craft of the Royal Canadian Navy are still scudding in, depositing their troops and slipping out again. Meanwhile, behind them is a formidable array of Canadian destroyers, assault craft and parent ships farther out in the Channel. Canadian motor torpedo boat flotillas are harassing E-boats [enemy torpedo boats] in waters swept clean by Canadian minesweepers for convoys, which Canadian corvettes and frigates are helping escort.

Canadian troops preparing to land.

That was the picture that presented itself as I stood on the bridge of Landing Craft 250, flirting with the coast of Normandy in the flush of D-Day noontime, while we awaited the order to crash onto the beach at Bernières-sur-mer and disgorge our troops of the Third Canadian Division. It was a picture of a Dominion burgeoning forth as a naval power, marshalled with the ships of the other Allied nations in the greatest display of unchallenged might the world has ever known.

What made the scene possible? I asked myself this question as we nursed our damaged craft back to England in the purple of that Tuesday evening. She was down by the bows, her forepeak filled with water, and we were a haggard and weary band of reservists. I raised my head and there to the west came our little sweepers, steaming proudly to sweep fresh channels for that unbroken procession of ships that crossed from England to France and back again to the westward. Beating up Channel came our Canadian corvettes, escorting new and strange devices which sailors hesitate to call ships. They were rocket ships.

In these two scenes I found the answer. These little ships had created this magnificent panorama. These little ships who in Britain's days of adversity had brought the convoys across the western ocean and ultimately won the Battle of the Atlantic. They had made it possible, because without victory in the Atlantic this great excursion to the shores of France could never have been accomplished. And the sweepers had played their part—*Georgian, Minas, Wasaga* and the rest of them. Now that the bigger ships could be spared they had reverted to the role for which they were first built. Britain had asked Canada if she could spare them. Now Canada could. So their sweeping gear was reinstalled and two flotillas of them sailed from Canada, manned fully by Canadians, to sweep the lanes for this gigantic landing. And if you ask any sailor who was there on D-Day which ships had done the major job he would tell you without hesitation, "Why, the sweepers did."

We in the landing craft flotillas went to France on the Monday afternoon that was heralded in official quarters as D-Day but which meteorological reports vetoed. There was something gala about the scene. Row on row of little craft and big ships steamed their way almost idly across the waters that separate England from the Continent. This kaleidoscope was accentuated as you sailed into the Bay at dawn of Tuesday, right under the noses of the Nazi batteries. It looked like the dawn that marked the opening of the season's regatta rather than the dawn of freedom. It was like Spithead all lit up for the coronation. Colored chandeliers dropped by enemy reconnaissance planes had flared all over the nocturnal scene, and now, as our little white-and-blue striped LCIs nudged each other along, with their jack staffs a galaxy of bunting, the bigger ships hoisted their pennants. "Good luck, drive on," they read.

We drove on and I could see Lieut.-Cdr. Harris Huston, Rossburn, Man., our flotilla leader, sweeping the horizon, looking for that speck on the chart which we were told at our briefing would be our landing spot. We pirouetted around that Bay almost endlessly, and suddenly you forgot about the regatta atmosphere for *Nelson* and *Warspite* and *Ramillies* were firing. They were stilling the coastal batteries and their accuracy was phenomenal. The cruisers *Scylla* and *Orion* and a dozen others were firing too. As we spun around on the coast side fringe of the armada we could see the Canadian destroyers *Algonquin* and *Sioux* smashing away at their land targets, and assault craft from Prince Henry and Prince David, loaded down, crashing through the waves on their way to the beaches. But the assault craft were having a hard time of it. The booby traps and submerged mines were taking their toll.

It was here that two of Canada's three landing craft flotillas entered the picture. It happened almost three hours after the first landings had been effected and the order, or, rather, the request to the Canadians was accepted without hesitation. The signal said, "Assault craft having a hard time at Bernières-sur-mer. Will you have a go, Canada?" We were driving around in line ahead when all of a sudden the flotilla leader's lamp flashed and in a second we were line abreast and striking for the beach of Bernières-sur-mer at full speed.

Those soldier boys from Galt and Kitchener and Cape Breton and Ottawa and Toronto and Brantford and a hundred villages and hamlets have courted death a score of times since we set them down that morning, but I doubt very much if the thrill of that drive

165

Disembarking from landing craft at Bernières-sur-mer.

through the sea to Bernières will ever leave them. We who had lived in cramped quarters in the ship with them for days and had eaten out of the same ration tins cried to them as they stood nearly 200 strong in our ship with their packs and their bicycles and their rifles ready to land. We cried to them, "Hold tight, we're going in." They held tight and in almost a split second we had crashed our way head on, right onto the sand, right over the mines and booby traps.

The Nazi death-dealing appliances were exploding all around us but these men of the 3rd Division never faltered. The ramps went crashing to the beach; the soldiers grabbed their gear and after wading ashore up to their armpits, with rifles and bicycles held high, were piped up the beaches by their regimental pipers. The enemy snipers to the west of us were kicking dust spots on the greensward above the sand and the enemy mortars were moaning as the troops took up their position. They were undertaking a job

166

to which they had not been assigned.

When the landing had first been planned this brigade was a follow-up unit. These soldiers were supposed to grab their bicycles and force their way into a certain rendezvous, there to dig in. But as we received our order to beach, which incidentally was not at the spot to which we had first been assigned, we could see that it was not being held by Allied troops. This brigade, therefore, had to create a bridgehead, and as we forced our way from the sand bars we could see them digging in at the beaches. From Bernières eastward there was a mass of smoke and flame, but we know that those rugged men of Canada counteracted all the obstacles of warfare and are now fighting their way well inland. We left three of our craft on the beach badly holed but our casualties were few.

Lieut. Charles Bond, RCNVR, husky Toronto policeman, was hit in the neck when a mine went up right under our craft and the shrapnel flew onto the bridge of his craft. Farther along to the eastward a flotilla under Lieut.-Cdr. Hugh Doheny, Montreal, was landing more Canadian troops and contending with the same hazards as we had, while the third flotilla under Lieut.-Cdr. Lorne Kyle, Vancouver, was operating with the United States Navy, beaching troops of another force.

We had little time to wait, but as we pumped our way out we stopped to look about us and lend a hand to other cripples if need be. You could see Lieut. Johnny O'Rourke, the red-headed Irishman who was at St. Nazaire and Dieppe and knows the coast of France like his home street in Calgary. You could see him on the bridge exchanging pleasantries with Lieut. Hugh McColl Harrison, Toronto.

In our craft there was still the same banter in the midst of all this. Some of us were going back for another load but others had to stay as their craft were too far gone. Lieut. Andy Wedd, Toronto, who won his DSC at Dieppe and went on to North Africa and Sicily, had another craft in tow and he took his place in that procession to sail back to England at four knots. It took him many hours but he got there, and he has since been back to the same beaches. You could see Lieut. John Shaw, Vancouver, a veteran of convoy work who was converted to landing craft, standing offshore, waiting for the word to crash his way in. And crash his way in he did, and we watched his men go down the ramps with lightning precision. You could see officers and men in other Canadian craft wading ashore to detach mines and traps from obstacles. These they piled on the beach, regardless of danger, and miraculously enough they live to tell the story.

We came back through that concentration of ships, to which no film or story will ever do justice from a descriptive standpoint. *Warspite* and *Nelson* were still busy at work, hurling their one-ton projectiles far into enemy-held territory. And far to the west of us two of Canada's outstanding ships, the Tribal destroyers *Haida* and *Huron*, in company with sister ships of the Royal Navy, were patrolling the middle reaches of the English Channel. They were guarding the western flanks of the invasion armada on its way across. Had any enemy destroyers, E-boats or submarines attempted to attack they would have had to pass through that screen. Enemy destroyers a night or two later did try to attack, and for their pains suffered the loss of at least one of their destroyers midway across the Channel. *Prince Henry* and *Prince David* passed us and the officers and men waved. Many of their assault craft had been lost on the beaches and the ships' decks looked bare. They were going back to their home port for a fresh supply of craft and a fresh supply of troops. They got them and back they went on the shuttle service.

Midnight found us in England, in a semi-sinking condition; but two days later the craft had been patched up and was in service again. I went over that same scene by air five days later and I could see the same warships hammering away and the same landing craft methodically discharging their troops. There were the same scenes of desolation on the beaches—stranded enemy tanks and burned-out homes all enveloped in smoke.

D-Day and H-Hour. We had waited for four months, during which time the ships of the Allied navies and of the Allied merchant navies had worked continuously in preparation. Now here was the aftermath. Still not an enemy plane in the sky and the land batteries had been silenced.

As I looked down from this reconnaissance aircraft I could not help but think of the words of the Chief of Staff at our last briefing prior to embarkation. He said, "What Philip of Spain tried and failed to do; what Napoleon would have liked to do but didn't do; what Hitler hadn't the courage to do, we are about to do, and by the grace of God we shall." We did, and we of the Royal Canadian Navy are proud to have been there.

A city editor of the Windsor Star *before the war, Commander MacRitchie went on to serve in the Far East and was present at the Japanese surrender. After the war, he worked as a journalist in Montreal and as news editor of the* Detroit Times. *He died at 84 in October 1992.*

ASSAULT ON NORMANDY

—July 15, 1944—
Lionel Shapiro

With the Canadian Forces in France— History is standing astride these rolling Norman fields and resolving its own direction for perhaps a thousand years to come. We mortals who sit below can only be awed by its mighty presence. But if I cannot write world history in its proper perspective, perhaps I can write a personal version of Canadian history as it was unfolded before my eyes during these last flaming days, because between the little seaside town of Bernières-sur-mer and the Caen battle front, Canadian troops have written an immortal story.

Landing with bicycles at Bernières-sur-mer.

Assault on Normandy

For me the story began on the weekend of May 28. The Sunday was gracious and warm, and over London hung an expectant hush. People knew something was in the process of happening. There were no troops thronging the streets and no holiday gaiety on Piccadilly. Like the rest of the assault correspondents, I had been cautioned to remain close to my telephone. Sunday and Monday passed slowly; the waiting was an excruciating ordeal. Then, early on Tuesday morning, the summons came. I was to report with full battle kit at a secret rendezvous at 4 p.m. Nine correspondents attached to the Canadian assault forces gathered excitedly at the rendezvous point somewhere out of London, and in a few minutes we were in jeeps rolling out of London toward a British port. At a halfway point, we were driven through a heavily guarded gate and in a huge manor house we found some 20 British and American correspondents awaiting us. A brigadier then read out our names and the assault units to which each of us would be attached. I drew a brigade of the 3rd Canadian Division.

We found our brigade in a marshalling area enclosed by barbed wire and heavily guarded by troops. Once inside, we were completely cut off from the outside world. We still did not know where and when the assault would take place, but the country was clearly indicated by the fact that the troops were playing poker with French five-franc notes.

Then on a certain evening early in June, we got into transport and rolled out of the camp. We were on our way. It was dark when we rolled through the gates into the enclosed port area and took our places among the thousands of trucks, tanks and guns inching toward the dockside. Then a wisp of dawn appeared in the east, and like a stage effect the light slowly increased over a beautiful and terrifying panorama on the harbor waters. There were ships— hundreds of them—riding at anchor. From great battleships to smaller landing craft, they were strung out as far as the eye could see.

At last it was our turn to board. Our vehicles rolled down a concrete ramp and into the open mouth of a tank landing ship. Within hours, the ship was crammed tight with fighting vehicles. The ship steamed to mid-harbor to take its place in the line of invasion craft. The deck was jammed with tank crews and brigade officers. Six of us were accommodated in a room snugly built for two bunks. We rode at anchor all day, apprehensive of the brisk wind that was blowing up the sheltered waters around us. And we wondered how treacherously the Channel waters would behave. It didn't help when there was a general issue of two vomit bags per person.

I was hardly able to sleep that night, so vast was my excitement. We rode at anchor the next day, all of us sniffing like seals as we sampled the wind. Early in the evening, the OC [Officer in Command] Troops walked into the wardroom, then said quietly, "H-Hour is at 7:35 tomorrow morning." I looked at the calendar. It was June 5. I went out on deck and watched the green countryside of Britain turn grey in the distance.

The armada carrying the 3rd Canadian Division plunged through choppy seas without incident. It seemed uncanny that the Luftwaffe should not have spotted the collection of ships in the harbor; and it was ominous that we should not yet have evoked an enemy reaction although we were already nearing the coast of Normandy. The ship plunged on, sometimes rolling heavily. The tanks strained at their cables. Some of the troops were sick.

"Flares to starboard." A lookout shouted the words to the bridge. The luminous dial of my watch made it 3:10—four and a half hours to zero hour. A single flare hung in the sky; suddenly there were three, four, five, 20, 50, 100! They burst in the sky in orange, yellow and red until it looked as though a gargantuan Christmas tree was rising in the sky.

The convoy rode through a dawn almost as sullen as the sea. The only sign of action was the roar of planes overhead. Below decks, tank crews were scrambling over their machines preparatory to landing. The officers stood on deck scanning the horizon for signs of the Normandy coast.

Suddenly, a low rumble reached our ears. "The naval guns have opened up," our skipper said. The ship moved on under a canopy of fighter planes. A few minutes later we moved into the battle area. The spires of churches could be seen sticking out of the smoke haze over the beaches of Bernières and Courseulles-sur-mer. Below the smoke, the first Canadian infantry units, accompanied by tanks, were moving up the beaches. To the accompaniment of

Assault on Normandy

Régiment de la Chaudière in Normandy, June 6, 1944.

the confusing thunder of war—at this stage one could not distinguish between our naval and tank guns and the enemy's shore batteries—our landing ship dropped anchors at its appointed place, about 2,500 yards offshore.

The leading infantry landing ships, carrying the first Canadian assault troops, were caught on the beach by the receding tide. They were empty of troops. The Canadians were already at close grips with the enemy and the long-awaited battle for the three-mile stretch of Hitler's vaunted coastal fortifications was joined. This is what was happening under the smoke and haze during the fateful minutes between 7:35 a.m. and 10 a.m.:

Two brigades of Canadians dashed ashore promptly at zero hour accompanied by Canadian tanks carrying heavy guns for use against the sea walls. At Bernières, the centre of the Canadian assault area, a strip of mined beach, 75 yards deep, was commanded by a low wall behind which was hidden half a battalion of Germans equipped with light automatic weapons. These Germans were

173

Captured Germans on D-Day.

already stunned by the half-hour's violent bombardment from warships and heavy bombers. Engineers and tanks rolled up to the wall and smashed breaches through which troops of an Ontario regiment swarmed to kill their first Germans and take more than 200 prisoners.

On both flanks of Bernières, towards St-Aubin-sur-mer and Courseulles, were situated the main German defences from which the Germans could pour devastating crossfire onto the Bernières beach. On these flanking positions, Canadians of eastern and western formations won their greatest glory. Here, there was only a 10-yard depth of sand beach, then a 15-yard depth of barbed wire and behind this the most modern German steel and concrete defences. On each flank, three big guns were entrenched underground, each capable of sinking a battleship. These gun positions were connected by underground passages.

174

Assault on Normandy

Under the covering fire of tanks, some still in their landing craft 50 yards at sea, the Canadians swarmed against the flank positions. The first wave of troops was caught by machine-gun fire and died on the barbed wire. Other troops leaped over the bodies of their comrades, and into the very mouths of the cannon, to fling grenades through the small ranging apertures.

Meanwhile, our troops and tanks, as soon as they smashed through a section of beach defences, rushed inland. That was Montgomery's most urgent order: "Don't fight on the beaches a moment longer than necessary. Break through and move inland as far as possible to peg out claims. Leave the still active German beach defences to follow-up troops."

Thus, the battle on the beaches continued for almost three hours, while the survivors of the original assault units were already four or five miles inland. Each succeeding landing party fought as briefly as possible against the German beach defenders still holding out, then swarmed inland by all possible roads.

By the time I landed, wide strips of beach were cleared, but the fighting was still violent on the farthest flanks. Carrying only a typewriter, I raced up the beach and into Bernières. In a dining-room of a small hotel, still miraculously standing, about 300 yards back of the beach, I wrote my first newspaper story. Then, I returned to the beach and followed parties of the Royal Marines who were "winkling" isolated German units out of camouflaged dugouts which had escaped the notice of the assault infantry. The scene was a nightmare of exploding mines, dead bodies, mostly German, and live Germans approaching with hands raised high in the air.

Ten hours after H-Hour, I found a Canadian officer who could give me the first report on what was happening inland. The western Canadian troops had pushed through almost eight miles inland to the outer defences of Caen. This proved to be the outstanding job done by any troops in the British-Canadian sector and it sealed the success of the assault in our sector.

I wandered as far afield as I dared. The town itself and the beach flanks were alive with snipers, and mines were still exploding. Our troops and tanks were coming ashore and racing inland.

175

The smoke of the battle still hung low over the ruined town. Desperately tired, I wandered back to the hotel. The blond and pretty daughter of the proprietor served wine, explaining that this had been carefully hidden from the hated Boche. Through a window I could see scores of German prisoners being marched to the beach, and at the roadside French residents were jeering at them with eloquent gestures.

Darkness was falling now and German aircraft were beginning to drop bombs on the beach. I went to a field and fell into a sleep of exhaustion. A great and historic day in Canadian history was ended.

Shapiro, one of Canada's top war correspondents, filed this report ten days after the June 6 invasion. The winner of a Governor General's Award for his 1955 war novel The Sixth of June, *he was Maclean's chief foreign correspondent for nearly 20 years. In addition to novels, after the war he wrote plays, short stories and screenplays, before dying at 50 of cancer in 1958.*

I

DROPPED
ALONE

August 1, 1944

Private Alexander Huton

(as told to Lionel Shapiro)

This is the story of a fabulous adventure as it was lived during the first dramatic days of the invasion of France by a 21-year-old Canadian private, Alexander Huton, Prescott, Ont. Sandy-haired and slightly built, Huton jumped with a Canadian parachute battalion many hours before dawn of D-Day. In order to record this story Lionel Shapiro crept to a front-line position. He and Huton sat under a tree less than 800 yards from the German lines and the parachutist's story was related to the constant accompaniment of shells whistling overhead and

Paratrooper jumping from Douglas Dakota.

mortar rounds dropping close. Two years ago Huton joined the Army at Prescott, Ont., and requested service with a parachute battalion out of sheer love for adventure. His peacetime occupation was machinist's helper in the Prescott Marine Works. He trained in Canada, the United States and England, making 17 practice jumps before the fateful 18th landed him in France. This is his story as he told it within 24 hours of his almost miraculous return to our lines.   —The Editor, 1944

Somewhere in France (by cable)—We were on deck and ready for the Big Show for about three days before it really happened. Maybe there were postponements. I don't know. But it was pretty nerve-racking waiting for the signal that the party was really on. We were confident all right, but you know how it is when you've trained for and thought about a certain day for two whole years. You sort of get impatient when you know it's pretty close, and you can't wait for it to happen so it will be behind you and finished with. Well, we sat around those three days and smoked and played cards, but mostly we cleaned our weapons over and over again and thought about the party.

Then on June 5 the company commander gathered us together and said, "Tonight's the night." I was glad, because it had been too tough waiting around. Anyway we went out to an airport about 10 o'clock that night and got our chutes and all our equipment ready. We had tea and the pilots of our planes talked to us and told us about their end of the show. They were wonderful fellows. The plane I was going in was an American-built ship and we had a British pilot, an Australian navigator and a British wireless air gunner. With us Canadians in it, it was sort of a League of Nations. When we were all ready the station commander came around to wish us good luck.

We pushed off some time before midnight. It was sort of a funny feeling I had as we raced down the runway. I felt numb and plenty scared. You figure to yourself you know you have to go and there's nothing you can do about it. I suppose that's what they call sweating it out. We had lights in the plane. We looked at one another and smoked without saying much.

I Dropped Alone

Suddenly the lights were turned off. We stopped smoking. I knew we were over the coast of France. We began talking then, kidding about seeing Berlin soon. Somebody said, "It sure's going to be an exciting day back in Canada tomorrow morning when they wake up and find the invasion has started." Then the flak started and we got bumped around. A big piece of flak hit us, going clean through the tail. Hot lead whizzed inside the plane but nobody was hurt. Why, I'll never know. Finally the air gunner yelled, "We're okay. Five minutes to go." We stood up—got ready. I had my rifle valise, my rifle and two rolls of assault cable strapped to me. The air gunner yelled, "Three minutes to go." We all pushed nearer toward the door.

I was the tenth man in the stick. Some of the battalion head-quarters party were in the plane, including Major Jeff Nicklin, Winnipeg, and Lieut. John Simpson, Toronto.

A red light went on, then a green light. That was it. We began jumping. The first seven men got out swell, then the plane lurched badly and the eighth man stumbled at the door. Lieut. Simpson, who was the ninth man in the stick, pushed him out and hit the silk right after him. Just as I was about to jump, the red light went on and the air gunner yelled, "We're off our DZ." That meant we had overshot our rendezvous area. The plane circled, the green light came on again and I went out. I was a long time getting down and I remember wondering how I'd find Lieut. Simpson, the offi-cer I was supposed to report to. I was plenty excited as I floated down. I looked around and I saw water below, then some trees. It looked like swamp area and I was scared. I went for a tree landing.

My chute caught in the tree and my rifle broke loose. I dangled there for a minute or so and then the chute loosened and I dropped into four or five inches of water. I kicked around in the water try-ing to find my rifle but I was getting into waist-deep water. Then I heard somebody shout, "Come on." The voice seemed to come from the next field. I crawled through some bushes and got onto a track but I couldn't see anything around me except water. I shout-ed in the direction of the voice and I got no answer so I went back, trying to find the rifle. It was too dark. I couldn't see anything. All I had was my fighting knife so I figured I might as well lay up for the night. I was plenty exhausted. The best place I could find was in four or five inches of water. I covered myself with a camouflage net, propped up my head to keep from drowning and went to sleep.

I was awakened by a pistol prodding me under the chin. A mud-covered man was staring me in the face. I thought I'd had it the first day. He asked me what battalion I belonged to—and boy, what a relief to discover he was a British parachute captain! He gave me a shot of liquor from a flask and led me across marshes to the place where he was hiding with eight British parachutists. By this time I'd lost my fighting knife but the captain gave me a grenade in case we got into a fight.

We didn't know quite where we were, although we could hear the sounds of battle a few miles away. Our party crept along a path until we sighted a farmhouse and barn. The captain and sergeant "recceyed" the barn and found it empty. We all crept in. We felt pretty safe there so we took off our wet clothes. "Come on, Canada," the others were saying, "pull out those good fags of yours." I carried about 300 cigarettes but they were all wet except one package of 50. I handed them around and we were pretty happy. Those British boys are pretty cool customers all right.

About an hour later two Frenchmen crept into the barn. They were Resistance men and they gave us a layout of the territory. We mounted guard all day because we could see Jerries moving along the road 500 yards away. That night we decided to get out. We formed up, with two Sten gunners in the lead and me carrying my lone grenade right behind them. We moved across about a thousand yards of swamp and came to an extra wide dyke. One of the Sten gunners tried to cross it and almost drowned, so we decided to return to the barn and figure out a new plan. Next morning the Frenchmen brought in three more Britishers and also food and wine. The Jerries went searching the area and we laid up in the barn for two days. The Frenchmen brought us as much food as they could but it wouldn't go around and we were pretty hungry. They suggested killing their dog and eating it but we wouldn't let them. It was a swell pup. We would rather go hungry than kill it.

On the third morning one of the Frenchman brought in a small radio and we heard the BBC news of how the invasion was going well. The Frenchmen were jumping for joy and we all figured it wouldn't be too long before we'd be rescued. We couldn't move out of the barn because the Jerries were still all around us. That evening a young French girl darted into the barn carrying a little food which she'd cooked for us. She was a pretty girl as well as a brave one. On the fourth morning the Frenchmen woke us up yelling, "The British are coming!" We were happy, but not for long. It was the Navy that was shelling the Jerries in our area and the creeping barrage was coming our way. Shells were bursting closer all the time and thank God they stopped just before they reached the area of our barn. That night four men, including the captain, decided to try to get away. They left around midnight and came back about four in the morning. They couldn't make their way through the swamp in the darkness, and the roads were being constantly patrolled by Jerries.

Just after the four came back, a British sergeant—his name is Lucas, and I'll never forget him—stood up and said, "Are you game to try it, Canada?" I nodded my head and so did seven others. That made a party of nine, including the sergeant, a corporal and seven privates. I was the only Canadian. We spent all next day making plans and at 11 that night nine of us started out. We hadn't eaten much for three days and we were pretty weak. But we figured we had a fighting chance of getting to our own lines. We formed up, with Sergeant Lucas moving out in front alone. He was followed by two men carrying Stens, then me with my grenade and the other five bringing up the rear. We decided to try the road and we crept along in the ditch at a very slow pace.

We moved along about a mile and suddenly we fell flat on our stomachs. About 50 Jerries came cycling by within four feet of us. They were blabbering away in German and laughing a good deal. We crawled another mile, then went flat again as a battery of German horse-drawn artillery clattered down the road. It was too close for me. I was getting a bit jittery but the sergeant was steady as a rock. What a soldier! He led us across the swamp and just as daylight was breaking we saw a barn. We hid in a hedge while the sergeant walked to the door and pried it open with his bayonet. He came back to get us, saying, "Quick, men, the place is full of chickens. Get in there before the chickens escape." Then he went to the farmhouse and woke up an aged farmer who brought us milk and a little butter.

We slept most of the day in an upper hayloft and pushed out at midnight. We were climbing over a hedge when we heard a rifle shot in our midst. We fell flat, hardly breathing, until one of our men sheepishly said, "Sorry, fellows. It was my rifle. The safety latch slipped." We moved again, this time over a cratered field, the sergeant always moving out in front. Twice he stopped and dug his toe in the dirt, then he led us around a mine. That was typical of the sergeant. He tried everything himself first before he would allow the rest to follow. When we came to wide dykes the sergeant swam across first to see if we could make it.

We moved up on the main road again, the sergeant stopping to cut the Jerry telephone wires with his bayonet and again we had to fall flat while Jerry field guns rolled past. The sarge was always taking note of their equipment and direction. He didn't miss a trick. We were cold and pretty weak from hunger. I passed around my emergency ration for everybody to have one bite. The sergeant had a flask with cold tea. We had one spoonful each.

We moved all night and just before first light we rolled into a deep ditch running behind a high hedge. It was the best place we could find to spend the day. Suddenly we heard a deafening roar and we discovered that a battery of German field guns was firing not 50 yards from us. The sergeant crawled away, saying it was his duty to mark the exact location of the guns so he could inform our artillery when we got through. He crawled under the very noses of the German gunners, noting the types of guns and the landmarks by which he could locate them on the map. While we slept most of the day in the ditch the sergeant was studying a makeshift map, trying to plan the night's journey.

At nine that night he awakened us, gave us a spoonful of tea each and ordered us to blacken our faces. We moved out at 10 o'clock, because the dusk was deepened by a heavy rainfall and it was safe to move at that hour. We joined a herd of cows and walked between them across high ground. Then we came to a ridge. We were doing a leopard crawl in the dark when machine guns burst all around us. I thought I must be hit and I pinched myself. I was okay, but the man next to me was dead and three others were wounded. Two had scrambled away in the darkness, leaving the sergeant, the corporal and me with the three wounded. They were groaning with pain and we figured Jerry would be on us in a moment, but for some reason they didn't follow up. We did our best for the wounded. One was badly shot up and was dying; the second was shot in both arms and the third was hit in the back. They told us to go on and leave them, saying they would call to the first Germans they saw at daylight. It was hard to leave the dying man. He was asking not to be left alone in his last moments. He knew he'd bought it. We stayed with him a little while until he became unconscious, while the two others lay there and urged us to get moving. We propped them up as comfortably as we could and slipped away in the darkness.

The three of us reached a tributary about 80 yards wide. We were very weak but we managed to swim across and then crawl along a dirt road. I'd lost track of where we were going but the sarge was leading us and we took his word for it. At first light we came to a house surrounded by a high wall. The sarge said, "We must be only a few hundred yards from our own lines now. But this looks like a German unit headquarters. Let's use the grenade and the Stens on them before we push on." I argued, "For God's sake, Sarge, let's get back to our lines and do some fighting later." But the sergeant was all for shooting some Jerries. He forced the gate, crawled up the garden path, pushed the door open with his foot and poked his Sten in the house. It was a tense moment—until an old Frenchman came clattering down the stairs shouting, "Welcome, welcome!"

The Frenchman gave us something to eat and said our troops were in a wood only a quarter of a mile away. While we were eating he darted out and in 20 minutes he was back with two huge British commandos. I could have hugged them I was so glad to see them. They took us back to their headquarters and the sarge told the story of our escape. The commandos said, "How about showing us where you left your wounded last night?" And what do you think the sarge did? He took a stiff drink and started back along the road with three commandos to rescue the wounded men. What's more they were back in six hours, carrying the two wounded. The third had died during the night.

Well, that's about all there is to the story. I got back to my unit yesterday and the sarge and the corporal went back to theirs. But there's one guy I'll never forget and that's Sergeant Lucas. He's all man and all soldier. Nobody can ever tell me the British haven't got guts. That sergeant has enough for the whole blasted Empire.

After the war, Alexander Huton returned home to Prescott, Ont., to finish high school. Later he became a federal customs officer, dying at 55 of a stroke in August 1978.

JONES
OF
JUGOSLAVIA

December 1, 1944

William D. Bayles

Jones (left) with partisan leader Marshal Tito.

As far north as Vienna posters were stuck up offering a reward of 50,000 reichsmarks—a small fortune to a German soldier or Balkan peasant—for the capture, dead or alive, of "The Notorious General Jones." The Nazi radio ranted against him and speculated on his identity, for naturally Jones was the patently obvious alias of some leading British general whose presence in Jugoslavia had coincided with daring raids and successful military thrusts in a dozen directions. Clod-minded German troops grew more uneasy daily, victims of their own propagandists, and German local commanders in the Balkans withdrew into the few garrisoned towns, fearful of the sudden onslaughts planned by this phantom leader.

Recently the mystery man of the Balkans turned up in London. A silver-haired, sparely built little man in British battledress came striding into a hotel lounge. His mustache, much darker than his hair, bristled defiantly, and his single good eye—the other was glass—darted around the room as though cautious from long experience. There was something about him curiously remindful of a coiled spring. About his reputation among the Germans he laughed heartily. "They've given me a whale of a promotion," he said. His battledress bore the single crown of a major.

Here was the phantom general of the Balkans—Major William Jones, who before the war dealt in real estate—whose ambition it once was to be a medical missionary, and who taught Sunday school in New Toronto's Century United Church until he sailed to Britain—and war.

Born 49 years ago at Digby, N.S., he had missionary ambitions from an early age, but these were interrupted by the First World War. In France he served in the 13th Battalion, Black Watch, and was promoted through all the ranks between private and captain before demobilization. He won the DCM and Bar. He was wounded five times—losing his left eye in 1917.

Deeply religious, he served after discharge in the Home Mission Field at Neil's Harbor, Cape Breton, and later attended Pinehill Theological Seminary at Dalhousie University. In summer holidays he was a merchant sailor. Later he did surveying, and still later, community welfare work for Price Brothers newsprint mill at Kenogami, where he organized Boy Scouts and Girl Guides. In 1925 and 1926 he came to the University of Toronto, where he took an odd mixture of courses, including premedical science— and military studies.

Money failed him and for two years he was partner in an unsuccessful grocery store. Then he became a real-estate salesman, establishing his own office in Toronto in 1933 and specializing in industrial and business real estate.

In 1935 he married Helen Scott, who at that time was taking a medical course at the University of Toronto. For the past three years she has worked in the Small Arms plant at Long Branch, Ont. They have no children.

Major Jones's fantastic military career in the mountains of Jugoslavia might never have started but for his inability to take "No" for an answer when medical authorities at the beginning of this war told him that he was both too old, and too incapacitated by the loss of his eye, for military service.

Once he almost managed to slip by the medical examination— by memorizing the eye-testing chart. But the doctor thought it odd that his left eye did not respond to certain stimuli, examined it more closely and found it was—glass.

Turned down again, he signed on a Britain-bound merchant ship at Montreal as an able-bodied seaman. After a hazardous crossing he managed to talk himself out of staying with the Merchant Navy and went to London to enlist. Again he was refused. For a while he worked during the Blitz as a demolition laborer and then, through Air Commodore Alfred Cecil Critchley, Calgary-born promoter of sports in Britain, he was commissioned in the RAF as an instructor in military drill.

A few months later he managed to get posted to Cyprus in the Middle East Command, where he organized defense works. In January 1943, he was transferred to the Black Watch in the British Army—he, an old Canadian Black Watch veteran—with the rank of major.

While flying to Alexandria from Cyprus he was able to pen a brief note to his wife, saying that he was making the transfer in order to go on "a secret and dangerous mission." He told her, also, not to expect any mail for some time. An American colonel, homeward bound, posted the letter in Washington.

After a stiff parachute and commando course in Egypt he left Derna by plane and on May 19, 1943, dropped in a parachute near the Croatian town of Bihac, his mission to make contact with the Partisans fighting under Marshal Tito and to perform liaison duties between the Marshal and the British War Office.

It was his first visit to that part of the world. He spoke no Balkan language, he knew no one there, and was entirely on his own.

In 1943 a unique situation existed in Jugoslavia. The Germans were officially in occupation and held all the principal cities, the railways and main highways. But invasion was nothing new to the tough southern Slavs and, following their time-honored custom, they had taken to the mountains to carry on the kind of warfare they knew better than any formally trained solider. Hundreds of square miles of broad mountains and valleys of Croatia and Bosnia, wedged in between the coastal mountains of Dalmatia to the west and the Serb territory to the east, had become a vast no man's land into which few Germans dared to venture. Here, under the dynamic leadership of Marshal Tito, a people's army numbering over 250,000 was fighting one of history's strangest wars of liberation.

Picked up and his identity established, Major Jones was welcomed by the Partisans as a fellow fighter. In fact, he said, there was no alternative to becoming a Partisan because there were no neutrals or noncombatants in the Balkan mountains.

Leadership was by natural selection; the man in a village best qualified to lead his neighbors emerged in battle. As Major Jones proved his ability in patrols and raids, the people with whom he fought simply accepted him as their leader. That he came from a faraway country, completely unknown to most of them, mattered as little as his glass eye or the fact that he couldn't speak their language. "Language was no barrier," he said. "It was amazing how many of those fighters had worked in Pittsburgh or Detroit. And there were hundreds of university students and professional men who spoke English. You could find two or three interpreters in any village or mountain station."

After six weeks in the Croatian headquarters of the Partisans, Jones went to Slovenia, where there was an important target for military sabotage. The Partisans assigned three brigades to do the job—and Major Jones got a message back to the Middle East Command, asking that six tons of explosive be dropped for their use.

Hard luck struck then. First, the Germans occupied the dropping point designated just the day before the British planes were supposed to come—and after that British aircraft were so occupied that for two whole months not a single sortie could be flown to Slovenia.

But Major Jones was busy at other things by this time and the Partisans destroyed a German armored train that was bringing four tank repair shops from France to the Italian front—an important loss to the Germans at a critical moment.

Major Jones, who has strong ideas on Christian ethics and believes ideals should mean something, had found a cause after the dictates of his own heart. Liaison became secondary, while Jugoslavia gained another fighter for freedom. "What I saw there," he said, "certainly has no parallel in history. It was a people down to the last ditch actually pulling themselves up by their own bootstraps."

The Partisans lacked everything except enthusiasm. Firearms were taken from dead Germans and Italians. A soldier was ambushed and his weapons taken. When half a dozen guns had been acquired in this manner a patrol was ambushed and a dozen firearms collected. As men became armed in a locality, enemy columns and convoys were attacked and stores of equipment grew.

It was a wild kind of will-o'-the-wisp warfare, requiring stealth and extreme courage. At one time, Major Jones related, he and a group of Partisans maintained a headquarters and courier service for 10 days in a cave within easy hearing distance of a large German force sent out to find and wipe them out. In the end it was the Germans who were forced to withdraw.

Many women are members of Marshal Tito's Army—on a basis of complete equality with the men and with sex completely submerged.

"Although this is contrary to the rules of nature," says the major, "it is a sacrifice they are willing to make to gain their freedom. I cannot recall ever having seen any indication of the usual man and woman attitude; not even to the extent of holding hands."

"In spite of the necessary secrecy," the major said, "the Partisans maintain the most complete information system imaginable. The mountains are dotted with courier centres into which messages arrive and are sorted and routed. To gain operational information a commander has merely to tap the nearest courier station and he learns not only what has passed through that station but what has been routed to it from all the others."

Thousands of boys and girls 14 and 15 years old slip along mountain trails day and night with messages. They are armed with a rifle and if they see that capture is imminent they know they must destroy their dispatches and then kill themselves. They may never be taken prisoner.

War in the Balkan mountains is waged with words as well as bullets, and Major Jones is particularly proud of the psychological campaign in which he played a prominent part. Through leaflets, posters and even released prisoners the enemy is constantly made conscious of his position as an invader. The ardent liberation spirit of the Partisans is contrasted with the serflike status of the German and Italian soldiers. The results are surprising. Thousands change sides, the biggest catch being General Cerutti, who commanded the Italians in the Ljubljana district.

"He asked for a conference," Major Jones said, "and offered to change sides and fight the Germans but insisted on his men retaining their equipment. This didn't suit the Partisans because they wanted most of all the Italian equipment for their own people. Forty-eight hours later General Cerutti agreed to hand over part of his equipment."

While this transfer was in progress the general attempted to escape to Italy in his car but he was stopped and the car confiscated. Instead of taking him prisoner, however, the Partisan leaders provided him with a foot escort and food. After walking for three days he decided to join the Partisans, and orders were sent out over his signature for the demobilization of the entire Italian Army operating in the district. "One of our easier victories," Major Jones commented.

Until the surrender of Italy, Italians who were captured and refused to join the Partisans were usually stripped down to their underwear and started off on foot toward Italy, but Germans who do not voluntarily join the group are killed in battle because the Partisans have practically no facilities for prisoners.

More important than the Partisan war, which has become a huge hammer dealing terrific blows at Hitler's southern flank, is the experiment in state-building that is going on simultaneously.

"It is a renaissance of democracy in the truest sense," Major

Jones declared. When a village is freed a people's committee is elected to deal with civic problems and maintain liaison with the Army. When a whole district is liberated the people elect a district council, which in turn sends representatives to the regional councils of Croatia, Bosnia, Herzegovina and the other states that comprise Jugoslavia.

At the top of the governmental pyramid is the Supreme Council of about 240 members, which governs the country. The military leaders are chosen in the same way as the district, regional and national representatives. The best qualified man in a village leads its troops, from among the village leaders are chosen district leaders, and the process continues to the top. Tito, upon whom the Supreme Council conferred the title of Marshal, worked his way to the top by sheer ability, but there are at least a dozen other leaders of almost equal ability who could carry on the fight.

"You can't fail to be impressed," Major Jones said, "by the singlehearted purpose and sincerity of these people. Factionalism has simply disappeared, the Quisling element represents a negligible minority, politics are rarely discussed, religion is no issue, and everyone is wrapped up in the vast experiment of nation building."

Native ability—and some of the tricks learned in Pittsburgh and Detroit—are fast overcoming the isolation into which the German invasion plunged the country. Alcohol, distilled from charcoal, is used as fuel for combustion engines which run dynamos, which in turn provide power for lighting, telephone and machine shops. Repair parts are made for equipment, clothes are manufactured, and hand grenades are turned out in vast quantities.

With practically two-thirds of their country now liberated, the Jugoslavs are also mapping their future. They admire the Russians as Slavic brothers who had to go through a similar experience in building their state, but they affirm to a man that they are not fighting the war to make Jugoslavia a part of Russia.

They have a deep regard for the British and American democratic way of life. Self-determination is their motto, and they want Jugoslavia for the Jugoslavs. They are even determined that the districts of Istria and Trieste, which Italy seized, shall have a plebiscite to decide whether they want to rejoin Jugoslavia or remain Italian.

Whether the country again becomes a monarchy will also be decided by vote. King Peter, they say, left the country in the hour of crisis and did not return to help them in their fight. Now they would prefer to have him remain away until peace has been restored and a plebiscite can be held. But even should the monarchy be restored it will never again be absolute, as in the pre-war days.

The Partisan leaders, Major Jones declared, mostly conceal their identities because many of their families are held by the Germans as hostages in the cities. But they include many men formerly prominent in the Government and professional men from all fields.

Before leaving Jugoslavia to come to London, Major Jones spent several days at Marshal Tito's headquarters.

"He was living in a huge natural crevice in the rocks, which had been turned into two rooms," the major said. Tito he described as a strikingly handsome man of remarkable ability and understanding, with kindness and strength combined in his features. He is utterly honest, has no dictatorial ambitions, is cautious and deliberate in his decisions but quick of action once his mind is made up.

Tito is intensely proud of the democratic state system the Partisans have built up and refers all decisions to the Government. He is Premier in the Government as well as commander-in-chief of the Army, and works in close collaboration with Dr. Ribar, the president. His popularity with the soldiers is immense and he accepts for himself the same hard routine and privations they must endure.

Before the war he was an ironworker, who fought in Spain against the Fascists and was outlawed in Germany, Italy and Spain. He was also imprisoned by the pre-war Jugoslav monarchist government.

Major Jones's optimism dims slightly when he speaks of the hardships the mountain fighters undergo. Everything, he says, is scarce, particularly food, clothes, leather and medical equipment. The livestock is mostly gone, seed is not available for sowing and cloth is so scarce that bandages are used as many as 25 times. At hospitals, hidden in the woods, doctors perform amputations without anaesthetic, the patients sing to keep from screaming from pain. Instruments include carpentry tools and kitchen knives, and salt water is often the only antiseptic.

But he is certain that with a normal amount of supplies, which could easily be sent by sea across the Adriatic, the present crisis will be overcome. Throughout the Balkans the Germans are sealed off in their defensive positions or on the run, and the Partisans are working more and more in the open.

One certain sign of impending victory is the amusement, instead of concern, with which the Partisans regard the Nazi notices offering 50,000 reichsmarks for the capture of "General Jones." Whenever they find them posted, on trees or house walls, they remove them carefully because they have become coveted collector's items. "They're selling them as souvenirs," he said. "I think the price is about 50 cents a poster."

ESCAPE

—*December 15, 1944*—
Flying Officer Alfred J. Houston
(as told to Geoffrey Hewelcke)

About me was nothing but blackness, with the even blacker walls of tall Breton hedges meeting in a corner directly behind me. The sky above was overcast. Below—I patted the freshly plowed earth with my palms. That earth smelled as good as any newly plowed field in Ontario. I wiggled my toes inside my wet flying boots and waited.

Presently I heard someone whistling in the distance. It was a jiglike little tune. Someone else picked it up a little closer. Then both whistlers stopped.

Suddenly there were men around me. They seemed to have grown up out of the wet earth. Many men.

"We're Patriots," a voice said at my shoulder. "We fight for France. We're the men of de Gaulle."

I shook hands with the owner of the voice. He was their captain. I'll call him Tony, although that was not his right name. I may as well explain immediately that I'm not going to give the right names of any of the men or women who helped me, just in case the Germans still hold some of their relatives as prisoners. The Germans would take revenge on these prisoners...I know that.

Tony fingered my RCAF battledress and shook his head.

"It won't do," he said. He snapped a few words in French and a bundle of clothing was passed up from somewhere behind. By touch I identified a pair of civilian trousers, a jacket and a pair of hobnailed boots, which later turned out to be a German Army issue. I changed right there in the dark.

Then somebody shoved a Sten submachine gun into my hands.

"Loaded?" I asked.

194

Escape

"Loaded," was the reply...I was now a member of Tony's group of Patriots—of what the newspapers later called the Maquis, though I never heard any of the men call themselves by that name.

Later that night Tony and my new comrades brought me to a barn in which it was safe to light a candle. I saw them then. There were 30 of them—hard-looking, weather-beaten men, most of them dark-haired. All of them were between 18 and 30 years old. All of them had gone "to the fields" rather than serve in the German forced labor corps. All of them were armed—either with the Sten guns and grenades dropped by our planes—or with German rifles and pistols. A German rifle in the hands of a Patriot, I got to know, meant that a German soldier was rotting in some shallow grave in a Breton field.

It was in the barn that I told Tony and the others that I was navigator of an RCAF Wellington that had been bombing a town with pamphlets warning civilians to stay off the highways when the invasion came; that we had run into a Junkers 88 on the way home and that our full gas tank was pierced by a shell from the Germans' guns. I told him that there were five more of the crew somewhere in a 20-mile radius.

Tony took down the names and their descriptions. There were Flying Officer Harold Brennan, my pilot. He came from Lindsay, Ont. Myself, I come from Toronto. Before the War I was a salesman for the chemical products of the A.S. Boyle Co. There were Sgts. Andy Elder, rear gunner from Vancouver; Ernie Trottier, Cornwall, the bombardier; Roger Dickson, Vernon, B.C., the mid-upper gunner, and Johnny Kempson, wireless operator, Surbiton, Surrey—the lone Englishman in our Canadian crew. The date was April 20, last spring.

I told Tony that I'd advised the boys to head southeast in the direction of the Spanish border when we bailed out, and he made a note of that too.

Within a few minutes a bicycle bell shrilled outside and Tony snuffed the candle while the door was opened. Then he lit it.

A little girl flung her pigtails back over her shoulders and stood stiff as a ramrod before him. She was one of the messengers used by the Patriots—and proud of her job.

195

Quickly she chattered to him in a language I could not follow. He nodded gravely. She spoke again. Of course she was speaking Breton—a language close to Welsh—quite beyond my comprehension.

"One of your friends has been found—severely injured." Tony turned to me. "A dark-haired young fellow with a thin face…"

For a moment I considered.

"That must be Johnny Kempson," I guessed. "What's wrong with him?"

"He's with a doctor 20 miles away," Tony said. "He was found unconscious among the rocks in some wild land. Would you like to see him?"

"Of course," I said.

Tony spoke to someone behind me. Again the candle went out when the barn door was opened. Again it was lit.

"I've told one of the boys to steal a car," Tony told me. "He'll be back soon."

He looked at me curiously—half enviously.

"It must be wonderful to fly in those—those *avions*," he said. "To shoot the Germans—to bomb them… We who have to crawl in the fields and ditches would give a leg to do the same."

"You have your job too," I suggested.

Tony nodded. "We have," he admitted. "We do it. Don't think that we're not soldiers because we have no uniforms. We've killed a great many Germans—and we'll kill more."

I was surprised at the ferocity of his voice. But I am no longer. I have found out what the Germans did to the Patriots when they caught them.

Next instant, though, Tony asked if I'd had any trouble in parachuting down, and I told him that I'd landed in a field singing at the top of my lungs, so happy to be alive. He grinned when I explained that my parachute had failed to open at first. He smiled approvingly when I told him of fleeing across fields and through hedges, across a river and back again to confuse my scent because I heard hounds baying in the distance and thought they might be leading Germans on my trail. I told him also of my wanderings that day until I finally met the man who had led me to the field in which I met him.

In an incredibly short time a car rolled up outside the barn. Five of the Patriots and I climbed into it, holding our weapons between our knees. The Germans had forbidden people to be out of their homes after 9 p.m. But that seemed to make no difference at all to the Patriots.

Presently I was standing by Johnny's side. His face was grey. A doctor and a lady were attending him.

"Johnny!" I cried.

He turned his head slightly but evidently could not see me. I dropped on my knees beside his cot. He put his arms about me.

"Get me home," he mumbled.

The doctor, a grey-haired man with a kindly face, shook his head. I drew him aside and he told me bad news. Johnny had been found by the Patriots among rocks. Maybe he had been dragged through them by his chute. Anyway he had a skull fracture besides internal injuries.

"Why can't we turn him over to a German military hospital?" I asked. "That would give him a chance."

The doctor smiled sadly. "Not now," he said. "I've already given him aid, and the Germans would know that…they'd shoot me, for their regulations are that any parachutists must be left where they fall if they're injured."

German patrols made frequent calls at this village so Tony decided that we must move Johnny Kempson and we took him in the car to a village about 15 miles off. Here we took him into a barn and bedded him in the straw. I stayed with him, as did two young Patriots.

In the next five days the rest of the Wimpy's crew were rounded up by the Patriots, who brought them to us, one by one.

During this time the doctor visited Johnny every day, bringing with him a specialist from a nearby town; a specialist in head injuries.

Despite our care, despite the daily visits from the two doctors, Johnny died on the sixth morning. We knew he was going and the Patriots brought a priest to him just before he died, though Johnny was a Protestant.

That night our Wimpy's crew gathered in the village. They'd spent the day digging a grave for Johnny on a hill some 15 miles off. They'd worked for nine hours on that grave—the ground was so rocky.

Early on the following day we buried Johnny, with our crew forming a guard of honor, a priest from the nearby village conducting the service and a group of ragged Patriots, leaning on their rifles, or holding their machine guns, in the background.

Six weeks later I passed that place again and found that the children of the village had placed fresh flowers on this grave that was unknown to them.

After the burial Tony called us aside.

"We're ready now," he said.

"Ready for what?" I asked.

"You want to get to the Spanish frontier," he said. "It is part of our duty as Patriots to help Allied airmen escape from the Germans … You are valuable fighting men … Much time and money has been spent on training you for your tasks … Very well, 15 men of our group will lead you southeast to the boundaries of the territory we know … We'll be your guides and your guard … We'll lead you and we'll fight for you—and we ask only that you don't risk your lives in unnecessary fighting … Leave that to us."

We started off—southeast.

Travel with the Patriots was easy—at first. Later, as the Gestapo closed in on us, it became a nightmare, and we became hunted men, leaving behind us a trail of blood and suffering. In the beginning, though, the Patriots knew what roads were safe from patrols … They knew what farmers would feed them with no questions asked … What woods were safe …

Besides they had their "service d'information" so well organized. Girls on bicycles—farmers' boys—would happen along every so often. At night somebody would be whistling a song in the dark … One of our men would whistle a few bars of another song … There would be a whistled reply—and a shadowy figure would step out and mutter a few words of information.

But the Germans struck soon; on the second night, some 40 miles from the place where we had buried Johnny, I woke at the sound of voices near me. I listened and was up on my feet. One of the speakers was a lad of about 17 who had taken spells with me in nursing Johnny Kempson. We had left him behind, but now he had caught up with our band and was telling a terrible tale. Somehow the Germans had heard about Johnny. They had heard about the doctor. They caught that doctor … They tortured him … They broke both his wrists and twisted them… Then they killed him.

The boy's voice was harsh and flat as he spoke. He told also that he himself had been captured but that he had managed to escape.

That was the first Frenchman who died for us; that gentle, kind-hearted doctor who knew that he was risking his life in looking after Johnny; yet came to see him every day. I never knew his name…

Tony called a meeting at once. It was obvious, he told us, that the Germans must know about us if they knew about Johnny. That meant the Gestapo would be alert ahead of us and on our trail behind us. We'd have to move with doubled caution.

We broke camp right away. The lad who had brought us the terrible news was sent on to another group of the Patriots.

Perhaps this is the place to say something about our guides. There was Tony, of course, tall, dark-tanned, profoundly efficient as a leader of men and the elected captain of the group. He had been "in the fields" ever since the surrender of France.

One of the other men was a barber, who plied his trade among us. Two were French sailors.

Others in our group were office workers, laborers and farm hands. They were all physically fit and thus sought by the Germans for forced labor. All had a burning determination to fight the Germans as long as they had a breath to draw. They considered themselves to be soldiers of France.

Groups of the Patriots were usually not too numerous—not more than 15 or 20 men or women to a group. Yes, there were women who served with them, although mostly they were not "in the fields." Each group had an elected captain. Each captain was responsible to a higher officer who had perhaps five groups under his control. Each one of these higher officers was responsible to a

199

still higher authority who was in touch with General de Gaulle's headquarters, received orders and transmitted requests for arms and dynamite.

There was a flexibility about the organization that was truly amazing. At the same time there was a control that worked perfectly.

We continued on our way, living off the country as much as we could by catching fish in the rivers; by snaring rabbits in the woods. Occasionally we bought bread from lonely farmhouses.

Shortly we received another warning. The Gestapo was definitely on our trail. We split up into small groups of two and three. My two guides looked after me for four days before we rejoined the others at a small town a good distance south.

That Friday night a doctor came out from the town. He invited us Canadians to visit his house over the weekend.

"You can have some home-cooked food," he said with a smile. "Besides I think you'll be wanting a bath and a sleep between sheets."

We had some doubts. "Won't it be risky for you?" we asked.

"I think I can manage affairs," he smiled.

At noon on Saturday we left our camp in couples: one crew member, one Patriot guide.

After a weekend of rest at the doctor's home we left just before the German-imposed curfew at 9 p.m. and were making our way to the outskirts of the town when the Patriot scout some distance ahead of us raised his hand in warning. Instantly our guides dragged us into an alley entrance.

"German patrol coming," they whispered.

A few houses from us a door opened and a little girl of five or six darted out to go home. She had apparently been visiting a friend and had overstayed the curfew. She was in the middle of the street when there was the flat smack of a rifle shot. The little girl spun about; fell flat. She kicked twice... She was still.

We airmen were stunned by the brutality of the act. Then we felt sick. Then we grabbed our Sten guns and made ready to charge around the alley entrance—but the Patriots held us back.

"Not good," they said. "Not good. If you keel that patrol the

Boches will keel 30 or 40 peoples in this town for *revanche*."

Cautiously we peered around the corner. At the street inter-section four steel-helmeted Germans were dimly to be seen. They were leaning against their bicycles. One of them held his rifle at the ready and was looking at the pitiful little body near us. But he didn't approach it closer. Presently the Germans got on their bikes and rode off.

"Thees is France as she is today," my guide whispered. "You see—there is not a window opened to see for why was the shooting."

"It's hell," I said.

"Eet won't last—I swear to you eet won't last," he whispered passionately.

Two days later we reached the borders of the territory familiar to Tony and his men. There we met another group of Patriots who were supposed to see us farther on our way. This group consisted of 13 men under a captain whom I'll call Jean. He was a former Army officer who had gone "into the fields."

We travelled with him for two days and then a messenger came, saying that the Germans had got wise to the fact that a lot of Allied airmen were getting out of France by way of Spain. They had thrown in whole Gestapo regiments to patrol the border coun-try. It was hopeless to proceed.

So we turned northward again, heading once more for Brittany, although not on the route we had followed before.

A week later we sighted a German patrol of 20 men. They saw us too. Immediately they started after us across the fields. The Ger-mans gained on us. Moreover they had rifles which had a longer range than the Sten guns with which most of us were armed. Their bullets were coming close. Soon we'd have to stand and fight—and they were more numerous and had better weapons.

We crawled through a hedge that seemed to be a good obstacle and one of the Patriots—a young fellow of 28, well-built, sun-browned—suddenly went up to Captain Jean and saluted.

"I demand permission to stay here and fight," he said. "With my Sten—and perhaps another—I can hold them for half an hour while the rest of you get away."

201

Captain Jean looked at him. Then he saluted.

"Permission granted," he said.

The young fellow borrowed another Sten gun and settled himself in a ditch, his weapons pointing through the hedge to the field on the other side. He started firing almost immediately.

"Come along," Captain Jean told us. "His sacrifice must not be in vain."

We ran on while shots sounded behind us—and then ceased. Presently in the distance we heard a man screaming. It was a horrible sound.

Later we heard that he had been wounded, captured—and promptly tortured to death.

A few days later we were crossing a field when bullets slapped the air about us. The flat reports followed seconds after. We all fell to the ground—but one of the Patriots remained still.

"He's dead," Captain Jean said. "Leo, Paul, Pierre, Jacques and André—you are appointed to take our charges to the wood by the stream that you know of. The others will stay here with me and we'll fight the Germans off."

We crawled to a ditch, wormed our way along it to an opening in a hedge. Behind us rifles cracked.

That night the captain and two men rejoined us. Three more had been left lying in the field—killed by German bullets. They thought that they had got at least two of the enemy, who had at last broken off the engagement.

We travelled north some 80 miles to an old mill. Here we were told that we'd have to wait some time until the Patriots found another way to take us to safety. In the meantime we were to live in a small room under the roof of the mill; to keep as quiet as mice because the Germans regularly used to eat in a room two stories down. We were warned not to smoke except when the coast was clear; to show no lights at night and to keep away from the single cobwebby window.

Our food was brought by a dear old lady, wife of the mill owner, and her daughter.

We stayed in this room for the dreariest six weeks I've ever spent. There were two beds in the room. There were five of us.

That meant that one of us had to sleep on the floor each night. There were a table and five chairs, a slop pail—and a pack of cards. Nothing more.

We played bridge—endlessly we played bridge. The close quarters, the monotony of existence, our whispered speech, worked on our nerves until we hated each other.

Here we heard that the doctor who had entertained us over that lovely weekend had been forced to go "into the fields" with his wife because the Germans had heard of the episode.

The Patriots visited us at intervals, bringing us cigarettes and pipe tobacco stolen from the Government warehouse in the district. French civilians at the time were rationed to 20 cigarettes a month… Each of us smoked more than that number each day.

We had time to think in this place and time to worry about our people—and the worry we were causing them. Naturally we had all been reported as "missing in action." They did not know that we were alive.

At times we seriously debated whether it was really worthwhile to keep on the effort to escape; whether or not we should surrender. But each time we thought of the men who had already given their lives—cheerfully, willingly—because they thought that in so doing they were saving trained fighting men… We couldn't quit. It was impossible.

June 6—D-Day—occurred in our fifth week in the mill attic. It was my night to sleep on the floor and I woke with the notion that an earthquake had shaken the building. I lay there on the boards and felt more tremors. I listened and heard distant guns. At once I woke my friends and we sat there in the dark, straining our ears.

We doped it out right. We figured that the noise was too heavy for ack-ack. It was naval gunfire. It was probably preliminary shelling before the landing operations were to start.

At 9 a.m. the miller's nephew came bursting into our room. Two bottles of wine were in his hands. Tears were streaming down his face.

"*Les Anglais* have landed," he cried. Behind him came the clatter of feet on the stairs. The miller and his wife and daughter were coming up. We opened the wine and drank silently to that glorious morning, while out of the window we could see Germans driving forced labor gangs at their job of planting timber stakes in the open fields to make glider landings impossible for our invasion armies.

That same night we heard grim news again. The Germans had surrounded and killed a band of 18 Patriots who lived two miles away. Four of the dead men had brought us cigarettes. Seven had been shot in the fight. The other 11 had surrendered—and the Germans had tortured them to death. They might have found out about us.

Next morning the miller came dashing up the stairs, screaming at the top of his lungs: "*Allez—allez—les Boches!*"

We dashed down in a split second and he led us around the back of the building and pointed to a swamp 300 yards off. The Germans were coming up the road. We made for the swamp and lay among the bulrushes while a German staff car drove up to the front of the mill and an officer got out. Presently we heard two shots.

We didn't know what had happened, although we feared that our hosts had been killed. That afternoon the daughter of the house came down to us with a stack of bread and butter and a jug of cider. She told us that her parents were safe. The shots had been fired by one of the officers when a farmer and his cart lumbered into the entrance of the mill as the German car was about to pull out. It was just the German way of saying, "Pull over—or else." More searches were, however, expected.

We stayed in the swamp that night and all the next day until midnight, when we were called back to the mill, fed and introduced to our new guide.

She was a beautiful girl of about 19—a smartly dressed blonde—whom I'll call Paulette. She was also one of the bravest and sweetest kids I've ever seen, and she was a Patriot who performed specially difficult missions.

From her we learned that the Allied beachhead in Normandy was a good 100 miles away and that it was too dangerous to approach it. Other arrangements had, however, been made, she assured us with a mischievous smile.

That first night she led us 10 miles. She stayed with us three days and three nights and then handed us over to another group of Patriots with whom we stayed for a week.

After a week Paulette returned to guide us on our next stage.

We walked from 8 a.m. to 2 a.m. the next morning, spending four hours in trying to enter a small town without being sighted by German patrols. It was the town in which Paulette lived—and further it was a town in which the Germans kept a garrison—right across the road from Paulette's house.

Finally we managed to slip in unobserved and met her mother—a grand old lady who had lost four sons fighting for France. The last son had gone to England and joined the RAF. He was now reported "missing." She had no sons left—but Paulette was doing a job for France… That's the sort of family it was.

We'd been in the house for an hour when suddenly we heard whooping and shooting in the street. It was a German patrol, acting like a bunch of movie cowboys. They battered down the door of a house next but one to us and dragged out some people. We never learned what happened to them.

Eventually we got to bed… Brennan and I in one room and the other three in another. Next morning we watched with interest as Germans came out of the barracks across the road, packed their belongings on farmers' carts and started off to the front. They seemed to us either young boys or old men. Some of the boys seemed to be crying.

Two nights more and Paulette told us the last lap was coming up. She led us toward the coast. On the way she groped under a bush and came up with a magnetic mine detector, complete with earphones.

Somewhere she had learned to use it—and use it she did, for now we entered a German mine field several miles deep. Paulette would take a step forward, sweep the frying pan on a broom handle apparatus forward and from side to side in what looked like a complicated dance. If she found a mine she dropped a handkerchief on it. We would just see the white of it, like a flower in the dark. Then she'd move forward another cautious pace—and another handkerchief would go down. The last man in the file following her picked up the handkerchiefs and passed them forward up the line.

205

Seven miles we travelled that way, slow, nerve-racking, pace by pace, at times passing so close to German trenches that we could hear the men speak, and thought it impossible that they would miss seeing us. Dawn comes early in June and yet we could not hurry. Ours was a snail's race against the sun—and discovery. Finally we got through the field and Paulette waved us on to the next step. Censorship will not permit me to say what that was— but I can tell you that as we stood with dawn approaching and watched Paulette moving back into the deadly mine field in that slow adagio dance with the broom handle and the mine detector, we felt dreadfully sorry that she couldn't come with us. We prayed—very sincerely we prayed—that she got through the mine field safely... More than enough gallant French blood had already been shed to make our escape possible. Much more than enough.

Five days later we were in England.

F/O Alfred Houston now reveals that with German guns firing in the distance, the underground took them by rowboat to a waiting submarine that brought them back to England. Once in England they were interrogated, since they had come unscathed through enemy territory, to ensure there were no infiltrators among them. For the same reason, the group was not allowed to serve in Europe. The war ended while Houston was training for possible service against Japan. After the war, he became vice-president of marketing and sales for American Home Products in Toronto and now lives nearby in Mississauga.

Geoffrey Hewelcke was an assistant editor of Maclean's *at the time.*

X FOR
ESCAPE

November 1, 1945

Flt.-Lieut. Tony Pengelly

(as told to Scott Young)

I spent almost one fifth of the first 25 years of my life—the time when most people go to university or begin otherwise to fit themselves to make a living—behind German barbed wire. I probably won't know for years, if ever, exactly how much that five years in a German prison camp cost me in normal progress. But if a prospective lifetime employer came up to me this minute and asked for my qualifications, I would be able to say only that I am almost 26 years old, have a high-school education, was recognized by my friends in Block 104, Stalag Luft III, as an

---

Flt.-Lieut. Tony Pengelly (bottom left) in barracks at Stalag Luft III, Sept. 1941.

excellent cook, a good female impersonator for the glamor element in prison theatricals; I showed early promise as a confidence man, and had wide experience as a supervisor of expert forgers.

I was shot down near Hanover, Nov. 13, 1940, trying to get my two-engined Whitley bomber back from the fifth Berlin raid of the war. I was freed near Lübeck, in northern Germany, May 2, 1945, by two men in a jeep. Between those two dates I ate a good deal of bad food, helped engineer numerous minor escapes and two major ones, and took part in the horrible winter march of Allied prisoners from Silesia into northwestern Germany as the Germans tried desperately to keep us from falling into the hands of the advancing Russians.

During much of my time in prison camp I was part of what I believe must have been one of the war's most efficient escape organizations. That our biggest job ended in tragedy—the barbarous murder of 50 of my friends—I never will forget, and I can only console myself with the knowledge that the escape was planned perfectly and that nothing we left undone cost those lives.

Active participation in the work, and planning for that escape, was the most important thing in my prison camp life. The two and a half years I spent behind barbed wire before we began to plan the big escape was all training for that opportunity—training that developed all of us, by trial and error, into a group possibly as expert in escape technique as any men in the world.

The trial and error period seemed terribly long. At my first prison camp—Barth, near Stralsund, on the Baltic—we dug 48 tunnels in about 18 months. Every one was discovered. That was because at Barth escaping was strictly private enterprise. Somebody would just decide he was going to escape and go up to some other chap and ask him to come in. Most of them didn't have a chance. A man can't forge his own identity papers, dig his own tunnel, make his own wire clippers, his escape clothes, maps, compasses and so on. He might do one or two of those things, but he couldn't do them all and do them well. So the chances were he wouldn't get far when he started out.

From our futility we knew we would have to organize to be successful. We were just beginning to realize that when we were moved, early in 1942, to a new camp in Silesia, between Breslau and Leipzig, Stalag Luft III. Within a few days X (for escape) Organization was born.

At the top was Big X, an RAF squadron leader called Roger Bushell. He had been shot down in June 1940. He was about 33, I'd suppose, and had been a lawyer. He could talk better German than most Germans, fluent French, and was infallible—or almost. I don't suppose it will hurt anyone's feelings to say that he was disliked by some of the men in the compound—the same reaction some people the world over have to people who make no mistakes.

Under him directly was the X committee, which was made up of heads of the various departments in the organization. One of the most important of these was Big S, head of the security group, under whom I worked as head of forgers and cartographers. Regardless of rank or seniority every one of the 2,000 men in our compound had an X job. They could be cartographers, forgers, tailors, compass makers, engineers, cooks, toolmakers, contact men or guards. Yes, we had guards too—against interference in the intricate plans that were taking shape.

Even after we reached this new camp it took about a year to build our organization up to the point we desired. In that year our tailors became skillful in making civilian clothes from odds and ends; our contact men, by a combination of psychology and bribery, got several Germans in the camp working for us; and we assembled—through materials smuggled in to us from England, by a means I can't disclose even now—a typewriter, which came in part by part, radios and other miscellaneous equipment we needed to forge identification papers for our escapers.

We all knew that the eventual result would be a big escape, something to free hundreds of us. Meanwhile, as exercise, we engineered a few smaller ones.

If I ever want to smile over some part of my time behind wire, I just have to think back to one of those earlier breaks, the time imaginary hordes of bugs fooled the Germans and set free 27 of my friends.

It was really our first big job under X Organization. We had the complete plan ready for weeks before Big X decided the time had come to spring it.

When lice, bedbugs or fleas were found in a prison block, our own medical officer would report it to the German M.O. Then the block's residents would be taken, in parties of 25, to the shower house, 400 yards through the woods from our main gate. Simultaneously, delousing parties would move into the block and disinfect it. For this escape we reported bugs in a certain block. The routine began.

At 2:10 p.m. on this Escape Day—10 minutes after the routine relief of every guard in the compound—a party of 25, carrying towels, left the block. With it were two German guards.

While the party marched smartly toward the gate a fencing match started over in one corner of the compound, between Bill Geiger, an American, and—if my memory is right—John Marshall, an RAF man. A crowd of us gathered, yelling and cheering. Both were experts. The Germans—who loved fencing—had only one eye on business. The delousing party reached the gate, its guards shouted something to the guards on the gate, and off it marched into the woods toward the showers. Although the new guards weren't familiar with how many delousing parties had gone out during the previous guard, it was an awful sweat-producing few minutes.

Our minds weren't on the beautiful fencing. It was all we could do to keep from looking down the road. If there was no commotion there we would know the 27 men were clear—25 who had carried various civilian outfits—wrapped in towels—and the two guards, our own men dressed as German soldiers.

Their escape clothes had been assembled laboriously by Big X's tailoring branch. Some were made from blankets sent into the camp in personal parcels from home. Others were adapted from sports jackets and other odd garments that occasionally reached us the same way. Some of the men would be dressed as railroad workers, others as businessmen or German soldiers.

It was not difficult to supply these different types of clothing. Big X had full control over everything that came into the camp. Each parcel received bore with it a list of contents, and from those lists Big X commandeered anything he thought the organization could use. Civilian shirts, sports jackets, plain blankets and sheets

X for Escape

were fairest game for the tailors. Big X always would try to replace from our backlog of service clothing—sent us in bulk by the Red Cross—garments taken in this way.

We normally were allowed sewing equipment to repair our own clothing, and with it our tailors could make literally any outfit needed. A good job might take weeks, but time was our cheapest commodity. Given the time, our tailors could turn out an authentic outfit for anyone from a businessman (plain suit) to a chimney sweep (top hat, black coveralls).

Their papers, turned out under my supervision, matched their clothing. Most had temporary identification cards forged from a type the Germans used for people moving from one area to another. Part of the work could be done on a typewriter, the rest on an improvised mimeograph we had made, using for a roller a piece of broom handle wrapped with fine rubber from the handle of a cricket bat. A man dressed as a factory worker would carry travel authority on an authentic German letterhead stating he was going to take a job elsewhere.

People have asked me: Where did you get those letterheads? My reply is this: How hard is it to steal a letterhead from where you are working now? Probably not hard. The Germans we controlled in the camp did that for us. A few times we even had actual letters from the firm's files, so our forgers could do their job right down to an expert signature forgery and the initials of the boss's secretary.

To make the subject matter of the letters authentic was the job of another part of the security branch—the linguists, who read every German newspaper (supplied to us from the German canteen). Reading them they would find that a factory in Stettin, for instance, was advertising for a lathe hand. Often the advertisement would give the name of the man to see about the job. Our letter thus could be addressed to a real German, in a real company, from a real German in another company. It minimized the chances of detection.

From our German agents we had train schedules. For our maps working parties going out of the camp would concentrate on details of the surrounding country, report them to our cartographers. Other details we could get in casual questioning of our

211

contacts. Thus the maps these escapers carried were good, usually to a scale of an inch to a mile for the area immediately surrounding the camp. If a man ever was to have a chance to escape he would have it under our organization.

Maybe we'd even give some passports. A good passport forgery took up to a month. We would get a guard who was particularly well tied to the organization, ask for his passport for an afternoon. We would guarantee he would not be caught without it and that he would get it back that night. He would stay in his contact's room while my men worked on it nearby, doing even the fine print by hand with India ink and pens also brought in by Germans. Men from our security branch would be on lookout nearby. If anyone appeared to be coming our way, or looking for our chum, the passport would be handed back until the danger was over. There were many interruptions, but in time the work was done.

It was as much that—the exhaustive detail with which we had planned the escape—as natural anxiety for our friends that made it hard to keep our eyes on the fencing match, even though we knew anything else would have been suspicious. But finally someone looked, and the word went around—nothing was happening! They were clear! The fencing match went on, and so did another plan we had hatched to follow the first.

Within a few minutes one of our men, dressed as a German *unter-offizier* (NCO), appeared from one of the blocks, accompanied by seven of our compound's wing commanders and group captains and an American lieutenant-colonel. They marched up to the main gate. They were, the *unter-offizier* said, bound for the *commandatur* to confer with the commandant.

The real *unter-offizier* on the gate looked the other over carefully. He never had seen him before. It was possible for one guard not to know another, but there were fewer noncoms than ordinary guards. The gate *unter-offizier* was suspicious. He telephoned the commandant.

That was the end of the second escape attempt. The commandant and some of his officers came burning down from their quarters, and were considerably intrigued by this attempt to spring our high officers. "How do you think of these things?" the commandant

212

asked, chuckling. "You British!" He laughed heartily. "But we were too smart for you." That gave him much satisfaction.

"Of course," he continued, "we'll have to put you in cells for 10 days. Rules, you know." But we could see he sort of regretted the rules. He made no attempt to suppress his admiration for our idea, his amusement at our audacity, and his joy that his men had found us out.

We could hardly keep our faces straight. While he was telling us how smart he was 27 of our lads were packing off across the country in several different directions. We could picture them ducking off into the woods, changing into the civilian clothes they had wrapped in their towels, then separating and moving off through the trees—slowly and carefully at first, until they were clear of the camp, then more rapidly.

It was almost worth being a prisoner to see the commandant's face when a guard came running up a few minutes later and said he had found towels in the woods—and that the shower party had disappeared! The joke was over. The commandant went deep red, then pale. He ordered a roll call, and sent an alert to all nearby railway stations.

Rain began. The commandant ordered us all out on the sports field so he could call the roll and find out how many had escaped. It took five hours, and we were all soaking wet before it was over. But so was he. Meanwhile, troops were catching up with our men. Twelve were taken from a train they had caught at a station nearby. Some got farther away. The search was difficult, because the Germans didn't know what kind of outfits our tailors had provided for the escapers. Eventually most of them were returned to the camp. But some were not. It was a big day.

As much as anything, that escape was a test for our techniques—techniques based on our hard-won knowledge that getting out of a camp was perhaps the easiest part of an escape. There were many more escapers caught after leaving barbed wire than before. Our organization was making every effort to smooth the path beyond the wire as well as through it.

All this, as I have said, was part of the broad plan for making X Organization wide and strong enough to make our big escape a success. The preliminary work already was under way. It had started in the spring of 1943, and the shower house escape took place in the summer. Our plans were shaping up. Where before we had hope, now we had confidence.

Big X and his committee had decided the best place for our main tunnel to start was Block 104, my home. It was only about 30 feet from the wire, halfway between the top guard post and the gate. But we didn't pin all our hopes on one project. In March 1943, we started work on three major tunnels, code-named Tom, Dick and Harry. From the beginning, the Block 104 tunnel, Harry, was the one we hoped to use.

It started in a fireplace in the corner of the second room from the northwest corner of the block. When the fireplace and a section of flooring were removed there was a drop of about 10 feet, with steps down. Then came a level space of a few feet, and another drop to the bottom of the first well, 27 feet below the surface. From there, digging on a plan drawn by our engineers, the tunnel moved out under the wire toward freedom.

The soil was pure sand, making heavy shoring necessary. Boards to line the tunnel came from our bunks, which had 14 37-inch bedboards each. Of these Big X took eight and left six for each man to sleep on.

Planning the starting points for our tunnels took time and heavy thought. The barracks blocks in which we lived were one-story affairs, set in three rows of five to fill roughly two-thirds of the compound and leave one end open for a playing field. Each block had 24 rooms, and we had to study every one of them for escape possibilities even after we had picked the block we wished to use.

The end rooms usually were shared by a couple of wing commanders, and were not so good for escape purposes because they were much smaller than the 16 x 16 affairs most of us slept in. We also didn't want to use the kitchen, because there was only one to each block, with each room allotted 30 minutes a day to use the top of the stove or the oven. The kitchen was always in use, without cluttering it up with a tunnel. The orderly room wasn't a hot possibility either, because of the traffic there. That left the toilets, bathroom and 17 big rooms, with eight to ten people living in each.

X for Escape

Tom started in the bathroom of Block 123. We loosened a cement block on the floor and made it removable. Beneath, we dug. Each time when we were finished working we would put the block back in place, tamp clay around the edges, sand on top, and sweep vigorously until there were no cracks or openings.

It ran under a new compound the Germans were building, and had gone well past our own compound's wire when it was discovered. I'm not sure exactly how the Germans twigged to it. One report was that a guard heard underground noises outside the wire. Another was that a workman dropped a heavy hammer and the ground sounded hollow. At any rate they got suspicious and dug a deep ditch along the wire, finally breaking into the tunnel.

Then they decided to blow it up. They brought in dynamite and some hot engineers. We stood around in an admiring group outside the block while they prepared the charge. Finally a German engineer, standing well back, threw the switch to blow the charge and—WHAM—our loosened concrete block in the bathroom blew straight up into the air and tore a great hole through the roof of the block. We got a terrific kick out of that. The boneheads hadn't tamped the dynamite properly.

By this time, through material smuggled from England, tools we improvised, and what the Germans brought us, we had all the requisites for the job ahead. I cannot explain why the Germans in our power did for us what they did, but if I tell you how we came to influence them originally perhaps you can understand.

It was a psychological approach—simple, because our subjects were not on a high intellectual level. It could begin, as it did with one of our involuntary helpers, with me giving a German a cigarette. A few weeks and several cigarettes later I asked him into my room for tea. I looked at his snapshots with enthusiasm. Two or three months later he told me he was going on leave. I asked him to my room again for tea.

We talked about his leave: how long he was going to get, where he was going, how long it had been since he'd seen his family. Then I asked: "How would you like to take a little coffee home?" The average German hadn't had real coffee since 1936. He jumped at the chance. Then I said: "And a little chocolate for your little

215

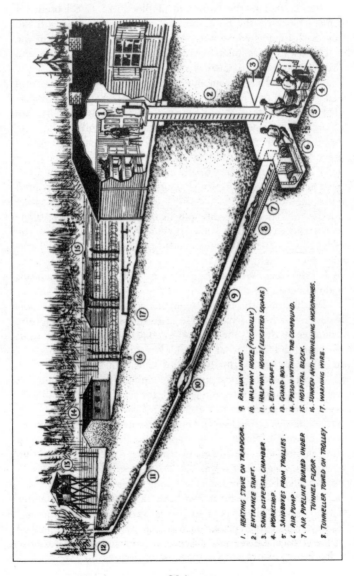

1. HEATING STOVE ON TRAPDOOR.
2. ENTRANCE SHAFT.
3. SAND DISPERSAL CHAMBER.
4. WORKSHOP.
5. SANDBOXES FROM TROLLIES.
6. AIR PUMP.
7. AIR PIPELINE BURIED UNDER
   TUNNEL FLOOR.
8. TUNNELLER TOWED ON TROLLEY.
9. RAILWAY LINES.
10. HALFWAY HOUSE (PICCADILLY).
11. HALFWAY HOUSE (LEICESTER SQUARE).
12. EXIT SHAFT.
13. GUARD BOX.
14. PRISON WITHIN THE COMPOUND.
15. HOSPITAL BLOCK.
16. SUNKEN ANTI-TUNNELLING MICROPHONES.
17. WARNING WIRE.

Reproductions of escape plan drawings by RAF Flt.-Lieut. Ley Kenyon. The originals were hidden in milk tins left in an abandoned and flooded escape tunnel. They were recovered after the war. Left: cutaway plan of tunnel. Top: hauling sand to tunnel entrance. Above: hacking away at workface.

217

Above: entering the tunnel.
Right: breakout with officer in foreground signalling all clear.

boy." Some German children had never had chocolate, so he went for that too.

You know how it is when someone gives you something. The guard wanted to know if there was anything he could bring me from outside. I said: "Yes, if you wouldn't mind, I'd like 100 tooth-picks." Anything inconsequential like that would do for the first time. You might never have used a toothpick in your life, and never intend to, but it was oil for the machine.

From then on, each trip I asked for something. In perhaps nine months we had him. His wife had grown to expect the coffee, his child was looking forward to chocolate every time he went home. He believed he had to take this little booty with him on every leave. Also, he had broken the rules so often that he would hesi-tate to deny any request for fear we told on him.

All these people didn't bite. Maybe one would decide the con-tact man was up to something and shake him off. Then he'd find that no other prisoner would talk to him or give him cigarettes. He'd see the other guards getting theirs. Often he would repent, come back and tell his contact man he'd play ball.

If you find it incredible that they would do so much for us, there's little I can say, because sometimes we found it incredible too. It was the psychology of binding a man with a thread and grad-ually strengthening the thread until it was far easier to submit to our bondage than to rebel. They never foresaw where it led until it was too late. And we paid them well in war-time Europe's best cur-rency—food that Big X commandeered from our Red Cross parcels in any quantity he believed necessary.

There were no repercussions when the Germans discovered a tunnel. The commandant recognized it was our duty to escape. He was happy as long as he could find the tunnels before we used them. So, after Tom was discovered, and while we were working on Dick and Harry, we used a system which was anything but shrewd, but worked rather well.

When we figured enough time had gone by without the Ger-mans finding a tunnel, we would start one in a small, crude way and then have a multitude of people dashing in and out of the hut all one afternoon, or leave sand or working materials where the

Germans would find them. Naturally they would figure we were building a tunnel, come in and make a search, and find it. Then they'd be happy for a few weeks longer. The Germans were quite stupid about tunnels. They thought it took much longer to build them than it actually did.

As the work on the main tunnel progressed tension grew. The excitement of playing a deadly serious game of cops-and-robbers, with freedom as the stake, made us want to work longer hours—get it over sooner. Our contact work with the German guards grew hugely in importance, because one disgruntled client among them could have given the alarm. Although they knew nothing whatever of the magnitude of our project, a really efficient search perhaps would have uncovered it.

We were helped immensely by close German observance of the international laws governing prison camps. There were no armed men inside the compound, unless an escape was suspected. We could talk together as much as we pleased; it couldn't have been otherwise with eight men to a room. There was no constant check on our movements, except the roll call late each afternoon.

That doesn't mean the Germans didn't try often to find out what we were up to inside. There were occasional attempts to plant spies among the prisoners. Knowing this we had an elaborate system for interrogating each new arrival, no matter how authentic he looked.

The interrogation, conducted by a security branch officer, would go something like this: "What squadron were you in?"

"Four oh one."

"What were you flying?"

"Spits."

"Know anybody from your squadron in here?"

The man might answer yes. Then, if he could be identified, he was all right. If not, the next question would be:

"Where are you from?"

"Vancouver."

"Know anybody from Vancouver in here?"

If he did, again he was all right. If he didn't, it went on.

A typical example was Charlie McCloskey, Toronto. He was

221

almost stumped. He didn't know anyone from his squadron in our camp. He didn't know anyone there from Toronto. The interrogating officer gave him the camp's nominal roll. McCloskey read it and stopped at my name. He said he recognized it. They called me along to see him.

I had never seen him before in my life, but he said he had gone to school with one of my sisters. He described her appearance, habits, and the school and district well. He knew that my mother was well known in Toronto musical circles. From it all he eventually was approved.

Until the interrogating officer was satisfied, each new man was confined to his room with a guard. One day one turned up who claimed to be a pro-Allied Turk. He said he had gone from Turkey to Cairo and had flown with the RAF in Italy. We kept him confined to his room for three weeks. One morning he wasn't there any more. The Germans had quietly withdrawn him.

In the early days the Germans used to string microphones into our rooms. We always found them. Some of them we purposely left open, to feed false information to the Germans. In others we merely would join the wires in the microphone pickup and blow the fuses.

Up until this last great escape plan was under way none of us knew how many were to go out in it, or who. When the time became close we drew lots, intensely, in small groups. Mere slips of paper they were, holding the yes or no of freedom—and, for the lucky ones, how long he would be after the first to leave.

I drew No. 93. Then I was faced with a major decision. Someone in my branch had to stay behind to check identification cards at the tunnel head as the escapers left. There was to be nothing left to chance, no man would leave with papers which didn't match his clothing or general escape plan. If I took my priority, someone else in my branch would have to stay behind. The few who could handle the job were all anxious to go. Because of my seniority as a prisoner and my major part in the escape organization, I could go if I wished.

I weighed the arguments. I hadn't seen my fiancée, in England, for more than three years. I hadn't seen Canada since 1938. I thought of home, the lights, the food, the shows, the people, the freedom to open a door and walk down a street. Against all that was the knowledge that because I had directed production of our escape documents I knew them better than anyone. Perhaps, if I left the job to another, there would be one vital detail only I would know, and I would be gone.

It was the greatest decision of my life as a prisoner of war. I was head of the section that forged those documents so I probably knew more about them than anyone. There could be only one way. I gave myself the appointment, thereby forfeiting my escape number—93—on the list of 375 prisoners we planned to release.

When I made my decision it was early in January of 1944—just a few days away from my 24th birthday, and a couple of months past the third anniversary of the black night I parachuted into enemy hands from a crashing Whitley bomber after the fifth Berlin raid of the war.

Big X was to be Number One on the escape roll, so we would have to reorganize. That was another reason for staying behind— we would need a nucleus of old hands to build up the organization again. But that was for the future. For the present Big X was still running the show.

Our main tunnel, code-named Harry, was just about complete. Nine months before we had started three major tunnels. One of them, Tom, had been discovered by the Germans. The others, Dick and Harry, were still our secrets. The entrance to Dick, which was farther from the wire than Harry, and therefore our second choice for eventual use, was a masterpiece.

As far as I know, it never was found. It started in a bathroom floor drain—a grate with a concrete well below. The well served to catch sediment, while water ran into a drainpipe on its wall. It also made a nice front door for our tunnel. We removed one of the sides and built a concrete panel which would slip in and out of place. The opening was about 27 by 24 inches and it was devilishly difficult to get through it into the tunnel. First you had to mop up all the water at the bottom of the well, so your clothing wouldn't suffer. Then, when the slide wall was moved, you would wiggle through the opening like a vaudeville version of someone getting into a girdle. For Harry's air conditioning we tried several methods before settling on a bellows made from kit bags. Worked by hand and operated almost constantly during work in the tunnel, the bellows was attached to pipes made from Klim (dried milk) tins, drawing in pure air and pumping out the bad. The pipes ran up under our barracks block, alongside an upright.

Starting at the first well was a small railway system for carrying back the dirt. Drawn by hand, the wooden cars ran in grooves in the traffic-hardened dirt floor. There were many extreme difficulties in digging the tunnel—engineering without proper instruments, the necessity of stealing or improvising every tool used—but dispersing dirt from Harry was the most difficult physical problem in the entire 12 months of effort.

I estimate it took 12 men on dirt dispersal for every man digging at the face of the tunnel. Approximately 25 men dug, in shifts that lengthened steadily through the months of labor. Usually about six worked at digging in each shift. In addition to the diggers there were men stationed at each well (marking the various levels of the tunnel) to help transfer the cars from one level to the next.

When the dirt reached the tunnel's main well (closest to the tunnel entrance) it was dumped in an auxiliary dispersal well. From there the dispersers—about 300 men working almost 100 to a shift—took over. One system was to strap long sausagelike bags (made from greatcoat linings) to their legs, go for a walk, pull the rip cord and let dirt dribble out as they scuffed along. Another method was to wear dirt-filled pouches under their greatcoats, find a blind spot in the camp—there were a few where you couldn't be seen by any of the guards—and dump them there.

In both cases the dirt could be kicked around until it mingled with the other soil—fortunately loose and sandy. I cannot estimate how much dirt we moved from Harry during that year, but the tunnel was 437 feet long at its completion, a couple of feet high, and perhaps three feet wide. That is a lot of dirt.

Our engineers, in the main, were enthusiastic amateurs—most of them with either an untrained aptitude for the job or some small preliminary experience. I can't think of one who had been an engineer before he joined the Air Force. But they did a fine, tight job,

X for Escape

wound up with a tunnel safe and well-shored with the bedboards Big X had commandeered from every bunk in the compound.

When we started work on documents, letters and identification cards for the big escape, there were four people in my outfit. I finally had eight working full time on forging and ten on maps, with a total staff of 137. I worked them only an hour or two every day at first, because it was absolutely essential they maintain high interest and accuracy. Intricate detail was necessary. Using the wrong color of ink on one of our forged rubber stamps could have undone a year's work. Rubber stamps can be made quite handily from rubber heels.

There was a terrific amount of this work which couldn't even be started before we knew the date of the escape, because certain German temporary passes we were copying always were stamped to be valid only for a month from date of issue.

We were extremely successful in keeping from the Germans all hints of our plans to escape. We caught any spies they tried to plant among us, foiled every effort they made to find out our inner organization. One reason for this success was that we were well-informed in advance on every German move. The camp commandant's secretary had a boy friend, a German guard we had tied up pretty well. The secretary would get correspondence files from the commandant's desk, give them to her boy friend, who would give them to us. Big X would read them, send them back along the same route.

There may be some who think that our complete organization of the science of escaping took a lot of the opportunism out of it. That wasn't so. Any prisoner with an idea could go straight to Big X and be on his way in half an hour—and instead of being out with only a good idea, he would have authentic German clothing, a compass, papers, money, maps, food and good advice.

Attempts to escape on garbage wagons were quite common. This could be tried almost any time. Big X would provide someone to distract the driver's attention while the escaper climbed into the cart and pulled garbage over himself. It wasn't such a good way to escape, though. At first the gate guards used only to jab into the carts with bayonets. But eventually they learned a man could get

225

under so much garbage a bayonet wouldn't touch him, so they began firing rifle shots through the garbage loads. That discouraged us effectively.

I have a considerable affection for the memory of one particular escape, a one-man affair. Every so often a chimney sweep came into the camp. Our tailors duplicated his outfit—the top hat, black overalls, high boots. One day, while the sweep was working on a chimney, one of our men decked himself out in this outfit, stole some of the sweep's brushes, and strolled casually out of the main gate. When the sweep tried to get out later the guards stopped him, thought he was one of us, then got him into considerable trouble when they found he wasn't. He was a very discouraged sweep by the time he got home that night.

But jobs like that were just marking time for the big one.

On March 1, 1944, tunnel Harry was finished to the point where our engineers figured open air was only about three feet away, an hour's digging. But we had to wait. There was a full moon then—bad escape weather. We wanted a night with no moon, a wind (to create noise in the woods to cover any we might make) and no snow. Only Big X knew, but we generally figured the break would be on the week of the 19th.

The morning of March 24 was beautiful and sunny. The ground was reasonably clear of snow, and there was an east wind—which we knew from experience usually held pretty well. I was pounding the circuit (walking around the wire) when one of X's runners came haring up and told me I was wanted. I had a feeling this was it. Big X had a meeting with the X Committee (heads of branches) every morning, and about this time each day it ended. I figured Big X had decided this was the day.

It was. I got my lads together and we started stamping "passes." Nobody was told except people who had work to do. We couldn't take the chance that someone would show excitement.

Late that afternoon the word went out. Everyone with an escape number was to be in Block 104 by eight o'clock, lockup time. That was a hazard in itself, because the block ordinarily would have only about 140 people in it. This night there would be 375 as well as those of us who were to direct the show. Although guards never entered the blocks at lockup, they always looked in the shutters. That meant we had to do a pretty good job of hiding the extra bodies. Nobody could be wandering around the corridors either, because that was unusual and therefore suspicious.

People going into the block did not carry their escape packs with them. Orders had been given to leave the packs in their rooms. Other prisoners had been designated to bring them over after dark.

In addition to clothing, these packs included iron ration kits which had been made up by our cooks. These were K-ration fruit bars from American Red Cross parcels, chocolate, raisins, Ovaltine tablets and a fudgelike business we made from oatmeal, sugar, cocoa, raisins and dried milk. Also there was some bread and meat—the latter mainly garlic sausage, of which very little came into the camp, all of it saved for the escapers. There were Americans in our camp during the last couple of years of the war, and their Red Cross parcels were made up mainly from service rations. That was handy, because K-rations in particular were built to give the maximum food in the minimum space—just the job for an escape.

Each man also had a compass, built in the camp. How? Take a small round piece of gramophone record. Paste to it a compass card. Heat the record, imbed a gramophone needle upright in the centre. Magnetize a sliver of razor blade, make a tiny hole about the point of balance, fit the needle to the hole so the blade can swing freely. Heat the piece of record again and bend carefully around a piece of glass about the size of a watch crystal. Result: a waterproof compass, about $1\frac{3}{4}$ inches in diameter. Our compass makers were so proud of their work they used to stamp our camp name (Sagan) and a phony patent number and date of manufacture on the bottom of each one.

The sun went down. Gramophones were going. People were reading, writing letters, acting naturally. All the tools used in the tunnel were taken and stored in Dick's first well, so they wouldn't be found in the flap that would be sure to follow the escape through Harry. I had to go and see that Dick was locked up properly after I put all my stamps, ink, paper and stuff away.

The tunnel was to break about nine o'clock. Diggers were sent down to knock out the last few feet. Other men who were to be stationed in the tunnel during the escape went to their posts. In the block, small escape groups gathered. Each had a leader, who wasn't going out. His job was to have the group ready on time. At the top of the tunnel was a timekeeper, to direct traffic.

There was a little more digging to do than we anticipated—about five feet instead of three. So it was after 10 o'clock when the tunnel broke. The diggers hared back, changed their clothes, and got ready to go.

On a word from the timekeeper, at the tunnel head in Room 23, a runner was dispatched along the barracks hall to a group commander with the terse message: "Get ready!" The group proceeded to Room 23 to be searched and have equipment and papers checked. Then it began to move through the tunnel. Big X was first man. The escape was on. It was 10:30 p.m.

I had a million things to do. Some people didn't understand their papers, wanted things explained to them. There were signatures missing on some papers. They had to be fixed. Some had the wrong papers altogether, and had to change with others or get new ones.

The tunnel head search was necessary. Every last detail of equipment had to be German. It was almost funny, if things hadn't been so tense, that we found an English nailbrush on Old Infallible, Big X. We found Gillette blades on others, and odd bits of stuff that a German wouldn't carry. It was all removed, naturally.

The tunnel opened into pine woods on the far side of the road north of the compound. From the mouth of the tunnel a cord stretched through the trees for several hundred feet. A man was stationed at the end of the tunnel. As each escaper reached that point his hand was placed on this cord. He felt his way along it to the end. There he gave it a sharp tug, and the next escaper would begin to grope toward freedom.

Against the wall near the end of the tunnel stood an external trap door we had built and camouflaged. If we were caught before the break was complete we were going to try and seal the tunnel and use it again. Or, if we got out the entire 375, we would seal it off and hope it was still our secret when the hubbub died down. We weren't overlooking any possibility.

The first 30 or 40 men went out without a hitch. The escape was running behind schedule, but everything was going well. Then, around midnight, we had a remarkable stroke of bad luck.

In the camp we operated our lights on the honor system. We put them out ourselves at 10 in our rooms, and in return were allowed to keep them on in the corridors all night. Because of this the only time the master switch would be thrown in the camp was in event of an air raid. We hadn't had a raid for months. But about midnight the planes came. All the camp's lights were thrown off. But we had been prepared, even for this. We had improvised a stock of candles—tins of boiled margarine with pyjama cord wicks.

In an hour and a half the timekeeper began calling numbers again and the escape went on. There were either 83 or 84 men out (I'm not sure which) when a guard, walking his beat up and down the road under which our tunnel ran, heard a noise. He stopped and looked at the tunnel mouth for a few seconds, then proceeded as if he were satisfied nothing was wrong. But when he came back he left the road and walked through the bushes. He was just in time to grab a man coming out of the tunnel.

Everyone else in the tunnel ran to the other end and scrambled back into the block. But the guard, for some reason, thought the tunnel had just broken. He took our chap to his guardhouse, and reported the escape. A guard was placed immediately on the tunnel mouth. But much to our surprise nobody came into the camp immediately. We were able to burn all our illegal documents.

About seven in the morning dozens of guards, carrying rifles, came into the camp and routed us out. The commandant arrived to call the roll. At first he didn't seem very worried. He couldn't quite understand why people were in the wrong blocks, but in the first block he took there were only three or four people missing. He thought things weren't very bad. But he got more and more worried as he went on. At the end, when he totted up and found there were more than 80 people out, he almost went mad. In fact, he did go mad as a result of that escape. When he had to report to the Gestapo how many people were loose, they removed him and we later heard he had gone around the bend.

The Gestapo took over the camp for the next several weeks. They were tough, hard men—small, usually a little on the stocky side—real gangster types. They established a first-rate reign of terror among the camp personnel. Interpreters were tried and shot summarily, and camp officers relieved. The Gestapo, perfectly thorough, searched the home of every guard, even if it was 300 miles away. If anything were found (food, soap, chocolate) to indicate the guard had been dealing with prisoners, it was worth his life. He either would be slated for the high jump immediately or would be sent to the Eastern Front. That was considered the same thing.

The Gestapo tore the camp apart. We were turned out of Block 104 for several days while they searched. When we were allowed back in, everything was wrecked. All our sugar, cocoa and other food had been turned out on the floors and ground into dirt and ashes. Our cigarettes were all broken, and clean laundry trampled and torn. However, apart from the inconvenience, it didn't cost anything. We were asked by the organization to report the extent of damage, then other people in the camp contributed to make it up. Even in adversity our camp was a communal project.

We heard why the Gestapo was taking this so seriously. They were afraid the Allies soon would land in the west, and that there would be a simultaneous uprising of the millions of foreign workers in Germany. They figured this incipient underground was being organized from England, but didn't know how. Then someone had a bright idea. He decided information and directions were being sent in to prisoners of war, who then were getting men out to lead the underground movement.

We didn't know it, but having decided that they determined to make an example of our escape.

About a month later a notice went up on the camp board. It read: "The following officers were shot while trying to re-escape ..." and gave the names of about 20 chaps we had sent into the black woods toward what we hoped was freedom. Other lists came later, until we knew that 50—six Canadians and 44 from other parts of the Empire—had been executed in all violation of every rule of warfare. We knew the Germans lied, because those men of ours knew better than to attempt escapes with armed men standing over them. They had been stacked up against a wall and shot out-of-hand. It was a lesson, Gestapo-style.

Some of the men who were caught near our camp were brought back to cells there, and later were among us when the first list was posted. I believe three of those who got out eventually reached England. Big X was not among them. His name was on the first list.

We were terribly shocked. The first day we gathered immediately in the theatre. There we prayed and sang hymns. It was forbidden for us to sing "God Save the King." We sang it, and felt better.

That was our last escape. Immediately news of the executions reached England, the Air Ministry told us over the BBC—yes, we had radios, smuggled radios—to stop escaping.

I cannot say what would have happened to us in the next few months if it hadn't been for the invasion of Normandy. Until then, with the incentive of escape work gone, many were losing the comparative peace of mind with which we had lived and endured the long years. Our morale was dangerously low.

The invasion gave us hope again. We set up a great marked map in one of the rooms—a map so accurate and detailed that Germans came in each morning to see how the war was going. It gave us infinite satisfaction to show them the ring drawing ever tighter.

From then to the end of the war none of us spoke to a German. And from then until our liberation on May 2, 1945, each of us wore on his sleeve a small diamond of mourning black, so that each time a German looked at one of us he would be reminded of what his people had done.

After being liberated, Tony Pengelly returned to Canada where he worked in sales and later in advertising in the Maritimes and Toronto. He now lives in Niagara-on-the-Lake, Ont., where he volunteers with the Shaw Festival, pursuing an interest in theatre kindled during his POW days.

Scott Young, an assistant editor of Maclean's *from 1945 to 1948, earlier served with the Royal Canadian Navy in Europe. A longtime columnist with the Toronto* Globe and Mail, *Young went on to write more than 40 books.*

CHARLIE MARTIN'S WAR

—June 6, 1994—
Anthony Wilson-Smith

Martin (left) with friend Lindy Lindenas.

For the 50th anniversary of the historic D-Day landing, Maclean's accompanied Charlie Martin of Mississauga, Ont., on an emotional return to the beaches he helped secure shortly after dawn on June 6, 1944.

Through the clearing mist, the French village atop the sable beach looked so unreal that Sgt.-Maj. Charlie Martin kept thinking, "It's like a picture postcard." As his Allied assault craft punched through heaving seas, not all the 28 men on board felt so benign about the tranquil scene one kilometre before them. For one thing, alongside the sturdy, three-century-old spired buildings were more recent, ominous additions: concrete pillboxes, machine-gun emplacements and gleaming, pitchblack 88-mm cannons. And in the water, Martin and his men saw a succession of round, rolling mines that could blow them and their landing craft to pieces.

Within the landing craft, the only sound was the undulating whir of the engine. Some men, like Martin, prayed. Others chewed gum and stared fixedly into space. Sea spray and waves washed over the bucking boat so that the troops, wearing heavy woollen khaki uniforms and weighed down further by 22-kg backpacks, were sometimes too sick and exhausted to think about how frightened they were.

It was shortly after 8 o'clock on the morning of June 6, 1944, a day that would become known in history as D-Day. For Martin and the other members of Toronto's Queen's Own Rifles, it was only minutes until the front ramp of their landing craft would drop, and they would be dispatched to the killing ground that lay ahead.

Fifty years later, Charlie Martin would remember virtually every sensation of those moments, including the wordless glances he exchanged with his second-in-command, Sgt. Jack Simpson. These two would lead the charge to the beach—and Simpson would be one of the first of the Queen's Own to die, cut down by a machine-gun burst just as he hit the sand.

Charlie Martin, three metres away when Simpson died, kept running with scarcely a backward glance at his fallen mate. There was no time to mourn that day. But the tears and the sorrow would last a lifetime.

No matter the time or season, a chill wind always seems to blow along the beach at Bernières-sur-mer. It whips up the sand and drives a constant spray of water from the English Channel, so that anyone walking across the flats is left half-blinded by grit and shivering in the damp cold.

It is not much different today than it was 50 years ago, when it was a most uncomfortable place for a young man to die. In the early morning hours of D-Day, that was only one of the considerations facing each of the more than 150,000 mostly Canadian, British and American troops as their landing craft approached the beaches of

233

Normandy. Other facts of life were how frightened and alone many of them felt, despite their numbers. While they would land together on the beaches, the prospect of imminent death was a solitary concern. Behind them, anchored eight kilometres from shore, the armada of more than 7,000 Allied ships that ferried the troops across the Channel receded into nothingness. Although there were more than 4,000 of the much smaller landing craft, the four-metre waves, grey skies and limited visibility meant the soldiers could see little on either side as they careered towards shore.

The vessels were such clumsy and uncomfortable contraptions that some of the men longed for the battle ahead because it promised relief from nausea and helplessness. The Queen's Own were used to being in close conditions, although nothing in their previous four years' service could compare with this. Most of the Queen's Own that day, members of Canada's oldest continuously serving regiment, founded in Toronto in 1860, enlisted in 1940. They stayed together through training stints in Newfoundland and England and knew one another almost as well as they knew their own families. Few had ever left Canada; many had never been outside Ontario until the war began. They included Martin, then 25, the company leader; Rifleman Herman (Chief) Stock, an affable Iroquois from the Gibson reserve on Georgian Bay; Henry (Buck) Hawkins, a 37-year-old rifleman with a wife and two children, who was also A Company's much-admired, undeclared father figure; Jim Catling, Bill Bettridge, Cpl. Jamie McKenzie and the feisty, always argumentative Bert Shepherd. Most were inspired to volunteer for the same reason Martin would express 50 years later. "Our country was at war, so we never thought twice about fighting for it."

A Company was among the first to hit the beaches that bloody day, just past 8 a.m. on the launch of Operation Overlord, the battle for the liberation of Europe and the biggest military operation in history. June 6 marked the beginning of the end of Nazi domination of Western Europe. Against an estimated 210,000 German troops spread along the coast, the Allies amassed eight infantry divisions and 14 armored regiments—156,000 men in all—to invade an 80-km front. Of the five code-named landing beaches, the Americans landed on two—Utah and Omaha—the British on two others—Gold and Sword—and the Canadians, part of the 3rd Canadian Infantry Division, on Juno, an unspectacular eight-kilometre stretch of sand sandwiched between the two British sectors. But for the men, the size of the operation and the enormity of its place in history were secondary to more personal concerns. "We never felt so alone in our lives," recalled Martin earlier this year, as he stood on the beach at Bernières-sur-mer and remembered the day his war began.

Charlie Martin is 75 years old now, with a limp and a cane and a heart that requires regular medication. He is a grandfather with a smooth, unlined face; a gentle, churchgoing man who never curses, seldom raises his voice and responds to compliments by immediately deflecting the praise to others. He has been married to his British-born wife, Vi, for 51 years and they move hand-in-hand through life with the quiet comfort of two people who have many memories and few regrets. "Charlie," says Vi, echoing words she first wrote as a war bride in England 50 years earlier, "was the love of my life when we married, and that has only grown since then."

They went back to Bernières-sur-mer earlier this spring, returning to the place where so many memories and fallen friends lie. Even now, there are reminders of war in the chilly peace of springtime Normandy. A German pillbox and rusting cannon—the same one that raked the beach with gunfire as the Queen's Own landed—remain as a memorial. A Canadian Sherman tank, decorated with the badges of the 14 "Normandy Landing" units that landed on D-Day, is permanently parked in the village square of nearby Courseulles-sur-mer.

When Martin stands on the beach, he still sees "two sights in my head: the way it was that day, and the way it is now." Among those French residents old enough to remember, the images are equally clear. "We must never forget," says Michel Chrétien, who has written a book honoring Canada's D-Day efforts, "and we must ensure that our children never forget." But that is not easy to ensure. Now, says a waitress in her mid-40s in Courseulles, another of the beach towns that the Canadians recaptured from the Germans, "the

Martin revisiting where he landed at Bernières-sur-mer, 50 years later.

kids growing up know little of the war, and care even less."

There is nothing on the Normandy beaches to mark where each of the men died. There were too many deaths for that: 375 Canadians, alone; another 628 were wounded. Total Allied casualties on June 6 were about 10,000, including more than 3,000 dead. Of the 124 men in A Company under Martin's command, Stock and Catling were among the first to wade through the water and among the first to die, killed by the same burst of machine-gun fire. Where they fell, there now stands a row of peeling, windbeaten wooden changing rooms.

As he prepared to take to the beach in 1944, Charlie Martin had a prayer in his head and a letter in his breast pocket from his wife of less than a year that said that whatever happened, "you will always be the love of my life." He also, he insists, held no particular worries about dying. "I guess the only thing we really fretted about," he says now, "was being wounded and severely disabled."

Looking at Martin today, it is difficult to see the traces of the

236

tough young man whose D-Day commanding officer calls him, half a century later, "the finest fighting soldier I have ever known." But it is clear why then-Maj. J. Neal Gordon holds that opinion. By the time of the invasion, Martin—four years removed from clearing fields on a south-western Ontario farm near Dixie—was a barrel-chested judo expert who also was a certified marksman and skilled knife-fighter. He appeared without fear and so instilled confidence in the men who followed him. "Every soldier who served with him just felt, instinctively, that Charlie was a person you could trust with anything, including your life," says then-Capt. Dick Medland, another of his former commanding officers and the holder of a combat medal.

The wake-up call came at 3:15 a.m., but few of the sleep-starved men on the Normandy-bound ships needed it. Outside, a violent storm filled the night; even if it had been calm, the fear of German mines laced at intervals across the Channel would have been enough to keep many men awake—and watchful. By 5 o'clock, they began leaving their transport ships for the smaller assault craft attached by ropes alongside. In practice, in calm waters in England, boarding had been easy. Now, they were burdened by heavy gear and a rolling sea. Anyone who fell was almost certain to perish quickly in the icy depths. Martin was the last to board. As he was lowered onto the deck by a rope, the pilot of the assault craft, impatient to be under way, gunned the motor. Martin almost lost his grip, but was hauled to safety by Hawkins and McKenzie.

Few Allied troops faced a more difficult landing than the Canadians. In *The Struggle for Europe*, Australian war correspondent Chester Wilmot wrote that Canadian troops landed "on the most exposed beaches, with the farthest to go, against what was potentially the greatest opposition." From the Queen's Own, two companies—A and B—landed in the first wave; C and D, each with up to 200 men, followed shortly after. When the first flat-bottomed landing craft ran aground, the Germans opened fire with cannons and machine-guns as the men jumped into the jarringly cold water and tried to spring through the heavy waves. One hundred metres ahead, at the edge of the beach, Martin saw a small gap between two manmade sand dunes. In the middle, a German soldier behind a submachine-gun shouted warnings to his mates. The sound of enemy gunfire, says Martin, was "like a constant cracking noise, and you could hear a snapping sound whenever a bullet passed near you." Alongside Martin, who was firing his rifle while on the run, Bill Bettridge ignored the heavy enemy fire, stopped, and took careful aim. The shots from one of the two guns—Martin is not sure whose—hit the German soldier and created an opening for the Canadians. That might have been the first time Martin killed another human being. "It may sound terrible," he says now, "but the fact I had to kill does not bother me. We were in a war."

Ever conscious of the time, Martin noted the landing time as 8:21 a.m. Later, he estimated the spring across the beach had taken less than 30 seconds—and cost the lives of a dozen A Company men. The fight for the beach was just the beginning. Martin, leading Bettridge, Shepherd and a dozen other men, raced across a railway line to a grassy field fenced in by barbed wire. Martin cut the wire, crawled under and advanced about 10 steps until he stopped abruptly. He had stepped on a hard object that he recognized from training as a "jumping mine"—a nasty mix of explosives, nails, buckshot and scrap metal that could, once detonated, shower debris with deadly effect over more than 60 metres. There was only one way to stop the mine from detonating. Martin—still under enemy fire—had to stand statue-like and maintain pressure on the mine with his foot. He did so until all his men were out of range. Then, to avoid the mine's upward spray, he dropped down quickly alongside it. At about the same time, a bullet hit the inside of his helmet and rattled around without harming him. Miraculously, this time, he received no wounds but experienced "one heck of a headache."

The rest of Charlie Martin's D-Day was less remarkable—but no less dangerous. He and four other men advanced, in extended single file, through Bernières-sur-mer. The winding streets and old homes, with their tiny windows and thick, brick construction, provided ideal cover for snipers. "You looked at every window," recalls Martin, "and wondered what might be behind it." Despite frequent fire, the group reached their first objective, the outskirts of town, without any casualties. By 8:45 a.m., 24 minutes after landing, the regiment had secured control of most of the town. By 9 o'clock, another member of the regiment later noted in his diary, "A cafe 100 yards off the beach [was] open and selling wine." The battle had been swift, but deadly. A and B companies lost 138 of 240 men—63 dead and 75 wounded—more than 50 per cent of their manpower.

But Martin's group still faced seven more kilometres of travel before their day was over. Much of it was through farmland and light underbrush, in which they and other Canadian troops took turns trying to draw out enemy guns by alternately jumping up, running erratically and then flopping for cover. The process saved them from ambush and injury, and helped them learn the location of enemy gun emplacements.

Meanwhile, C and D companies, which had landed 15 minutes after Martin, began a drive towards the regiment's first-day objective, the town of Anguerny. The survivors of the four companies met there late in the afternoon: of all the Canadian forces, the Queen's Own was the only one to meet and hold its ultimate D-Day objective. That was cause for pride and satisfaction, but it was also time to recognize the pain. As dusk fell, Martin had time to collect his thoughts. He wandered away from his fellow soldiers to a solitary place behind a waist-high stone wall. There, he knelt and remembered all the men killed that day whom he had known so long, and so well. Then, Charlie Martin wept.

Martin did not cry again until after the war. He fought with extraordinary bravery for another 10 months through the Allied liberation of France and Holland, and sorties into Germany. Many times, Martin led three-man patrols into enemy lines, with the objective of capturing a prisoner to get information on German troop movements. Once, under heavy enemy fire, the five-foot, seven-inch, 128-lb. Martin half-carried, half-pulled a six-foot, 200-lb. wounded comrade back to his own lines. At the same time, the wounded mate was himself dragging along a German prisoner.

On another occasion, Martin and a partner went out overnight and dug a concealed trench in a cabbage patch less than 150 m from a German gun emplacement holding down the company's advance. The two lay there for more than 18 hours until dusk fell again. Then, they emerged from their hole, shot and killed the two German gunners and spent another three hours huddling under a bombardment from an enraged enemy. Martin survived countless other close brushes with death, including one incident in Germany where a Gestapo officer who had just been taken prisoner suddenly produced a hidden pistol and opened fire at him from five metres away. One shot drew blood on Martin's right ear; the other went through the mesh of his helmet. Martin drew his own pistol and disabled the Nazi by shooting him in both shoulders. On another occasion, Germans encircled and ambushed his platoon. Martin decided the route to escape lay in leading a bayonet attack against the ambushers. In the ensuing battle, he was stabbed over the left eye and broke a finger fending off an attacker—but led his men to safety.

Charlie Martin's luck ran out on April 16, 1945, when he was trying to cross a bridge near the village of Sneek, Holland. Midway, he sensed a movement—and turned as a German soldier opened fire at close range. Bullets hit Martin in the right leg, chest and left arm even as he fired back, killing the German. He passed out from loss of blood and remembers nothing again until May 8, 1945, when he came to in a military hospital in Ghent, Belgium, in time to hear Winston Churchill on the radio, announcing the end of the war.

At the time he was wounded, Martin was the last man still serving in active combat from the original group who came together five years earlier in Toronto. The figures tell the horrific tale of the losses suffered by the Queen's Own. In a regiment that had an official strength of 800 men, from D-Day until the end of the war 11 months later, each man was replaced because of death or wounds an average of 3 1/2 times. By the war's end, 453 had died and more than 1,000 were wounded—and the average time experienced in combat before either happened was less than six weeks.

In short, by the time Charlie Martin's war ended, he had outlasted the average Queen's Own combat service span by more than seven times. For his efforts, Martin now wears proudly on his jacket lapel a Distinguished Conduct Medal and Military Medal, among Canada's highest awards for bravery in combat.

The bodies of 2,049 Canadians lie in the immaculately kept Canadian War Cemetery at Beny-sur-mer, five kilometres inland from Bernières-sur-mer. The graves are almost all marked by identical white stone crosses. Elderly local French residents sometimes come and leave flowers in memory of the young men they never met. Occasionally, there are wreaths and bouquets accompanied by personal messages—reminders that some of the sons and daughters of the dead still come to visit.

Even for those born long after the war, it is a wrenching place to visit. Some of the dead were in their teens: had there not been a war, they could still be working, enjoying grandchildren, pondering retirement and the future. The worst thing about those deaths, says Martin—who wrote to all the families of the A Company dead—was dealing with the parents. "I knew that the widows were young and could start life again," he says. "But for a parent who lost a child, a large part of themselves died with them."

Other losses were painful for different reasons—such as the enlisted men in their late '30s and early '40s who left behind half-grown families when they went to war.

One of them was Martin's 37-year-old friend Buck Hawkins. He was an easygoing but decisive character whose size, age and maturity made him a natural leader—but who always rejected promotion from his rifleman's rank because it would have taken him away from his friends in A Company. He was killed on July 18, 1944, while providing covering fire that allowed wounded members of his platoon to retreat from a heavy German attack. His gravestone at Beny-sur-mer says that Rifleman H.H. Hawkins "gave his life for his friends."

Tears still fill Martin's eyes when he looks at Hawkins's grave or talks about him. "I can see him today just as he was," says Martin. "A big, handsome so-and-so with a devilish grin, so quick with a joke and a smile."

On June 6, Charlie and Vi Martin will return to Normandy for

241

official ceremonies. This, the veterans agree, is likely to be the last large commemoration. Age and disease are gradually achieving what war could not, and it may be a final chance for many to formally honor the memory of those they left behind. "We had the chance to live our full lives, and they did not," says Martin. "It falls to us to remember who they were, and what they did."

History, it is often said, is written by the victors, but memories belong to those who lived the event. In the memories they share in their autumn years, the veterans of the Second World War learned a more fundamental lesson: there is never a comfortable place for a young man to die.

Charlie Martin returned to the Normandy beaches for the last time in June 1997. Martin died four months later, on Oct. 13, 1997, at age 78, after a brief illness.

SECOND WORLD WAR
—Asia—

ESCAPE FROM HONG KONG

—June 15, 1942—
C.E. Ross

C.E. "Ted" Ross was born in Winnipeg twenty-nine years ago. He joined the C.P.R. in Vancouver in 1929, was sent to Shanghai in 1936 and transferred to the Hong Kong office four years later. When the Empress liners were removed from the Oriental service due to the war he was granted leave of absence and joined the British Ministry of Information staff. This story of the last tragic but courageous days in Hong Kong from Dec. 8 to the surrender on Christmas Day, and of his thrilling escape with a small party of officials from Hong Kong to Chungking,

Aberdeen fishing village, starting point of the escape.

CANADA AT WAR

Maclean's presents just as Ted Ross set it down in a long letter to his mother, written as he waited for a plane that was to carry him from Chungking to Calcutta.   —The Editor, 1942

Well, here I am at last, away up in Chungking, China's war capital; and believe me, I've just been through the greatest adventures of my life—and there's still more to come. If all goes well I'm off to Calcutta tomorrow night by plane, so must get some part of my story into the mail and on the way to you.

It seems so far back now, back to December 8, the date of the outbreak of war in the Pacific, and so far as I'm directly concerned—Hong Kong. It has probably changed my whole life (and that of many thousands of others, for that matter).

I've often wondered if my last letter written about the beginning of December ever reached you. I sent it air mail, and enclosed a little Christmas gift for you both. Do so hope it arrived. Also did you get my two cables? One sent from Hong Kong about the middle of the fight, and the other from Waichow (first point in Free China we reached that had a wireless station). Hope you got them both, especially the last one, as it cost me four hundred dollars.

Mac and I (Davis MacDougall, he was my boss in the Ministry of Information in Hong Kong) made for the wireless station just as soon as we found out where it was, dashed off a cable each (incidentally Mac's wife and child are in Vancouver, too—he evacuated them to Canada from Hong Kong long before the trouble) and when we got the bills later we almost collapsed. Of course we had nothing like that amount with us and had to borrow from the Admiral. Anyway we were feeling so good to be alive and free once more, we'd have spent many hundreds more at that time just to let the world know about it.

Well, I'd better start at the beginning. Shortly after five on the morning of the eighth, I was awakened by a phone call from the Defense Secretary. He said things looked mighty serious and to get down to the office as quickly as possible. I got in touch with Mac and started into town. It was a beautiful morning, and the drive in from Repulse Bay just like any one of a hundred similar drives I'd made since moving out there, except I was stopped every once in a while by sentries posted along the road.

Nothing happened for a while after we arrived at the office until a force of about thirty Japanese planes appeared over Kai Tak, our one and only airfield, on the Kowloon (mainland) side. They got quite a few of our planes on the ground. Mostly big passenger planes. Also a couple of our military reconnaissance planes—we had only three all told. We had no fighters or bombers. Well, that started it, and from then until our surrender at 3:15 p.m. Christmas Day seems just like a dream now.

There were an estimated million and a half Chinese (civil population) on the Island, in addition to approximately twenty-five thousand Europeans, mostly British. Our job was to keep them informed of the military position. To that end we had to see to it, as far as possible, that all English and Chinese newspapers kept publishing. We made three trips a day up to Battle Headquarters for official communiqués. These were passed to the press, in addition to a multitude of notices that were required to be promulgated as necessity arose. These notices covered everything from warnings not to drink water unless it was boiled first, to appeals for warm clothing for Kowloon evacuees; and from instructions covering air raid precautions to appeals to the populace to remain calm and not to listen to rumors and scaremongering.

There was a large and very active fifth column operating. They spotted our gun positions and troop concentrations and flashed information across to the Japs, but worse than that they were actively disseminating alarmist propaganda and false rumors. We had to combat them by newspaper, radio talks, leaflets, posters and having our own counter-rumormongers mingling with the crowds in air raid tunnels and shelters. It was a great game, and with the valuable aid of pro-Chungking organizations and volunteer Chinese writers and translators, we definitely won out.

Battle Headquarters was a splendidly built string of military offices about eighty-five feet underground, having its own power plant, telephone system, etc., so when eventually our lights went, headquarters carried on unhindered. It felt so safe and secure away down there, but going and coming three times a day was no joke. The naval yard was just below and there were gun batteries above, so there was usually quite a hail of fire to go through.

The newspapers, both English and Chinese, worked marvelously. When the power went, on December 18, they turned out their editions by hand press, and on one occasion an English newspaper editor ran over to our office when his hand presses were knocked out and got out a last edition on our mimeograph machine. Right up to the last day there were three English newspapers and about five or six Chinese newspapers still publishing. Mind you, due to severance of all outside communication, and with the power gone so that we couldn't even get radio news broadcasts, the editions of the last week were simply single sheet affairs carrying local news and special notices.

Keeping the internal situation under control was just about as urgent as the actual fighting. If ever those million civilians became restless and got out of hand the military position would have been hopeless. Fifth columnists were actually sniping with pistols and rifles from the upper stories of downtown buildings, but not to any great extent. It was their job to create as much disturbance as possible, and to aid them the Japs kept flooding the place with anti-foreign leaflets from the air. They also set up loudspeakers on the Kowloon shore, and on boats moving up and down the harbor at night, exhorting the Chinese and Indians to turn against the Europeans. Also telling the Canadians to lay down their arms and they would be well treated.

The Japs have a funny mentality. Do you know, for several nights they played gramophone records of all of the old tunes (Home Sweet Home, Swanee River, etc.) in an apparent effort to make the troops feel homesick, and perhaps give up the fight. It was, of course, all to no avail. Most of their propaganda was directed to the Indians to "throw off the foreign yoke"; but, by golly, the Indians fought magnificently, never conceding a single inch.

The Japs broke through on the Kowloon side much quicker than had been expected, and we had to withdraw all troops to the Island by the morning of the twelfth. The invaders fought very well indeed and appeared to follow a well-formulated plan. Their numbers were estimated at 45,000 men with a further division in reserve. We numbered less than 12,000, made up of British regiments, Indians, Canadians, local volunteers and Chinese sappers. Our actual strength was made up of roughly a regiment of Royal Scots, a regiment of the Middlesex, a regiment of Punjabis, a regiment of Rajputanas, two Canadian regiments and the balance local British, Eurasian and Chinese volunteers.

As I see it, the Japanese had a reasonably simple problem before them. They knew the number and exact position of all our huge, fixed defense guns. They knew the exact strength of the garrison, position of pillboxes, etc. And they knew the huge problem we had on our hands housing and feeding the large civilian population. It was simply a military problem of how many guns of each calibre to bring up to overcome ours, how much light artillery, mortars, etc., and how many men. They had control of the sea, and knew we could get no reinforcements, either of men or materiel. As fast as we knocked out their gun positions they replaced them, but as they knocked out ours, we had no replacements.

Finally our remaining forces, depleted by heavy casualties, were almost fighting in their sleep. After seventeen days of continuous conflict, their physical exhaustion was something that could not be overcome without large reserves, of which we had none. The Japs, on the other hand, kept bringing up their fresh reserves. The end was inevitable.

The first two days passed reasonably quietly. We made no attempt, according to plan, to hold a line out on the border; but slowly and steadily withdrew to prepared positions in the hills beyond Kowloon. Our company of Chinese sappers did very good work with their demolitions. Roads and the railway line were blown up and blocked, railway tunnels blown in, and all bridges demolished. The Japs were then forced over the hills, dragging their equipment with them. There was very little fighting during those two days, beyond skirmishing between their advanced patrols and our rear guard.

It was generally believed we could hold that line behind Kowloon for some weeks; but by a very heavy night attack on the Castlepeak flank, they turned the line and began to filter in behind our positions. That made the whole line untenable, and immediate evacuation to the Island was inevitable. Their officers were in the thick of it all the time, and suffered very heavy casualties, losing twenty-three out of thirty officers in one group. The Royal Scots, the Indians and the Hong Kong Volunteers were fighting on the mainland, keeping the Middlesex and the Canadians on the Island in reserve and to ward off any attempted landings. The Volunteers did very well, and suffered practically no casualties in that mainland fighting. The Indians fought magnificently throughout.

All troops were evacuated from the Kowloon side by the morning of the twelfth, except for a small group of Indians holding out at Devil's Peak. That's opposite Lymun, the entrance to the harbor. The essential services (medical and nursing staffs, food control staffs, air raid precautions staffs, etc.) were recalled on the afternoon of the eleventh. A large number of the medical and nursing staffs (many of them women, and some with husbands on the Island) refused to leave, and remained at their posts until the Japs arrived.

In all fairness it must be admitted, apart from one day, the Japs confined their fire as much as possible to military objectives. In addition to armed positions these included the naval dockyard, all main roads, government house, the police station. The day after the evacuation of Kowloon they sent a peace mission across under the white flag to ask our surrender. They brought two British women with them, and when questioned they stated so far they had been quite well treated and were confined to the Peninsula Hotel.

When their peace offer was rejected they pushed off, and the next day (or the day after that, I forget which) they simply cut loose point-blank with everything they had. This appeared to be the only intentional indiscriminate firing, and was intended to scare us into an early surrender. Shells and bombs fell everywhere. You'll remember several of the places hit, mum. The Hong Kong Bank received several hits. We had three heavy shells in the Gloucester, one right on our third floor. It was a big baby, looked about nine point two, but fortunately for us it didn't explode. Just plowed through the outer stone wall and penetrated a couple of rooms.

The police station was badly smashed up, and darned if they didn't move into the ground floor of the Gloucester. I didn't like

The author, Ted Ross.

the look of that, knowing the Japs were after them; but apart from those three hits, and one incendiary bomb that landed on the roof, the Gloucester wasn't hit further. Glass and debris littered all the main streets, but none were completely blocked.

At noon a dead calm settled down, and in the afternoon a second peace mission came over. This time the Governor refused to have any dealings with them, and when they returned the siege started in earnest. They systematically pounded away at our gun positions, and their planes dive-bombed the dickens out of them. Our big siege guns were well protected by heavy concrete emplacements and stood a good deal of pounding. For this reason casualties among the gun crews were comparatively light, as their plotting rooms, etc., were quite well protected. However, one by one, our guns were being knocked out.

The enemy made their first landing on the Island during the night of Dec. 17–18, and when we failed to force them off the

251

following day, it was fairly certain the jig was up. They laid down a heavy barrage all the previous day, and on into the night, knocking out all our pillboxes along the shore in the North Point area, and blasting our strong points just behind. Then, either by luck or intentionally, some shells set fire to a large oil dump near the waterfront. The wind was blowing down the harbor, and the dense, billowy, black smoke from the burning oil tanks made a very effective screen. This screen, together with the darkness of the night and their heavy covering fire, enabled them to get a foothold.

How many they got across that night is not known, but there must have been a considerable number. Dozens of small groups of about ten men each quickly filtered through the streets into the hills behind and set up strong machine gun and trench mortar positions. When we counterattacked early the next morning along the sea front to attempt to clear the Jap bridgehead, these hidden positions in the hills above proved very effective, and were, to a large extent, I think, responsible for the failure of our attack. During the following night the Japs simply poured across by the thousand. They must have suffered severely as we had every gun we could fire blasting away at them; but in the dark of night it was difficult to tell just how effective our fire was.

The power station went out on Dec. 18, and we had to carry on by candlelight after that. Then the water mains were smashed, and the large reservoirs captured, and water became very scarce and dangerous to drink. Long unused wells under some of the downtown buildings were brought back into use, but the water was salty and brackish. We worked and slept in the office.

Up to the night of December 17th, I had been getting out to Repulse Bay each evening for a good night's sleep, as it was very quiet there and comparatively free from bombing. That night, however, the Japs captured Wongneicheong Gap, the gap through which the Repulse Bay road runs, and when I tried to get through next morning I ran into a hail of machine gun and mortar fire, and was forced back. Got to the office by going right around the south side of the Island, which was still in our hands.

All motor cars were commandeered by the Government for use by essential service workers only. Gangs were sent around the streets to pick up all cars and drive them to car dumps, the main reason being to clear the streets for essential traffic, and secondly so that those authorized to drive could go to the dump and pick up a car. In effect, as cars were damaged by shell fire or collision, got flat tires or run-down batteries, they were simply left for wrecking crews to pick up, and the drivers went to the dump for another one.

I went down and picked myself a peach of a big new Buick Special. Boy, it was a honey. I drove it right through the siege, through streets littered with debris, broken glass and hanging trolley wires, and never even got a puncture. We used it in our final escape, and left it standing beside the wharf intact and full of gas. Gosh, it broke my heart to leave it! We used it for everything; dashing up to headquarters three times a day for communiqués, distributing leaflets and pamphlets, picking up gasoline, oil and food supplies.

The Japs continued to pour men and materials across, and before long had control of the eastern half of the Island, excluding Stanley. The fighting was continuous and casualties on both sides severe. We damaged all our big guns on that part of the Island before being driven out, so that the Japs could make no use of them... (*four lines censored*).

Repulse Bay Hotel had quite an exciting time. The Japs finally surrounded it, and we had a motley gang of volunteers, Canadians, Indians and I don't know who else trying to hold it. As our men were cut off up in the hills a good many of them filtered down to the hotel and finally formed quite a garrison. Unfortunately a large number of women and children had taken refuge there, so it was impossible to make a last ditch stand. The women and kids were put down in a shelter under the hotel, however, and the troops hung on as long as they could.

The Japs scrambled down the hillsides, and climbed through the windows. Our fellows cleaned them up with hand grenades and Tommy guns. During one of the first dark nights, when they realized the Japs were trying to get down the hillside, they fired flaming arrows into the bush and started fires so they could see the Japs coming. My room was on the ground floor right up against the hillside, so I'm afraid there was nothing left of all my stuff. The Japs slunk down to the windows and heaved hand grenades in, blasting

Canadians arriving in Hong Kong, Dec. 1941.

down the doors, so my poor old radio, typewriter, clothes and everything must have been blown to bits. I had given them up for lost long before anyway.

By the 24th, things looked pretty well hopeless. The Japs had landed an estimated twenty-five thousand troops on the Island, and our defenders, pitifully reduced by casualties, were nearly dead on their feet. It's impossible to tell, but we probably had about five thousand men left to meet the twenty-five thousand fresh Japanese. Surrender seemed inevitable. Mac and I talked it over and decided to prepare for a break if an opportunity presented itself after the surrender was final.

We carried on the work right up to the last minute and in the meantime prepared a couple of well-stocked packs. I was driving from headquarters one afternoon and noticed that one of the army stores had been hit and evacuated, so I stopped a moment, dashed in and picked out two brand new army knapsacks. We filled these

254

with a change of underwear, socks, razor, toothbrush and as much concentrated vitamin food and chocolate as we could cram in—enough to keep us going a couple of weeks once we got into the country and could get a little rice.

The big problem was how to get off the Island, and where to land if we did manage to get off. The Japs had complete control of the water, as our poor little navy had been shattered. They also had a few troops placed on nearby islands, and held the mainland for a depth of about thirty miles. Beyond that were pro-Japanese puppet troops, and scattered here and there were bands of pro-Chungking guerillas—the latter on our side if we could find and convince them we were friends of Free China. We at first decided to risk a journey at night in my canvas canoe to any place off the Island of Hong Kong where we could hole up for a day or so, and have a look around. But the Japs captured Repulse Bay and we couldn't get the canoe.

Then we contacted some daring Chinese junkmen and made tentative plans to have them smuggle us out at a thousand dollars a head. This plan failed because we couldn't leave until after the surrender (above all, we couldn't leave our work so long as the fight was still on). The junks couldn't hang around waiting indefinitely as the Japs were capturing one place after another along the coastline, and we could give them no indication when or where we'd be when the white flag went up.

Finally we decided to hide in the hills of the Island until dark, then sneak down to Deepwater Bay, find a sampan, or as a last resort swim out to the Yacht Club, grab a club rowing boat (if there were any still intact) and row out to any island as far away as we could paddle. Our problem of how to make a getaway was finally solved (so we thought) when we learned that one of our few remaining motor torpedo boats had orders to stand by just before the surrender and take off some high Chinese officials in an attempt to dash to the safety of the China coast to the north. The order to leave had to be given before the surrender, as, apparently, according to military procedure, once the surrender order was given, if it were an unconditional surrender such as ours, all property immediately became that of the victor.

How, then, were we going to contact the boat when we could only leave the centre of the city some time after the surrender? Well, we decided to take the chance that the boat would still wait a while. In other words, the order from headquarters to go would be given, but the commander of the launch could use his own discretion after that.

At 3:15 p.m. on Christmas Day the cease-fire order was given. That had been a terrible day for the last remnants of defenders. The Middlesex had been ordered to hold the streets leading into the centre of the city from the racecourse. The street fighting was intense, and the Jap casualties heavy. By sheer weight of numbers they finally overran our troops, and I'm afraid our casualties during those last few hours must have been very heavy.

To those essential workers and civilians carrying on in town, it must have seemed just like any of the preceding days. I believe very few realized the end had come. Of course Mac and I, being in constant touch with headquarters, knew it was coming fast. We got in touch with the Colonial Secretary and asked to be released from duty after the surrender was final. (We didn't want to make our break, and be called deserters at some later date.) He gave his sanction and wished us the best of luck. We were then in the clear, and on our own. We stayed around the office cleaning up the last few things, telling the Chinese staff to clear off home and stay indoors for the next day or two until the situation stabilized a little.

My thoughts strayed back to the night before—Christmas Eve. We had had dinner with some of our Chinese friends, those we had been working very closely with throughout the siege. It was a queer little celebration by candlelight in the hallway of the fourth floor of the Gloucester. I had managed to buy a small tinned Christmas pudding, someone else had brought some Christmas sweets, and we could still buy drinks from the hotel. Just as we were about to sit down, one of the chaps produced a paper parcel—a small roast chicken he had brought along as a surprise. Well, we had a great old dinner and enjoyed it all immensely, even though the atmosphere was strained.

You see, after dark it was almost impossible to move about on the streets. There was not a single light showing anywhere, and you were challenged every few yards. Those last two or three nights it was more than risky as the poor fellows on patrol were dead tired and were usually a little too quick on the trigger.

We had a watch kept on our telephone, and slipped upstairs for the dinner. Mac and I knew things were coming to a head fast, and without spoiling the party by blurting out bad news, we managed to convey to our Chinese friends, especially those who had worked most openly against the Japanese and would stand little chance once the Japs got their hands on them, that it would be very advisable to obtain old dirty coolie clothes next morning, and keep them handy to slip into quickly if and when the Japs should break through. I'm glad to say they nearly all heeded the advice, and on Christmas Day about noon we were able to give them the tip to slip quickly into their coolie outfits and mingle with the crowds in the densely populated areas of West Point. We all went to sleep about 8:30, most of them sleeping on the floor in our office.

At a quarter to four we could delay no longer. The Japs were advancing right into the centre of the city. We dashed out onto Queen's Road, where the trusty old Buick was parked just in front of the King's Theatre. There we were joined by the party of four official Chinese (they had not contacted the torpedo boat before the surrender, and our hopes rose that perhaps the boat would still be waiting) and five British officers who realized the jig was up and were anxious to attempt the escape with us. There was an RAF Squadron Leader, an Army Major, two Captains and a Captain of Police from India who had been caught in Hong Kong when the trouble started.

I drove the Buick with half the party and the rest followed in another car. We sped through the street out the west end of the city as the Japs poured in from the east. Tore past the Queen Mary Hospital onto the south side of the Island, and into Aberdeen.

We couldn't see any sign of the boat and our hearts sank. Although the white flag had been hoisted nearly an hour before, there was still heavy rifle and machine gun fire to be heard all around, and an occasional burst of artillery. Jap planes overhead were still dropping bombs. Every once in a while heavy explosions shook the island, as our troops apparently blew up ammunition and oil dumps. The fighting continued, I'm afraid, until dark, and our casualties during those last few hours must have been terrible. You see, communications had broken down badly toward the end, with so many pockets of our men being cut off and isolated, and there was no means of getting word to them that the surrender was on. In any event, the Japs, after fighting and losing heavily all day, were in no mood to stop at the sudden appearance of a white flag.

We scouted around and finally located the naval officer in charge of the harbor out there. He was surprised to see us, and said the boat had been ordered to leave more than an hour before. We hadn't a moment to lose.

At any moment the Japs might appear along the road and cut us off. We dashed out onto a little pier and found a few naval volunteers trying to start a small launch. It had no battery or gasoline. Another chap and I jumped back into the Buick and tore down to the naval store just along the road a bit and managed to dig up a battery and sixteen gallons of gas. By the time we got back the other chaps had located a food dump and had filled the boat with water, canned food of all kinds, rifles, pistols and ammunition. We finally got the battery and gasoline in and pushed off at a quarter to five.

It was certainly a crazy attempt. It was a bright sunny afternoon and the ocean was as calm as a millpond; visibility was perfect and the Japs could spot us miles away. The boat was a flimsy wooden affair, with a speed of about seven miles an hour. Our party had now grown to sixteen, the extra five being naval volunteers who had been working on the boat and others who had just happened to wander along and decided to make the dash with us.

Well, we hadn't gone much more than five or six hundred yards when we were spotted from the shore, and the Japs let fly at us with everything they had—rifles, machine guns and small shells. The bullets simply whizzed through the side of the boat as if there had been no side there at all. Several of our chaps were hit, and soon a shot put the engine out of commission. That capped it. There we were, just sitting like ducks on a pond. The machine gun bullets kept tearing in. Mac got one right through his tin hat, another cut through the sole of his shoe, and just as he was saying how close they were coming he got one right in the back.

Some shouted, "Jump over!" and everyone started plunging into the water and swimming toward a small island about four hundred yards away. Two or three men were lying about on the bottom of the boat, and I didn't know whether they were dead or wounded. For a moment the fire into the boat lessened somewhat as the Japs turned all their guns on the men swimming. I took a quick look over to see how far away the island was and the water was simply a maze of splashes where the bullets were pouring all around the swimmers. One man was either wounded or he couldn't swim and was drowning noisily. I kept saying to myself, "Now don't get too excited, there must be some way out of this," and decided it was far better to pause a moment and get all my clothes off so as to swim faster.

By the intensity of the fire on the water I figured only about three or four would get through. I can remember so clearly throwing my clothes on a seat out of the oil and water in the bottom. The bullets were once again tearing through the boat and believe me, I stripped in nothing flat. The pockets of my jacket were bulging with last minute things I had tried to save, including two thousand Hong Kong dollars I was carrying to see us through if we ever made the guerilla country. Threw my pistol off—a dandy little 32 Colt automatic given to me by the Assistant Police Chief just at the start of the war. Gosh, it was hard to lose absolutely everything. As I hit the water I can remember feeling my wrist watch, and thinking, "That's the last thing I possess, now it's ruined."

By golly, taking my clothes off made a whale of a difference! I was one of the last off the boat, but the first to reach the island. I had such a funny outlook during all that time. Right from the moment the first bullet crashed into the boat until I was trying to get a handhold on the rocks of the island it never seemed important to me that I might be hit. I kept thinking, gosh, these poor fellows all getting wounded in the boat, and those poor fellows swimming out there, they'll probably drown. Only when I was about twenty odd yards from the shore did it suddenly strike me. Then something inside kept shouting, "You've missed everything in the boat and in the water, now wouldn't it be awful to be hit within just a minute or two of safety." I dived and swam as far as I could under water, and finally got to the partial shelter of a rock on the shore.

The Japs sprayed the rocks with machine gun fire as the survivors arrived and began to climb up. I was hit a couple of times with fragments of stone. The walls of rock were quite steep and I decided to cling on until it became dark in about another hour, and then climb over to the other side of the hill. Other fellows swam in to where I was, and after a long time Mac came floating in on his back. Can you beat it—he's not a strong swimmer at any time, and here, fully clothed and with a pistol strapped around his waist and a bullet in his back he had successfully made the shore after half an hour in the water. He was completely exhausted and it was all I could do to help him up onto a small rocky ledge. He had tried to get his clothes off as he had almost drowned several times, but couldn't manage in the water.

What a Christmas Day! For the first time I noticed how cold I was, and my fingers became numb and wouldn't grip the rock. I thought about you all and wondered if you were just sitting down to Christmas dinner. So many thoughts passed through my mind, but they were mostly thoughts of anger at the stupidity and futility of our suicidal attempt at escape. I cursed the luck that had joined us to this party, when Mac and I alone could have hidden in the hills until dark and had a much better chance of a successful escape.

The bullets continued to crash all around and Mac was still partly exposed. The back of his coat was covered in blood and he was cold and exhausted, and it was apparent he had reached the stage where he just didn't give a damn any longer. I tried to pull him up a bit but there was practically no room. Two or three times I made a half-hearted attempt to start climbing up to the top, but was so cold and miserable I couldn't make up my mind whether it was worse to climb and probably get shot, or continue to shiver on the wet rocks.

Just about this time we heard a chug-chug, and peeping over I could see the dull grey lines of a motor launch. Gosh, if our hearts could fall any lower they certainly fell then, as we thought it was a Jap launch sent out to finish us off. We waited and waited, and I looked out again and again and the launch seemed to be moving very slowly. Finally it turned out to be a derelict drifting in with the tide and the chug-chugging apparently came from some boat on the other side of the island.

That was enough for me. The Jap firing had eased up a lot, and I set off up the hill, telling Mac to hang on somehow until I got back. I had nothing on but my underwear, and it was covered with oil from the water. A lot of boats had been sunk or damaged around there, and there was a film of oil on the surface. My feet soon became cut and bruised climbing through the rocks and undergrowth, but it wasn't very far to the top, and once over the crest I ran into several others of our group who had swum to another more sheltered cove. Suddenly we spotted what looked like three launches tied up in a little cove on the sheltered side of the island and, as we watched, two of them pushed off and out to sea. There was a good chance they were British, as we knew four or five of our torpedo boats had still not been sunk by the Japs. However, there was more than an even chance they were Japanese. The rest of the fellows started making their way down to investigate, and I dashed back to help Mac along.

It proved to be longer and slower than I had imagined, and by the time we got back up to the top the other fellows had disappeared. Just then a Jap sniper concealed somewhere on our small island began popping away at us. We jumped from rock to rock and tried to take cover as best we could, while those darned bullets kept kicking dirt up all around us. My feet were very bruised and sore by now. However, we kept making our way down toward the boat, when suddenly it let blaze with its machine guns in the direction of the chaps who had gone ahead.

That was just about the last straw. Mac and I crouched down behind a rock freezing with the cold, feet all cut up, and apparently a Jap boat just below.

It was getting dark and I made up my mind there was only one thing left to do. Hide, if possible, until it was completely dark; climb back down to our original ledge and swim out to our

261

abandoned boat; put my clothes back on, and then try to swim back to Mac waiting on our rocky island with at least one of our packs, and especially with my two thousand dollars. We could make our way along the island in the direction of Aberdeen (Aberdeen was not so very far off across on the Hong Kong Island) and bribe a junkman or sampan man to take us back to Hong Kong. There I intended to try to get Mac up to Queen Mary Hospital.

My plans after that were indefinite, but I had a hazy notion of sneaking back to Aberdeen and trying again to bribe some sampan man to take me off to some farther away island, where I might have a chance of holing up for a day or two until I could make the mainland. It was a crazy plan as the Japs would probably have nabbed us the moment we set foot back in Hong Kong, but it seemed no more crazy than what we were just going through, and I certainly could see no way of escaping over miles of water and land clad only in wet, oily underwear and no shoes, and with Mac wounded I didn't know how badly.

While these thoughts were running through my mind Mac decided to hail the torpedo boat again. No further shots had come from it, and I was afraid our first group of fellows had been shot down. Mac apparently had got past caring. He simply stood up in the open and started making his way down to the boat, shouting as he went. I followed, taking what cover I could.

Nothing happened until we were almost down to the water's edge, when suddenly a voice in beautiful English shouted, "It's okay, come on down." I don't believe I've ever heard anything so beautiful and gratifying as that voice. We scrambled down and they picked us up in a small rowboat.

The explanation of the burst of machine gun fire was this. One of our chaps away ahead of the rest spotted the boat first, and without any thought that it might not be British, dashed down the hill, dived into the water and swam out to it. He was so excited and exhausted when they pulled him aboard he shouted, "There are ten chaps following, being machine-gunned." The crew misunderstood him to say, "There are ten Japs following me with machine guns," and when our advance party came into view they blazed away at them with their Lewis guns, luckily hitting none. The mistake was quickly realized and our fellows taken aboard.

Now I must go back a bit in the story. One of the Chinese officials who started out with us was Admiral Chan Chak. He was a grand old chap of about fifty, and had lost a leg while serving in the Chinese Navy. He had his A.D.C. and a bodyguard with him. The A.D.C. was a young Chinese whom we all called Henry, an excellent athlete and one of the champion swimmers of Hong Kong. When the order was given to abandon the boat they put a life preserver around the bodyguard, who couldn't swim, and pushed him off.

The Admiral ordered his young A.D.C. to beat it as he was going to make his own way to the shore. Henry dived overboard and waited to help the Admiral, but was again ordered to save himself. The old boy then threw his wooden leg over and jumped in after it. Just before he jumped a bullet smashed into his arm and fractured one of the bones. With only one leg, and now with only one arm in use, he made the shore. He had lost a good deal of blood, and before we first started off to explore the island we told him to lie still behind the rock and we would come back for him later.

By the time Mac and I were pulled aboard the torpedo boat it was quite dark and a small rowboat was immediately put back ashore to find the Admiral. He was not behind the rock where we left him and they searched and searched and finally found him right on top of the hill. He had heard the sniper after Mac and me and decided he was too exposed where he was, and had pulled himself, dragging one leg and one arm, right up to the top.

When they got him back it was almost ten p.m. and it was decided to push off to run the Japanese naval blockade. The sailors had dug up old dry clothes for our wet group and given us a good nip of rum each. When we finally all assembled we were amazed to find eleven out of our sixteen had got through, including the two wounded. And of that eleven, ten were of our original party that left the city together. We had lost one Chinese, a grand fellow and a high official, and four of the five naval volunteers that had joined us at the last minute in Aberdeen. That so many got through seems an absolute miracle.

263

We pushed off about ten p.m. and the throb of those powerful motors was music to our ears. About an hour later a Jap destroyer (or light cruiser, we couldn't tell which in the darkness) heard us and got us in her searchlights. She fired four shots at us, but they all fell wide and we continued on.

The next problem was where to land. It was decided to make a landing on a small island near the shore about thirty-five miles up the coast. We knew most of the coastline was held by the Japanese and the problem was where to slip through their lines. Someone knew there was a small Chinese fishing village on the island we selected, and the idea was to slip ashore quietly, shoot up any Jap garrison there might be (we thought at most there could be only a dozen or so Japs) and then get the villagers to guide us to a safe spot on the mainland.

By now we presented quite a formidable force. Including the crews of the M.T.B.s there were now about sixty of us, all armed to the teeth. I've never seen a party better armed. We had eight Lewis machine guns, six Bren guns, two Tommy guns and every man had a rifle or a revolver; most had both. A little after one a.m. two boatloads put ashore on the island chosen. Luck was with us again.

There were no Japs on the island, and the villagers were pro-Chungking and were very pleased to see us. When they heard the powerful throb of our motors they expected a Japanese raiding party and had taken to the hills, but rushed back on learning our identity. They sent two guides with us and we pushed a little farther along the coast and landed on the mainland right smack at the guerilla headquarters. The guerillas also heard our motors and took to the hills; but there was great rejoicing when they discovered who we were, and they simply couldn't do enough for us when they learned the Admiral was in our party.

We landed about three a.m. and they at once provided the best of biscuits and boiling hot milk. By golly, they were well stocked up. The very best English blankets, cigarettes, tinned goods, camp beds, etc. Regular bandits, with guns and bandoleers of bullets draped all over them. They're violently anti-Japanese, but don't let that interfere with their own private looting. On learning the Admiral was with us there was a great show of patriotism and they at once offered to provide us with an armed escort and guides to get us through the Japanese lines. We, in turn, told them they could strip everything off the M.T.B.s but that they must be sunk before daylight. (If left afloat, Jap planes would quickly spot them and be on our trail in a flash.)

They got some lovely equipment off those boats. Radio transmitting and receiving sets, and all the vast quantity of gear that goes with those well-equipped craft. They began to sink at dawn and it seemed such a shame to destroy them, with their huge powerful Napier engines. They were very reluctant to go down and the villagers had to pile them high with rocks to keep them under the surface. At dawn we marched a few miles into the hills and rested all day in a small village.

Oh, I forgot to mention, just before dawn a motorboat came cruising along and ran on a rock almost beside us, in the dark. It turned out to be another group of British naval chaps, seven in all, who had also escaped at dusk from Hong Kong. They were not quite sure where they were, and it was sheer good luck they stumbled upon us and safety. They had had an uneventful trip, having left Hong Kong after dark. We now had quite a distinguished party—the Chinese Admiral, a British Naval Commander and two Lieutenant Commanders in addition to our original little party of eleven. After resting all day we set out at dusk and marched in single file by moonlight. We had to be careful of Jap planes (a real danger had we marched by day), and also of any puppets who might spot us and inform the Japs ahead. We were indeed fortunate with the weather; clear and cold, with a bright moon for several nights.

We carried on and finally passed around the last Japanese stronghold, a Chinese city with a Jap garrison of four thousand, and five hundred cavalry. The guerillas knew the exact strength and positions of the Japanese for miles around. They were certainly to be admired. Their intelligence work was perfect, and occasionally we would spot one or two away off on some hilltop, threading along on our flanks to prevent any surprise attack.

We had one ticklish moment getting past this last stronghold. It was about one a.m. and we were creeping ahead in a long single file, not making a sound, when a wretched dog in a small village we were skirting started barking, and a villager took a shot at us. That shot sounded like a cannon blast. However our guerilla escort got hold of the villager and scared the wits out of him and we crept away with the nearby Japs apparently quite unaware.

Finally on Dec. 29 we arrived at the first Chinese city of any size on our route into Free China. We were a bedraggled-looking lot. Unshaven, uncombed, clad in odd bits of clothing picked up in the motorboats. The worst of all was marching for days with old borrowed shoes that didn't fit. Boy, our feet were in bad shape. I was bitten from head to toe with vermin picked up in the filthy Chinese huts we slept in by day. Three or four of our chaps were ill, one with dysentery and another suspected of having cholera. It was no wonder, when I think back on the food we had been eating.

It was indeed fortunate we were travelling in the coldest part of the year, when disease was at its lowest ebb. We almost froze each night, but that was far better than falling sick. I kept in the best of health, and was feeling better than I had for years. Kept thanking my lucky stars I had done so much swimming and hiking all summer, it was just what was needed.

What a reception! Word had been flashed ahead we were coming and they sent a fleet of bicycles for us to ride the last fifteen miles. And were we glad to see them! A small force of Chinese troops was drawn up just outside the city to salute us as we came by and I don't mind saying I was never so glad to see a Chinese soldier. We couldn't enter the city right away as there was an air raid on, but we got in about three in the afternoon and were given an evacuated hospital to stay in. Real beds and everything. Boy, it felt good to get a bath once again, even though it was only from a wooden bucket.

Mac had stood the trip remarkably well. It amazed me how he ambled on mile after mile with that bullet in his back and with the original dressing still on. There was only one Chinese doctor in the town, and after messing around for some time until he almost had poor Mac fainting, he announced he couldn't find the bullet and we would have to carry on to another city about five days away. The Admiral's arm was beginning to swell, and he was feverish; but they could do nothing much for him either, except change the dressing.

The whole city was a wreck. Bombing after bombing had produced rows and rows of burnt-out streets, and all the bridges were down. There were no roads or railways serviceable for transport and it was decided we would push on by river junk. We stayed and rested for two days, and bought a few necessities at outrageous prices. The shops simply had no stocks. What they did have had all been smuggled through from Hong Kong before the Jap attack and most of that had been bombed out. So at six p.m. on New Year's Eve we set out in four river junks for the interior of China.

Travelling by junk was slow, but not unpleasant. We made only about three miles an hour against a strong current. The boats had automobile engines, run on charcoal burners instead of gasoline. (Gasoline was $150 a gallon.) We chugged slowly along, having frequent engine breakdowns. Our junks were crowded to capacity with Chinese regular soldiers and some of our own guerillas with us as guards. We slept head to toe, on straw strewn on the floor.

Some of us wanted to go ashore and walk along the river bank for exercise, as the boats made their way along; but that whole countryside is unsettled and dangerous, and they wouldn't let us land. And so we went slowly along, until on the fifth day we came to quite a village where the first motor road linking with Free China began. (You must remember that after almost five years of war with Japan, the Chinese had thoroughly destroyed all roads, railways and bridges to hinder any attempted Japanese advance into the interior.)

Here again we had a great reception. After a huge dinner provided by the community, speeches were made from a platform draped with British and Chinese flags. Beef is scarce, and by government decree can be killed only three times a month; but by special dispensation they were allowed to kill a cow for us and, boy, it was good.

They provided five trucks for us and a car for the Admiral and Mac, who were feeling the strain by now, and we set off at four-thirty next morning for a two-day trip along the most mountainous, bumpy, narrow, dangerous road we had yet struck. We were bounced around and covered thick with dust, but it was a hundred per cent better than walking. After two days we arrived at Shiu-kwan (pronounced Shoo-gwan), quite a large Chinese town, and the first we had struck that had telephones and electric lights, although both were uncertain in the extreme.

We were met a few miles out of the city by the governor, the mayor and several generals. There were troops drawn up taking the salute, and a line of boy scouts and girl guides and small girls dashing around pinning rosettes on us. They were written in Chinese, of course, and the translation read, "To the brave defenders of Hong Kong." From the very first contact with the Chinese after our getaway I was struck by their friendliness and good will—one would have thought we had saved Hong Kong instead of losing it—and this show of good will never abated. It was amazing how well they took care of us.

Mac got a telegram off to the Ambassador in Chungking offering our services and he replied immediately congratulating us on our safe escape, and telling us to proceed immediately there as there was plenty of work to be done. Mac and the Admiral went into the Mission Hospital where it was found the Admiral's arm was broken. They removed the bullet and dressed him up but he became quite ill and was still in hospital when we left six days later. They still couldn't find the bullet in Mac's back, but he was feeling much better after a couple of days in bed, and it was decided he should proceed to Chengtu by plane where is situated the Canadian Mission Hospital—the best equipped in Free China.

We had a round of big dinners and receptions and I'll swear I've never shaken hands with so many generals in all my life. They were certainly good to us. Mac still had a bundle of Hong Kong dollar notes, soaked with salt water but otherwise none the worse for wear. The Central Bank of China cashed them for us and we were able to buy pants, shoes and shirts and began to look human once more.

After six days Chungking finally managed to get a plane down for us and seven of us lucky ones climbed aboard, leaving the rest to continue the long, arduous journey by train and truck. One of our original party got malaria and had to be left behind. It was my first long journey by plane. We took off in pitch darkness at nine p.m. and landed in equally pitch darkness at about four a.m. in Chungking. The plane was a peach of a big Douglas, the same type used on the American commercial routes; and the American pilots are tops. My gosh, when it became light and we saw where we had landed in the dead of night we were almost bowled over. Towering cliffs on both sides, with high-tension wires strung across the top, and we had slid right under the wires and between the cliffs and landed on a sand bank in the middle of a river. And these pilots do it night in and night out, flying planes that haven't been serviced for thousands of miles.

Now I must hurry; it's almost two in the morning and I have to scoot to the airfield in another hour, for Calcutta.

WE LEARNED ON OKINAWA

—*July 1, 1945*—
James A. Maclean

Okinawa—Plaster rattled down from the shaky blue upturned tile roof of the moss-covered stone Jap house. Marine Long Toms, their barrels poking out from under a camouflage net dotted with scarlet hibiscus, were at it again from their pits farther up the winding mountain road.

Below, almost hidden by the stunted wind-swept trees and the blackened mouths of gaping Jap hillside hangars, spouts of orange flame lit the base of a towering column of black smoke from one of our oil dumps.

From the sparkling blue bay the wind-borne mutter of ships' anti-aircraft grew heavier, and the broken glass in the gaping village windows rattled as stubby, barrel-bodied blue Corsair fighter planes rocketed low overhead, propellers screaming as they clawed for altitude, heading out to sea.

The kamikaze boys—Jap suicide planes—were coming in again, just as they had almost daily since our landing. But not so many this time. Maybe 20 or 30.

Outside, a white kid, not much bigger than a rabbit, grazed unconcernedly on the ivy leaves on top of a flame-seared stone wall bordering the narrow street. A column of shrivelled, aging civilians shuffled past in the dust, their drab black and dark blue kimonos stained and torn, their few effects, the ones they'd carried with them into the caves, bundled on their backs. A leper with a crutch brought up the rear. None looked up.

They never did, not until the Jap planes got overhead. Then they just stood there in the roads, unmindful of the spattering of spent machine-gun bullets, staring at the whirling blue and brown dots locked in dogfights thousands of feet above them.

"Well, here we go again," the Canadian observer, deep-chested, redheaded Capt. Gordon Eligh, 20, RCASC, of Vancouver, said as he ducked out through the low door. Standing on the planks in the red dust outside, absently lathering his face, he watched the Marine planes circle over the bay.

"Damn the Japs! They're worse than the Jerries. Always catch me shaving, with my helmet full of water."

Veteran of Sicily and Italy, Eligh didn't look particularly worried. Nor did his companion, another Canadian observer, Capt. Samuel J. Simon, 25, Toronto, another of the 20 Canadian Army officers attached to the American invasion force.

Others attached to the marines with whom we jolted ashore over the coral reef on Easter morning in the face of the abandoned shore defenses, included: Lt.-Col. Gerard J. Charlebois, CIC, Acting-Capt. Dudley B. Dawson, RCA, and Capt. Fred B. Palmer, RCSC, with the First Marine Division; Major Robert D. Murray, RCOC, and Capt. Robert S. Richards, RCR, with the Second Marine Division.

Ten other Canadian Army officers had been assigned to land with American Army divisions on the southern beach. I never did catch up with them. It took the better part of one day to locate Simon and Eligh, and another Canadian with them in the Sixth Marine Division, Acting-Major Lawrence D. McBride, RCEME.

All of them specialists in their field, these Canadian officers and a score or more in the Philippine theatre were sent into the Pacific by Ottawa last summer with the task of sending back full reports on the progress and manner of the war. Reasons behind these reports were obvious. Canada even then was taking the measurements of her job in the Pacific, a role still not fully disclosed or developed.

Outside, the roar of the Marine day combat patrol planes died away, and the ack-ack had slackened. Eligh, sweat rolling down his husky frame, staining his undershirt, grunted and bent to lace his high leather combat boots.

Although only 350 miles from the Japanese home islands, and

271

the airfields of Kyushu, Okinawa was plenty hot—hot enough to be almost tropical for Canadians, and tropical enough to nurture three kinds of deadly snakes. That was one reason why the invasion forces paid so much attention to their boots. A thousand Okinawans died a year because of those snakes, their grass sandals weren't proof against fangs. Also we'd accidentally bombed out the Okinawa anti-venom factory a few days before we landed, a factory which produced the only serum we were sure might work in case of bites.

"Our job is almost over now," Eligh said. "At least as far as us observers go. We expect to go home in August. It'll be up to the rest of the boys after that. I can't honestly say I am sorry. You can have my share of this for a bottle of Canadian beer," he added, waving his hand generously toward the southern end of the island.

I felt I knew exactly what he meant. War in Europe was one thing. But this Pacific business, typhoons and stuff, well, it was different, a lot different.

Down south, where U.S. Army troops were locked in desperate, hand-to-hand battle with the grim defenders of the enemy's year-old Naha-Shuri-Yonabaru defense lines, it was a flaming, savage struggle of a type never seen in Europe. Cave-hidden Jap 75s fired point-blank on their own machine-gun positions attacked by American troops, heedless that the Japs in those positions were still alive and struggling. Sherman tanks floundered and burned in the cabbage patch, the crews unaware that Jap sea mines had been planted there with curved detonating horns hidden by hollowed-out heads of cabbage.

Then, too, a machine gunner and his mate sat back to back on a ridge, the gunner blasting away at screaming, charging Japs attacking through their own hellish hail of mortars, while his buddy poked black Jap grenades back off the other edge of the ridge. These grenades were lobbed by three Japs in a hole a few feet down the slope—a hole the Americans had sat over for an hour and a half, not knowing it was there.

And always there were those honeycombed hills, innocent-looking but deadly, Japan's "secret weapon" against the mightiest bombardments of the Pacific war. Two cleverly hidden observers' holes, shoulder wide, somewhere on their summits, leading down through blast-stopping angled tunnels into caves five metres wide and big enough to hold a platoon, from which a third tunnel led out through another foot-wide hole somewhere in the bushes at the hill's base.

The deadly job of fighting up each hill under withering Jap support fire from cave-hidden Nambu machine guns, artillery and mortars in surrounding hills, then the immediate eruption of charging crack Jap troops from their hidden gopher holes underfoot. Savage hand-to-hand fighting again, and the eventual bloody victory. Then the cleaning out of most of the caves with flaming oil dragged up in barrels, with grenades, bazookas and flame throwers after most of the exits had been located and watched. The sealing up of those in which survivors still held out, ignoring demands to surrender, or the caves so badly messed up by the flames that their contents were dangerous for sanitary reasons alone.

And always, the one or two Japs bypassed in their holes somewhere on the hill. The ones that stayed hidden for days, firing the occasional bursts at targets of opportunity.

"Yeah, she's different all right," Eligh said. "Italy and Sicily were never like this."

Somewhere southeast of the airport a lone gun barked and was silent. That was "Old Mountain Joe-Pete," a lone Jap 75-millimetre cannon hidden in one of the hundreds of caves in the centre of territory we'd held for a week. They'd hunted for him for the first two days after the landing, when he started cutting loose with his two or three daily rounds from within our lines. But Joe-Pete was pretty elusive. He just kept changing caves at night, and he never hit anything anyway, so the hunt petered out. His crew would either starve to death or come down and get caught while looking for food. In the meantime the gun was kind of a mascot. That is it was until yesterday morning, when, with two inaccurate shots, it pinned a high Navy officer and his pilot beneath their plane on the airport for 15 minutes.

That wasn't showing respect for high rank. So they're out to get Joe-Pete now, and they will, unless he suicides first.

Earlier that morning I'd been down to the plateau airfield at the base of this mountain. On the airfield, which the Japs abandoned without a fight, was equipment valued by the Americans as worth $100 millions—to the Japs.

"Except for the aviation gas, which we could only use in our trucks, it wasn't worth a tinker's damn to us," one expert told me.

To protect that airfield the Japs had employed 40,000 labor troops to dig miles of intricate fire trenches, had built hangars sunken into the sides of hills, constructed supply sheds and thousands of storage caves and tunnels around it for an area of 70 square miles. It was an airfield on which they had propped up 70 dummy guns and 35 dummy planes, woven carefully from straw and set on top of oil barrels amid the wreckage of genuine fighters they had abandoned the day before we landed.

I'd walked over that airfield, more than a mile from the beach, the day we went ashore with Maj.-Gen. Roy S. Geiger, silverhaired commanding officer of the three Marine Divisions. We hadn't expected to get there in less than three days of heavy fighting, and for Geiger a virtually unopposed landing was something new.

"I've never before been on a battlefield like this," was the way he phrased it, as he walked bareheaded across the 4,000-yard-long Jap runways, while his personal guards fanned out ahead like quail hunters, scouring the spider-trap foxholes and fire trenches for possible enemy snipers.

The defenses were deserted, except those littered with children's schoolbooks, the odd fountain pen or two and a broken phonograph. No guns, no food, no shells were left behind. Around us the field still smoked from the initial rocket, bomb and naval barrage laid down before the landing.

"Nope, you can't figure the Japs out. That's for sure. They'll do something unexpected every time," Eligh said, slipping into his sweat-stained Marine greens.

He was right. There were the Baka bombs, for instance—the seven we found undestroyed by the retreating Japs, with their detonating wires still attached, and the 17 gaping 25-yard-wide craters where the rest of the deadly brood had been stored.

We Learned on Okinawa

Not pleasant to look at, those slim, rocket-propelled suicide bombs, with a fuselage not much longer or thicker than a freight canoe and a speed of roughly 500 miles an hour. The American gunners who shot down the first ones dropped on our invasion forces complained about that speed. "You hardly get time to see the ornery little things," one gunner said. "But we got 'em, and we got the bombers that dropped 'em, too."

"It's hard to imagine what goes through a kamikaze pilot's mind," said Eligh. "I can understand the Japs getting their kids so hipped up on the glory of dying for the Emperor that after a few flying lessons they'll take off from an airfield and dive their planes, bomb load and all, into our shipping. But I can't understand the guys that fly these Bakas.

"You get told—if you are a Jap—that you will be automatically commissioned an ensign for making such a flight. Okay, so to a Jap that's an honor. An ensign is a big shot. So the ground crews wheel out your Baka on its little three-wheeled dolly and they fasten it to the belly of a Betty (twin-engined bomber). You climb into the bomber, and you stand there, all four feet of you, jabbering away to the pilot, until the time comes. Over Okinawa you climb down into the Baka through a hatch in the floor of the bomber. Then you pull the teardrop cover over your head and sit there, waiting. Maybe you fiddle around with the oxygen hose. You're at 30,000 feet. Then the light flashes on your dashboard. It's time to drop...

"Nope, I still don't know what a guy can be thinking of when he yanks that switch."

Neither did I. Nor how the pilot was able to keep from blacking out, once he had dropped the 10,000 required feet, until he was travelling fast enough so that the Baka answered to her tiny controls.

For that matter neither did the little Jap pilot we captured two days later, his face all puffed up and bruised and his arm badly wrenched. Sullen and dazed when he was pulled from the sinking wreckage of his plane, which had crashed while attempting a suicide dive on a ship, he brightened and smiled when by gestures a correspondent induced him to sign his name to the correspondent's short snorter [an autographed one-dollar bill].

275

He signed his name all right, in English and Japanese. And sure enough, he claimed the title of ensign for the flight on which he'd failed. But beneath his signature he wrote a syllogistic little poem, bewailing the disgrace he felt it was to be a captive of the Americans. The fact that he was an officer seemed to make his humiliation all the deeper.

Okinawa, in reports we'd had before we landed, wasn't exactly healthy, what with the snakes and the diseases, some of which we had no serums to cure. Diseases like liver flukes and scrub typhus, for instance. Then, of course, there were the lepers, one or two in every village. Most Okinawans were tubercular, a high percentage had syphilis, and all were suffering from malnutrition. In one arm I had had these injections: cowpox, triple typhoid shots, triple tetanus shots, double plague shots and two cholera shots. I'd skipped the yellow fever ones.

No, Okinawa wasn't healthy when we landed, even without counting the 30,000-odd crack Japanese Manchurian troops and the 450,000 natives—about whose loyalties we had been very doubtful in view of past experience.

But the civilians had offered little trouble, except in nuisance value. They were always underfoot.

Hundreds lined the roads in refugee columns in the first few days, being herded, from the holes in which they had hidden, to the rear of our lines. One or two I saw were dressed in full Japanese Army uniforms, but they were neither soldiers nor labor troops. The Jap garrison on Okinawa, as we found out later, had for years made a practice of selling castoff military clothing to civilians too poor to buy clothes elsewhere.

"Did you hear about the conscripts?" Simon chuckled. "About 10 or 11 Okinawan men apparently had been ordered to report to their draft board on April 1, the day we landed. They'd been issued uniforms and had been up north chopping trees for tank traps and road blocks. Comes April Fool's Day, and although they'd heard our bombardment of the beaches they didn't know we'd landed. So out of the woods and down to the village they scampered—six miles—with Marines taking them for soldiers and firing at them all the way. They were scared silly, but they made it all right, and reported in as ordered. Only, an American colonel was sitting behind the Jap officer's desk.

Then there was the woman who strangled her two babies when the Marines closed in around her home.

"She was just scared crazy by the atrocity propaganda the Japs had fed her, I guess," the Marine who prevented her from strangling her third and last child told me. Like the gaunt, aged crone screaming and writhing, completely unclad, down by the beach yesterday, while two young, tall embarrassed Marine youngsters held her arms and clumsily tried to rewrap her in the dirty black dress she'd torn off while trying to escape. Finally, they had to tie her arms and legs with the dress, and carry her down to an enclosure along the beach.

I saw her five hours later, her blackened, decayed teeth showing in a huge grin as she munched on a can of American rations.

But then you could never be sure who were civilians and who were not. Take the case of the suicide swimmer the morning we landed. I was standing on the bridge of our transport, talking to Gen. Geiger, then clad in a New Zealand-made battledress jacket with the coiled yellow-red dragon patch on his shoulder, and his battered brown-stained helmet low down over his ice-blue eyes.

He was staring intently at the beach, listening to the incredible radio reports about lack of resistance as our first troops hit the shore. An hour passed and not a Marine casualty had yet been reported. "If this keeps up," he told me, "you'll have wasted your time."

Then came a delayed report from an LCM. "Suicide swimmer sighted at 0816, but escaped." That was 16 minutes after our initial wave had gone ashore. A Jap soldier, dressed in civilian clothes but wearing the familiar split-toed Jap army sandal, had staged a one-man amphibious counterattack, swimming alone out to sea with a bundle of grenades.

As it turned out later, that Jap did not escape, as the skipper of the landing craft had believed. Someone, probably one of the ship's guard posted to watch for attacks by suicide speed boats, had shot him before he got where he was going. We found his body, sprawled face up and bloated, on the coral next day, after the tide went out. His grenades in their bundle lay beside one split-toed shoe.

277

That one little incident, one Jap swimming out to sea to meet our fleet of more than 1,300 ships, the biggest invasion fleet of the Pacific war, convinced me that from now on all Japs will fight a suicide fight. Nothing that has happened since would indicate anything else.

Later, I left Okinawa to go on the invasion of Ie Shima, where we seized still another Japanese airfield. When I got back to Okinawa after that short-lived campaign in which Ernie Pyle was killed by a Jap machine gunner, things on Okinawa had changed.

Passenger planes and transports were flying off the Yontan field on clocklike schedules. All over the island new American-built runways were being slashed and gouged out of the once green countryside. Onion and beet crops had disappeared in the upheaval. The Canadian observers had moved on too, down to the south where bitter hand-to-hand fighting raged for Naha, Yonabaru and Shuri. Simon and Eligh were down there someplace, making notes—notes on the way the desperate Jap garrison, repeatedly driven into their deep burrows and two-decker caves, charged out again and again, once the barrage let up. Notes on how the heaviest bombing, naval and artillery shelling, of the entire Pacific war served only to drive the Japs into their holes once more, where they holed up and reduced the fighting to a basis of man to man—flame throwers, burning oil and bayonets, against Jap grenades.

For the Canadian observers, their job, as they said, was almost done. They'd passed full notes on the development of the fighting, and on the Jap and American techniques, back to Ottawa for use at some future date when battle-wise Canadians storm ashore to avenge Hong Kong.

James A. Maclean was a British United Press correspondent.

25,000 MILES TO BATTLE

—July 15, 1945—
Lieutenant Stuart Keate, RCNVR

On board H.M.C.S. *Uganda* in the Pacific—*The Uganda Tar Paper*, a news bulletin published daily on board H.M.C.S. *Uganda*, Canada's new cruiser, recently reported a story which its editor claims to have overheard on the boat deck of the ship.

Two sailors were gazing thoughtfully out to sea. Finally one turned to the other and said: "You know, this Pacific Ocean is a lot bigger than the Atlantic."

His shipmate considered this statement for a moment, took a second look, and then, with a thoughtful nod of the

H.M.C.S. Uganda firing on Japanese-held Pacific island, May 4, 1945.

head, assented: "Yep, it sure is."

This realization—that they are now fighting in a vaster and much more complex theatre than ever before in their lives—is but one of many which have dawned on the ship's company of "The Fighting U" since she joined up with the British Pacific Fleet. The juncture was effected after a 25,000-mile voyage via the United States, Halifax, the British Isles, Gibraltar, Malta, Alexandria, Suez, Aden, Colombo, Fremantle and Sydney, plus some volcanic islands which look like a setting for a Dotty Lamour–Bing Crosby–Bob Hope musical. Fundamentally the boys have learned that the days of ice-laden minesweepers and bucketing corvettes have gone forever, for them, and that they are involved in a brand-new kind of shooting match.

Able Seaman Roy Gallagher, Winnipeg, summed the situation up rather neatly not long ago when he wrote home:

"Dear Mother—This is a stinking war out here. First you fight the heat. Then you fight disease. When you're through with them you've got to go out and fight the Japs."

To this heartfelt lament A/B Gallagher might have added the more technical problem of supply, which is basic English for what the more formal treatises call "logistics." The British Pacific Fleet, it may be recalled, has undertaken to fuel, feed, ammunition and repair its ships independently in this theatre, and this is an undertaking which presents spectacular headaches for the Navy's white-stripers.

There can be no doubt that the British Pacific Fleet, of which *Uganda* is a proud unit, is presently maintaining the longest supply lines in the world. The Americans, when they first moved to the Pacific, faced the difficult task of supplying their forces over a 6,000-mile route from California, but the British are now obliged to sail their materials from the mother country through the Suez, down around Australia and up north to the "forward areas," a distance of some 12,000 miles.

The Yanks, as is their custom, did a thorough, speedy job, finding time (as one of their own officers observed) to "put in concrete foundations and Coke machines" as they advanced. The British, arriving on the scene after five years of war in the North Atlantic, home and European waters, attending to the emissaries of Herren Hitler and Doenitz, are confronted with the somewhat tacky assignment of the switch over to tropical conditions in a few weeks. That the Americans spent three years perfecting their system, and evolved a pattern from which the British can learn many lessons, is fortunate indeed.

The young men, from all over Canada, who are trail blazing the Pacific sea lanes for our country, have had to revise a lot of their concepts about how a war should be fought. The idea of them running from a submarine, with their background of weary hours of stalk and sink in the North Atlantic, is unthinkable, yet that is precisely what they have had to learn in the new cruiser. The answer is simply one of economics. Why risk a costly warship and more than 700 men for the sake of a measly midget submarine?

If, of course, *Uganda* surprised a Japanese submarine, midget or standard model, on the surface, she would expect to blow it out of the water with her six-inch guns. But she would not permit herself to become involved in any of the hide-and-seek games so familiar to North Atlantic veterans. She would hightail it for more lucrative sea pastures, detailing the job of stalking the sub to accompanying destroyers, whose speed and manoeuvrability fit them for such sport.

In the Pacific there is little of the monotonous plodding of the North Atlantic area, where patience and tenacity are cardinal virtues of the escort skippers, and ships sometimes go two or three years without encountering the enemy. Here it is a business of planned operations and attacks against a known enemy force or objective; a "clobbering" (as the Royal Navy's Fleet Air Arm boys have it) of Japanese airfields, wireless stations or railroads, or a lusty bombardment of an enemy coastal position. This is followed by a regrouping of forces, a short period of refueling and reammunitioning, and back to the "front" for another rub at the foe, with the anti-aircraft crews constantly on the alert for the Japs' "White Eagle" suicide bombers and such other tasty items as a piloted bomb which kicks up 500 knots.

It can be seen that this type of warfare has its advantages. Lieut. E. Maurice Chadwick, an Elizabethan character with an arresting beard and an eye to correct accoutrements, recently observed: "This is civilized warfare. A man can bathe, put on clean linen and dress properly before he goes into action. Consequently, he can die like a gentleman."

The Japs didn't give the *Uganda* time to observe such niceties in one of her first actions, a strike against airfields on northern Formosa on Friday, April 13. That date in itself should have made the Canadians apprehensive, for it was on Sept. 13, just 18 months previously, that the ship had been hit by a glider bomb, off Salerno, and badly damaged, with 15 casualties.

The plan called for the ship to go to "action stations" at dawn and the men had no sooner reached the upper deck, attired in anti-flash gear, which made them look like "Hooded horrors" of the wrestling ring, when things began to pop. From overcast skies and a dark horizon on her port hand there came the rumble of what many thought at first was thunder.

Then a brilliant white flare floated down over the Fleet, and it was obvious that the Japs had come to call. As destroyers on the outer screen began to open fire, red tracer latticed the sky in a brilliant display of pyrotechnics. In the middle of it there was a resounding "Whumph!" from back aft in *Uganda*. Lieut. Eric Makovski, RCNVR, Vancouver, had got one of the enemy planes in his sights and let fly with a barrage from his six-inch gun. This was the first shot fired by a Canadian warship against the "new" foe.

A few minutes later what appeared to be a flare drifted down toward the sea ("... in glorious Technicolor," the boys observed later). But for a flare it was doing unusual things. It was, for instance, moving upwind. When it crashed into the sea, with considerable force some 1,000 yards from *Uganda*, it became apparent that it was a Japanese plane, a belief which was confirmed in an official signal from the admiral commanding aircraft carriers at the conclusion of the strike.

His report revealed further that two other Jap planes had been "splashed" by Corsairs of the Fleet Air Arm after a rousing chase some miles to the north. This action resulted in a signal being sent by Admiral Nimitz of the United States Navy, who commands the Pacific naval theatre:

"The report of your successful attacks on the enemy is most gratifying. Congratulate you on the illustrious manner in which the forces of your command initiated their operations in the Pacific."

When, in subsequent operations, *Uganda*'s gunners (who were fast becoming "trigger happy") complained of inactivity, it was a tribute to the skill and daring of the Fleet's interceptors, who refused to let the enemy within striking distance. They had the satisfaction of hearing, at the end of the operation, that "all enemy airfields had been rendered unserviceable," and when the Fleet commander signalled Admiral Nimitz, saying that we still had enough bombs left for another run, and couldn't we please have another go at them, the American C-in-C signalled back:

"This spirit is in keeping with the high traditions of the British Navy."

Uganda's crew, schooled on the Newfie-to-Derry "milk run," came to the Pacific with the idea that a trip of 14 days, covering perhaps 1,800 miles, was a good fortnight's work. Now that they have crossed seven seas and four oceans just to catch up with the enemy, and done 5,000 miles in their first operation, they are becoming inured to the vagaries of big ship schedules. At this writing they have been more than a month without going ashore, and their commanding officer, Capt. E. Rollo Mainguy, OBE, RCN, Duncan, B.C., has warned them they can expect to remain at sea for much longer than this. This is a sobering thought for the Alumni of the Atlantic.

Another factor of war in the Pacific which they find hard to get used to is the way in which Allied and Jap positions are all intermingled. In the North Atlantic you knew that Newfoundland was one sanctuary, Iceland another, and the Azores another, with no German-held island in between. Here the picture is somewhat different. You can't even say that the front is "fluid." It's checkerboard, the result of the Yanks' spirited policy of bypassing key Jap bases in their drive forward. In the advance areas are New Britain, where the Aussies and Japs are slugging it out, and New Guinea, where a similar situation obtains. Similarly in the Philippines the Japs were tentatively installed at Mindanao.

The result of this, of course, is a more or less constant tension, a state of readiness for action at any minute. One night the Canucks were looking at a movie of Jimmy Cagney in *Johnny Come Lately* when the action bugle was sounded and the signal flashed: "Air attack imminent." After about half an hour the all clear was sounded and the boys went back to their picture, moaning bitterly about the interruption.

One aspect of war in the tropics which the Canadians have found agreeable, if incredible, is the fact that they were able to acquire suntans in February.

Around the equator the heat becomes stifling for men brought up on the biting cold of the prairies or deep snows of the Laurentians. In the engine room temperatures range around 110–124 deg., and up under the deckheads, above the turbines, they have reached 140. The steel ladders are usually so hot you can't touch them with bare hands. As the men sought relief in showers and at the taps of water coolers, fresh-water consumption soared to 110 tons a day. Since the evaporators can produce only 60 tons daily, serious drains were being made on reserves, and an appeal was made to use the water as charily as possible.

The ship's official photographers, Lieut. Gerry Moses, RCNVR, Toronto, and Leading Photographer John Turner, RCN, Edmonton, soon found that it was impossible to keep emulsion on their negatives under these excessive conditions. Accordingly they were obliged to lug buckets of water from the refrigeration system to their darkroom, so that they could get the temperature down to around 80 deg. and get some developing done.

Two branches of the service get a bonus, in the form of "tropical pay," amounting to 35c. a day, for working under particularly onerous circumstances. These are the engine-room ratings, whose coat of arms includes a sweat rag rampant, and the cooks, who must laugh hollowly when they think of their wives back home "slaving over a hot stove all day." It is impossible to prepare food in advance on board ship in the tropics. A 60-gallon tub of potatoes will begin to ferment in less than five hours if the water isn't changed from time to time. Similarly, you can't leave cooked meat in a container without it spoiling.

284

25,000 Miles to Battle

Chief Cook Ted Mundy, Edmonton, feels he is entitled to his extra 35c. a day. One morning when he and his staff were frying up some potato chips the thermometer in the galley registered 148 deg. On another occasion, when the ship was passing through the Red Sea at night, it touched 159!

As the heat rises, efficiency drops. Similarly, the longer a ship stays at sea under these conditions, the faster the food deteriorates, and both these factors impair the fighting efficiency of the ship.

To date the *Uganda* has had no trouble with tropical disease, but it is an ever-present menace. Mosquito nets have been stocked for each man, and 100,000 atabrine tablets are carried to combat malaria. Salt tablets are issued regularly to those who need them, and have the effect of making up for deficiencies caused by excessive sweating. Excessive humidity makes for fungus growth, and there are always a few sailors walking around the ship with what appear to be purple feet, undergoing treatment for the common "athlete's foot."

Each man has been vaccinated against smallpox and given injections for typhoid-tetanus, diphtheria, typhus and cholera; so much so, in fact, that Surgeon-Lieut. Bob Lennox, RCNVR, Montreal, who administers the needles, is looked upon with grave suspicion by the entire ship's company. In fairness to Lennox, who studied in the tropics before joining *Uganda*, it must be said that he has perfected his art to the point where he can inject "on the run," and on one occasion got a cholera shot into an unsuspecting fellow officer before that worthy realized he hadn't been stung by some exotic tropical insect.

Since the *Uganda* was the first Canadian warship to engage in a strike against Japanese territory, her men are not insensitive to the fact that theirs is, to some degree, a historic mission. Their feeling is somewhat akin to that of the rookie hockey star from Last Gulp, Sask., who suddenly finds himself in the first-string lineup with the Toronto Maple Leafs. He knows his past record is good, but isn't quite sure whether he can score in competition with this new, high-priced talent.

The man entrusted with the care of the new cruiser, Captain Mainguy (pronounced Ming-y), is regarded by both his officers and

285

men as an ideal choice for the job. Like all good leaders, his first thought is how he can bring his six-inch guns to bear on the enemy. His second thought is for his ship and its company. His last thought is for himself.

Captain Mainguy, who is called "Rollo" by his intimates, is a big, husky man of 44, who looks remotely like a refined edition of William Bendix. He paces his bridge stripped to the waist, and, often as not, despite the blistering decks, in bare feet. On each of his forearms are slightly faded tattoos, one of them a dagger and the other a coiled snake, and these lend a salty touch which his highly engraved seamen can appreciate.

Capt. Mainguy pursues a policy of directness in the conduct of his ship. One of his beliefs is that the men under him are entitled to know what's going on, and every time the *Uganda* goes on an operation he takes a hand microphone to the bridge and gives them a short, punchy briefing, with a few words of advice and encouragement tossed in for good measure. During a recent broadcast he wound up with the admonition: "I hope none of you will have any compunction about killing a Jap. Good luck and good night."

Capt. Mainguy came to the *Uganda* with an excellent record of service in the North Atlantic. In 1941 he was mentioned in dispatches, and in 1943 he was awarded the Order of the British Empire.

Capt. Mainguy's chief assistant in welding *Uganda* into a fighting unit has been Commander Hugh F. Pullen, OBE, RCN, of Oakville, Ont., who is serving in the cruiser as executive officer after a distinguished record as senior officer of a sub-hunting flotilla and an escort group in the North Atlantic.

Traditionally, in a big ship the commander is the one who must "tear off strips" or "tie on the cans," as the Navy's mess deck litterateurs have it. He is responsible for the cleanliness and efficient operation of everything on the upper deck, and it is a dirty job, calling for all manner of disciplinary action and the meting out of punishment to defaulters. It was one of Cmdr. Pullen's jobs, for instance, to convince *Uganda*'s crew that they couldn't walk around in leather jackets and dungarees as they had done for years in corvettes; in a cruiser, they had to turn out in "the rig of the day," and it had to be spotless. Once, when he routed a number of officers out of their bunks at 6:30 in the morning, the *Tar Paper* headlined the incident: "The Commander Strikes at Dawn."

It soon became apparent to officers and men that they had to dress a good war as well as fight one. In the wardroom officers were obliged to attend mess dinners four nights a week while in harbor. This called for wing collars and bow ties or, after passing through the Mediterranean, "Red Sea rig," which is a tasty ensemble consisting of white dickey jacket, cummerbund and dark trousers. As the *Uganda* neared the fighting zone and became—in the commander's phrase—a "useful member of society," this regulation was relaxed, to the accompaniment of fervent sighs of relief from the officers, whose laundry and tailoring problems were becoming almost as complex as their orders for arming, fueling, storing and fighting.

A zealous traditionalist, Cmdr. Pullen insists on his master-at-arms, Wilfred Thompson, Halifax, carrying a lantern for his nightly round after the manner of Admiral Lord Nelson.

The personalities of captain and commander, complementing each other as they do, have made an impact on the ship's company, which is gradually getting shaken down into a fighting whole. There was surprisingly little evidence of "stagefright" when *Uganda* began working with the mightiest British battleships and carriers afloat, and one Royal Navy captain commented after the first operation: "You fitted in as if you'd been with us for years." After the *Uganda* executed a tricky bit of seamanship in her first hour with the fleet, a British carrier sent a signal saying: "Nice work—well done," and the Canadian lads appreciated this pat on the back from their august senior.

Uganda's men are united in one determination: to "do their bit" to end this war, so that they can hustle back home. In spite of tropical moonlight, swaying coconut trees, great stretches of sandy beach and the fabulous Australian hospitality, Canada still looks better to them than anything they've seen in their 25,000-mile quest for a fight.

CANADA AT WAR

A reporter before the war, Keate served as a correspondent in the navy for three years during the Second World War. Afterwards, he resumed his journalism career, becoming publisher of both the Victoria Daily Times *and the* Vancouver Sun. *An officer of the Order of Canada and member of the Canadian News Hall of Fame, Keate died at 73 in March 1987.*

KOREA

WIN OR LOSE, THE RUSSIANS MAY GET KOREA

—January 1, 1951—
Blair Fraser

Behind the Australian war correspondents' camp north of Sinanju stood an empty Korean farmhouse. It was quite undamaged, but for some reason the owners had moved out. The reporters preferred to sleep in tents because the house was full of fleas.

The main room of the little mud cottage was papered with old North Korean newspapers, and I didn't have to read Korean to know who'd been in charge here. Every page was splashed with pictures—muddy photographs of Stalin and Molotov and the Red Chinese dictator,

---

Seoul's ancient south gate.

Mao Tse-tung; line drawings of Lenin and Karl Marx.

A small Korean boy saw me looking at this wallpaper. He ran over to a big picture of Stalin and made a great show of punching it in the nose. That is the fashion in Korea now that the Americans have taken over. I wondered what the boy would have done a month or two before when the Communists were still in control.

Did the little fist in Stalin's face indicate a real hatred, previously suppressed? Or was he merely doing for his own protection what he thought the new foreigners would like?

It's probably too soon to know the answer; perhaps the boy himself doesn't know. But, if the second interpretation turns out to be right, 5,000 Americans, several hundred Britons and Australians, and uncounted Koreans will have died to no purpose.

The United Nations put a tremendous war machine into this battered peninsula. It was a magnificent effort. Countries like Canada, which took little or no part, have no right to complain that in military terms there were many reverses and in political terms the Americans were too busy fighting the war to give much thought to winning the peace.

Syngman Rhee's government in South Korea was no great credit to democracy. Under a thin facade of liberty it set up a police state, run for the benefit of the privileged in an archaic society—a state in which arbitrary imprisonment and political assassination were used to keep the government in power. General MacArthur himself, talking to a visitor last May, made some acid remarks about Syngman Rhee's habit of classifying every political opponent as a Communist and clapping him into jail.

The prospect of victory didn't seem to have changed Rhee's line of thought. He made a speech recently deploring criticism of his government and branding such criticism as "disloyalty."

Just before I visited the 345 men in the advance party of Canada's Special Force at Pusan, the seaport town on the southern tip of Korea, I stopped in Seoul where I was billeted with a British correspondent. He was pecking out a story on a portable typewriter. "I'm supposed to be doing some light feature pieces," he said, "but the Koreans invited me out this afternoon to watch some executions. I don't feel like writing light features now."

Win or Lose, the Russians May Get Korea

It's fair to say that even when the shooting was at its lowest ebb, Korea was still in a state of violence that made due process of law an expensive luxury. Even when Seoul was 300 miles behind the front lines, we were warned not to go out after dark alone or unarmed. An estimated 15,000 to 20,000 guerrillas were still under arms in the hills, supported by heaven knows how many secret aides in the towns and villages.

Reprisal and repression, though, are double-edged weapons, and it was disquieting to think of the pools of bitterness and vengeance that were being replenished in this country. Ample publicity has been given to atrocities by North Koreans. For military reasons, atrocities by South Koreans have been played down. Most people here seem to think the story's about the same on both sides—except, of course, that no white men have been victims on this side of the line.

You had to visit Korea in winter to realize what a singularly unpleasant country it is. North from Pyongyang, the former Communist capital, you drove through a dreary succession of bare brown hills enclosing little flat valleys—a land without landmarks. Each hill looked like every other hill, each town and village was uniformly drab and poverty-stricken. Dust lay along the rough narrow roads in opaque clouds; often you couldn't see 30 feet ahead. Temperatures were low, winds high and cutting.

Campaigning here needs no enemy to make it daunting. I stayed with the British Commonwealth Brigade just south of Pakchon, and the whole front was quiet; the only shots I heard were fired by UN artillery a mile or two behind us. Nevertheless, it was no picnic.

It was the first real cold snap of the North Korean winter. As the sun came up you could hear mechanics all along the line trying to get jeeps and trucks started. Only about one in five would go. We didn't know it at the time, but the same thing had happened to weapons. Bren guns wouldn't fire, tanks wouldn't start. Only the artillery would function at all because it had been firing all night.

There was no thermometer in the open-ended tent where we slept on the ground, but we knew it was cold. When I washed in

293

an upturned helmet that morning I wet my hair before shaving; five minutes later I was combing flakes of ice out of it. The colonel of the Argyll and Sutherland Highlanders set down his shaving brush while he applied his razor; when he picked it up again it was a solid stick.

I had four blankets, a sleeping bag, long underwear and a fur-lined parka. I wore it all to bed and I was cold. Men of the forward companies were posted on windswept hills ahead of us, still wearing tropical underwear they brought from Hong Kong and supplied with two blankets apiece. They slept with no shelter but a tarpaulin, in shallow foxholes stuffed with straw.

"I'm not afraid of the North Koreans or the Chinese either," a British officer said. "I am afraid of the weather."

All over Korea, north and south alike, the people seemed chilly too. Maybe that is the liberators' own fault, but it's not one that can easily be corrected. It's true that the G.I. refers to all Koreans as "gooks," that he shows contempt for the native at every turn. But let's not be smug about it. Canadian troops developed some of the same prejudice within a week of their arrival.

Near the Argylls' battalion command post I saw a pathetic little arch of triumph made of evergreens. "Welcome to United Nations Troops," it said. Behind it was a large black patch and that was about all—the little hamlet had been burned flat in the battle. Korean villages burn like paper. I heard of one case where a lighted cigarette, carelessly tossed into a thatch by an American soldier, destroyed a whole settlement as effectively as a fire-bomb raid. Small wonder that Koreans regard liberation as a doubtful blessing.

Americans, on their side, don't fancy a country where you can't tell friend from enemy. We drove up to the front one day when an American truck convoy was ambushed by an innocent looking crowd of Korean peasants.

"Don't go wandering around the country alone," an American war correspondent warned me. "You can't trust anybody here. You may see an old woman washing clothes on a river bank. If you're in a group and armed, she goes right on washing. If you're alone she may pull a Tommy gun from her pile of laundry and shoot you."

That's why even chaplains bear arms in Korea.

Win or Lose, the Russians May Get Korea

The ruins of Seoul.

Down at Pusan I visited 345 Canadian soldiers who were badly browned off for different reasons. They were in a state of complete bewilderment as to why they were here, what they were supposed to do, what other Canadians were coming to Korea, and when.

They had been assembled as an advance party for Canada's Special Force, a brigade of three infantry battalions with its own artillery support. Elements of 18 units were included in the advance group—medical, dental, ordnance, signals, army service corps and so on, as well as some officers and other ranks from the combat battalions. They sailed on October 21.

When their troopship docked at Yokohama, Major-General Hume, of the U.S. Army medical service, went aboard to greet the Canadians—"Glad to have you with us," he said.

295

"Glad to be here, sir," said the Canadian officer commanding, Major Roy Bourgeois of the Royal 22nd, "but we're afraid the show is all over."

This was a couple of days before the Chinese Communist intervention that renewed and prolonged the war.

They weren't so well prepared for the next news. In strict secrecy officers were told that only one battalion, the Princess Patricia's Light Infantry, would be coming to Korea; the rest of the brigade would continue training at Fort Lewis. Next day the Tokyo newspapers carried an official announcement from Ottawa broadcasting the secret to all ranks.

Canada's advance party was badly confused. If only one infantry battalion was coming, they had nothing much to do. Preparations for an arrival on that scale would take only 48 hours, and they'd arrived more than a month ahead of time.

Only a few of them were infantrymen, so officers and men alike were wondering what they were supposed to do when the Pats arrived. Join the infantry? Many haven't got even the physical qualifications, let alone the training. Go home to Canada? That would be an ignominious finish, but they couldn't think of any third alternative. Certainly a lone battalion would have no use for the establishment that the advance party represented.

When I visited them at Pusan, the men were playing softball in the schoolyard where they are billeted—they did this two afternoons a week. The rest of the time they spent at infantry tactical training.

"That's the only part of our training we'd pretty well completed," an officer said glumly, "but there's nothing else for us to do. It keeps the men busy."

What about the officers? What were they doing to pass the time?

"We make plans," was the reply. "We have plans for everything. Plans for one battalion, plans for a whole brigade. Plans for landing and training at Pusan, plans for going to the British Commonwealth Training Centre at Taegu, plans for the British Commonwealth mustering point at Suwon."

Where would the Canadians actually be going?

"That's just it—we don't know."

Win or Lose, the Russians May Get Korea

This uncertainty was part of a general pattern of snafu that ran right through Canada's Korean adventure. Nothing apparently had gone right.

Actually this confusion about destination and size of force was not Canada's fault. There has never been good liaison between the Canadians and General MacArthur's headquarters.

Canada had military observers in Korea from the start, and Brigadier Frank Fleury went to Tokyo in August. That was when the Special Force was being recruited. All its operations and equipment were planned on the assumption that the job would be to hold the small perimeter around Pusan and Taegu in the warm south. General MacArthur's brilliant landing at Inchon in mid-September broke the back of the North Korean forces and changed the whole course of the war. But the first any Canadian knew about the Inchon landing was when it appeared in the newspapers.

External Affairs Minister L.B. (Mike) Pearson protested to Washington and was told it had been a military secret. True—but the press reported it later as "the worst kept secret in military history." Apparently it was open gossip in half the bars of Tokyo days before it happened. But nobody thought to tell the Canadians.

In October, about the time the advance party sailed, it looked as if the Korean War was about over. In Washington, plans were being pushed for a unified European army with North American components and Canada was expected to make a contribution. Ottawa asked if the Special Brigade had better be held at home.

Washington thought that was a good idea. General Mac-Arthur, consulted in Tokyo, said he wanted to broaden the scope of his UN force as much as possible and would like to have some Canadians; but he was quite content with one battalion.

Then the Chinese Communists came in and the war picture altered sharply. Reinforcements were rushed up, battle-weary troops sent back to the front. It looked like the start of World War III.

On the day the Chinese Reds joined the fight, Canadian Brigadier Fleury was packing to leave for Ottawa. Nobody told him about the Chinese intervention; he heard of it by pure chance from a Canadian reporter. It's not surprising that Canada appeared slow in adjusting to the various dramatic developments of the past six months.

Even as the Chinese Communists launched their big attack in late November, no final decision had been made about the disposition of Canada's Special Force. It was announced that the Princess Pats would sail, and they did so; it had not been announced whether the rest of the brigade would follow them or not. If General MacArthur wanted them he had only to ask for them.

Whatever the Supreme Commander thought, I think the troops in Korea would be glad to see the Canadians—the more the merrier. War or no war, there will be rough and dirty work to do in Korea for some time.

Somebody will have to rebuild Korea, too. The Americans made a thorough job of "strategic bombing."

Canada offered to send a corps of specialists—engineers, medical personnel and so on—last October, when everyone thought the war was over. It was not accepted. Canada's contribution was to be troops or nothing, plus our share of the cash required to restore Korea.

If that job falls to Canadian troops, it will be a pretty dull and miserable job. There's no comfort in this country. Even in undamaged Pusan the first thing Canadians had to do was put wiring into the school building where they were billeted and build toilets to replace the filthy Korean latrines. With every evening free, the boys ran out of things to do within a fortnight of their arrival.

They may not get much thanks for coming here, either. Latecomers are not allowed to forget their tardiness in Korea.

Blair Fraser, who drowned in a canoeing accident at 59 in May 1968, was Ottawa Editor at Maclean's from 1943 to 1960, and edited the magazine from 1960 to 1962.

CORPORAL DUNPHY'S WAR

—June 1, 1951—
Pierre Berton

Cpl. Dunphy relaxing.

The lives of nine men depend a lot on Karry Dunphy, a corporal of the Princess Pats. So, ultimately, does the cause of the United Nations, for the war in Korea is a section leader's war. Here, at the slit-trench level, is the story of the first Canadian ground troops to go into action.
—The Editor, 1951

On the weird cone-shaped hills of Korea, scarred by shovel and blackened by fire, there is no room for armies in the mass. The war is being fought not by divisions or even battalions, but by tiny handfuls of weary men clawing their way up to the high ground. It is not a colonel's war or a general's war as much as it is a section leader's war, and it is on the shoulders of hundreds of section leaders that success or failure inevitably rests.

A section, normally ten men, is the smallest infantry unit in the army and a section leader the most common casualty. A corporal gets only four dollars a month more than a private but his chances of going for the long sleep are infinitely greater (the Canadians had seven killed and wounded in the first three weeks of action). He has some of the responsibility of a commissioned officer but none of the privileges. In action, the lives of nine men depend to a great degree on what he does.

Section leaders are chosen for a variety of qualities: ability to lead, efficiency, general savvy. Cpl. Karry Dunphy, leader of No. 1 Section, No. 4 Platoon, Baker Company, 2nd Battalion, Princess Patricia's Canadian Light Infantry, was given his chance because he has a knack of keeping up morale. Although he is not yet considered a truly first-rate NCO, men will listen to him and follow him because of his personality.

Dunphy is the kind of man who emcees all battalion parties, writes a column in the battalion paper, can sing all the old army songs to the fiftieth verse and make up new ones on the spur of the moment. After taking over his section he dubbed it the Leper Colony—a steal from the movie *Twelve O'Clock High*, and his slogan, "Once a Leper Always a Leper," worries his officers because it tends to make Dunphy's section a tight clique within the platoon.

But it was these very qualities which stood Dunphy in good stead when his section came under fire for the first time from the Chinese Communists who were slowly retiring to the 38th parallel early this spring.

The section was advancing along one of the thousands of nameless ridges of this washboard land, crunching through spring snow in the shelter of the queer flat little pines that clothe the red hills above the winding tiers of rice paddies.

They were strung out behind him—the lead section of the battalion three men under strength, a cross section of the Army: all of them under thirty, only one married, none except Dunphy with more than high-school education. They came from towns as widely scattered as Fruitvale, B.C., Brandon, Man., Arnprior, Ont., and Charlottetown, P.E.I.

Dunphy, who had lived with most of them for five months, knew them as well as he knew his own family.

There was Burger, the bookworm: comic books, pocket books, magazines—it didn't matter: Chester Burger read them all in slit trenches, tents, latrines and lorries.

There was Bill Wilmot, known as "Wandering Willie" because he'd seen the world in the merchant navy. He was a strong B.C. booster and liked to sing off key. "I'm no canary," he'd say each morning, "but I got the crows all beat."

There was "Trigger Jim" Lacy, the Bren gunner, a blond, dour one-time master plumber, the only man in the section besides Dunphy who'd seen action in the last war. He was champion horse-shoe pitcher of the battalion. He was also champion army-beater in the rest areas, but in the line he carried twenty-seven pounds of gun and also twenty-one pounds of ammunition—the heaviest load in the section—without complaint.

There was Charlie Doyle, No. 2 on the Bren, a blond, rasp-voiced, pink-cheeked Irishman with a gift for a colorful phrase ("as dark as a squaw's packet") and an excitable temper which once brought him a severe drubbing at the hands of a sergeant.

There was young Alex Fairfield, a reinforcement who was constantly telling the others they had nothing to worry about. "There's nothing to be scared of," Fairfield would say. "All you got to do is lie back and figure where the fire is coming from. Then you fire back."

And there was L/Cpl. "Chicago Bill" Denne, second in command of the Leper Colony, a long-nosed former steel rigger and Dunphy's closest friend. Whatever Dunphy did or said was okay with Denne, who was inclined to imitate his section leader—even to the same relaxed way of walking, as if, in the words of one officer, "they were both strung on coat hangers."

Dunphy was pretty sure how each of his men would react under the test of their first fire. Doyle, the excitable Irishman, would be a bit jittery; Lacy, the veteran, would be impetuous; Denne would be scared as hell but alert, and the others would hit the dirt and wait for him to tell them what to do. He was right in all but one instance.

The shots came high and into the pines, shaking the needles

and cracking over the heads of the section, a burst of light machine-gun fire from the hills that seemed so empty. These were the first rounds fired in anger at Canadian troops in Korea.

Dunphy looked around at his section. Denne, very pale, was down on his haunches, rifle to shoulder. Lacy was on one knee like a sprinter, Bren at the ready. Doyle, forgetting his job with the Bren for the moment, was flat on his stomach. Fairfield, white and nervous, was shouting, "Where's our support?" The others were off the trail and down on the ground rolling out of position, as they had been taught, and waiting for Dunphy.

It was Dunphy's job to spot the fire, estimate the range, relay this to his officer and keep his section moving forward and under control. He saw that the bullets were high and therefore not dangerous so he exposed himself to view for a few seconds, drew another burst, estimated the range at fourteen hundred yards and began to coax his section forward.

Trigger Jim Lacy had already rushed up shouting, "Lemme get a whang at them!" but Dunphy restrained him. He moved cautiously through the section, kidding them along to get them moving. He had promised Denne a steak at Letros' restaurant, Toronto, if they got out in one piece, and he now remarked to Denne, with a grin, that he hoped they'd both be around to eat it. That helped break the ice. He had also promised five dollars to the first man to kill a Chinese and he now shouted, "Stay down, you bastards—don't crowd for that five bucks!"

Burger, the bookworm, was the first to answer: "Make it an even ten and I'll go over the ridge." Then the tension eased and the banter began. The section began inching forward, taking cover as it could.

When the section began bunching up, Dunphy kidded them some more. As each bullet struck the ground he'd shout, "There's a spot they got pin-pointed. We know where that is!" Gradually the section began looking at these places and forgot to be afraid.

The first man to kill a Chinese was Fairfield, who moved up the trail, got down on one knee, carefully brought his rifle to shoulder, practiced breath control as he'd been taught, got three shots away and knocked a sniper over at a hundred yards.

Then a weird thing occurred. Fairfield stood up. His whole face changed. With his rifle over his head he began to run back through the trees, screaming and shouting, his pack and weapon catching in the branches. "I gotta see the major," Fairfield shouted. "I'm in no shape for this! I gotta see somebody."

That was the last the section saw of Fairfield. He was boarded out of the Army with an S-5 category. S stands for Stability; five is as low as you can go. (Editor's note: The name Fairfield is fictitious for obvious reasons.)

In the platoon attack and the company attack that followed, Cpl. Dunphy and his men found little glamour and not much excitement. Most of it was hard weary slugging uphill, providing fire for attacking sections that moved past them. That night, the objective still not attained, they dug in one hundred yards from the enemy. They had thrown away their entrenching tools, which turned out to be useless, and used shovels. They wore wool balaclavas instead of the steel helmets you see in war bond ads. As for "wild bayonet charges," as far as Dunphy's boys were concerned these existed only in the newspapers. As L/Cpl. Denne said: "Why use a bayonet when you got a bullet up the spout?"

The Lepers have killed Chinese at long range, but some of them have yet to see one. "I'd like to get my hands on one of them Chinks just so I could choke him and know he exists," said Wilmot, explaining the frustration of everyone at an enemy who camouflaged himself into the very soil, then slipped off at night, burying his dead so the advancing forces hadn't even the satisfaction of seeing the results of their fire.

In the days and weeks that followed—weeks of slow remorseless plodding from ridge to ridge, of clearing mud huts, of firing round after round into apparently empty hills, of long patrols by day and longer watches by night—Cpl. Dunphy learned a great deal about being a section leader.

He learned that the country itself was as great an enemy as the yellow men in the hills. The slopes are so steep that the padre has had to omit the fine old hymn, "Unto the Hills Around Do I Lift Up My Longing Eyes," from church service. Tactics dictate that whoever holds the peaks holds the country, so the infantry is always climbing. On the first climb in training, half the company fell back exhausted. Now Dunphy has learned to rest his men, letting them lean against trees on the broad base of their small packs.

In the line the section lives in slit trenches, two to a slit. It is Dunphy's job to locate these slits, under the guidance of his platoon commander, a dark young lieutenant from Kelowna, B.C., named Murray Edwards. (There are three sections to a platoon.) The Lepers live, sleep, eat and on occasion fight from these holes in the ground.

The first night in a slit was the worst Dunphy has ever spent in his life. "That night," he recalls, "I reached my lowest ebb." The trenches, waist high, two and a half feet wide and five feet long, were dug in deep snow and frozen soil. The section was hardly dug in before the rain, mixed with sleet, began to fall.

The next ten hours were a nightmare. Even Wilmot forgot to sing. The men's parkas, battledress and underwear became soaked and then froze. They crouched in a foot of ice water. Dunphy and Denne tried to stand up and found their trousers frozen to the earth, which came away in a chunk. Blankets turned to sopping rags. There was only one ground sheet in the section. Dunphy kept everybody awake; he'd come around every half hour, haul men from the slits, walk them around and kid them about how silly they looked. One man in a neighboring section shot himself in the shoulder—nobody knew whether it was accidental or whether he did it on purpose through depression. But as Doyle, only half jokingly, says: "If the guns woulda worked I guess I mighta put a bullet in me." Three days later the troops' battledress was still wet.

In the days that followed, the Leper Colony learned a good deal about trench life—some of it from the Chinese. They learned to build a sleeping ledge above the mud base of the slit, to line the trench with straw and fir boughs, to cover it with logs and boughs on an angle for drainage. They learned to build fireplaces in the walls, using bazooka tubes as chimneys, to put hot charcoal in washbasins as braziers, to bury hot stones under their beds for warmth, to wrap their feet, boots and all, in straw.

Dunphy makes sure his men change their socks each night and that they are always clean. When the enemy is close his men sleep in sitting positions, each with his foot in his partner's crotch so he can wake him wordlessly. Dunphy sees that they keep their heaviest clothing off by day so they will appreciate it more at night.

In the line the Canadian soldier carries only his towel, toilet kit, ground sheet, one blanket and three pairs of socks. The Americans and some of the British take sleeping bags into the slits but the Canadians don't because they believe a man in a sleeping bag is too vulnerable to surprise attack. They have not forgotten the chastening and grisly sight that met them as they went into the line: some sixty bodies of American Negro troops, slaughtered in their sleeping bags in a surprise attack at night. Dunphy's men sleep with their boots on.

Dunphy has discovered many things not found in training manuals: how to build a smokeless fire from small roots, fine grass, dry pine needles and dry boughs from the undersides of trees; how to shave and wash in two ounces of water in a tiny jam tin; how to wash socks so they'll dry quickly—by rinsing just the feet in a mess tin.

Dunphy treats his men with scrupulous fairness. He sees that each gets an easy watch, from 7 to 9 p.m., and each an equal number of hard ones in the early hours. He takes a watch himself and tries to see that each man occasionally gets a night free from watches. He has never put a man on charge. "I have nine favorites in my section," he likes to say.

He believes that pay stoppage or detention is tougher on a man's family than on himself. But on two occasions he has used his fists to discipline men who wouldn't follow orders. One man had slept on sentry duty during training. Dunphy told him he'd shoot him if he lost a man in action through this negligence. Then, in his own words, "I clobbered him." At the beginning Dunphy told his men that if they followed orders he'd see they got through. At this writing he has had no casualties.

Dunphy's strength—his ability to get on with his men—is also his greatest weakness from the Army's point of view. "You can't win a popularity contest as an NCO," his company commander, Major Vince Lilley, has repeatedly said, but sometimes Dunphy seems to be trying hard. His men seldom call him "Corporal" but use the more familiar "Dunphy." His officers feel that he associates himself too openly with the gripes of the troops. "He doesn't always take hold of his men," one of them says. "It's as if he was afraid of hurting their feelings."

Dunphy is a six-footer with lean, dark good looks and a good deal of dash. In Pusan, out after hours, he took a swing at an American MP and got badly beaten. "I woke up with a couple of carrying handles on my head," he recalls.

On the boat coming over Dunphy was the first man to shave his hair off, thus starting the Cueball Club that swept through the battalion. He wrote "Little Benny Writes Home" for the ship's paper and is the author of innumerable songs, most of them bawdy. One of them satirizes the first battalion of the Pats who, during training at Wainwright, Alta., never tired of referring to their part in Exercise Sweetbriar up north. The phrase "Sweetbriar was never like this" has become a byword in the Leper Colony and one of Dunphy's verses goes:

> Up in Sweetbriar we played lots of games
> We built big fat snowmen and jumped out of planes.
> And when we were frozen almost half to death
> We packed up our gear and we bloody well left.
> Look away! Look away!
> Sweetbriar was never like this.

Dunphy, who is 27, served a three-year stretch on the North Atlantic during the last war as a radar operator in the Navy. After the war he tried to get into pre-medical school at McGill, but settled for Dalhousie in Halifax. He quickly became a big man on the campus, went in for rugby, Canadian football, basketball and track and field.

But Dunphy was a trial to professors and coaches alike. He played a good game of football even after all-night drinking bouts, but didn't bother to learn all the rules. In his second year he switched from medicine to law, but attended few lectures. Instead, he took a hotel room downtown, threw a two-week party and ran through all his savings. He quit the campus and lived a restless life as clerk, surveyor and free-lance writer. (He sold a verse to the *Saturday Evening Post*, but nothing else.) Last fall he joined the

Corporal Dunphy's War

Korean Special Force. He intended to write a novel with a Korean background, but "it's tough to find anything exciting to write about," he says. "I've become too insulated to this whole life."

The responsibilities of his job have had a steadying influence on Karry Dunphy. Some of his superiors feel he may make officer material with another six months of experience. Meanwhile, he is slowly being cast in the Army mold.

Like everybody else, from colonel to private, he peppers his speech with a single obscenity which serves him as verb, adjective, participle and noun. Like everyone else, he calls the enemy "Chinks" and lumps all Koreans as "gooks." He dislikes the Americans for a series of reasons too complicated to go into here.

On the other hand, he has no particular hatred for the Chinese, whom he has seldom seen and whom he considers "sporting soldiers." Even when the Chinese were withdrawing beyond the 38th parallel, he was under no illusion that the UN had beaten them, and he was irritated by the newspapers back home which carried such headlines as "Pats Hurl Back Reds." He knew the Reds had not been hurled back, and he was convinced that if they wanted to they could have held the hills of Korea almost indefinitely.

In many movies about war there is usually a point toward the last reel when the ordinary soldier stands up and makes a little speech about what his particular war is all about. There are no such speeches in the Leper Colony. Although they volunteered to participate in it, all the members of Dunphy's section are confused and cynical about the Korean "police action"—a phrase they sometimes use as a gag.

Dunphy himself once thought he knew what he was fighting for. "I thought it was a good thing that the UN was sticking its neck out," he says. Now he professes to be as baffled as Bob Perley, a Maliseet Indian from New Brunswick who recently joined the section and who, incredibly, was under the impression that he was fighting Chiang Kai-shek's troops until somebody corrected him.

The attitude of the Lepers is undoubtedly conditioned by the stupefying, unending vista of waste and destruction in which they move. Almost every bridge in the land is destroyed, locomotives and freight cars are wrecked and tossed over the sidings, rails are

307

ripped up, buildings gutted, roads reduced to impossible ruts, rice paddies flattened by tenting armies, villages turned to black and steaming sores.

All this destruction, with no hint of reconstruction, bothers Dunphy. He can see no evidence that the war has benefited the people on whose land it is being fought. "No schools, no churches, no progressive farming—nothing," he says. "Why, they're still tilling the farms with little sticks." In an environment like this it is not hard for a soldier to lose sight of the high principles for which he is fighting. And the fact that the mass of the Korean peasantry neither knows nor seems to care what is happening maddens Dunphy still further.

"They don't know or give a damn who runs the country," he says, and his buddy Denne adds: "To them we're not here as liberators, we're just the white race fighting on their ground to save our own face."

The Koreans—even the "friendly" ones—have tried to steal almost everything from the troops. Once, putting up a tent, the section lost four of seven shovels to thieves. Dunphy saw one wiry little woman make off with a tent which four Canadians had been carrying. In Pusan ragged Korean children sold bottles of what they said was wine to the Canadians. It turned out to be urine.

"I love kids," says Dunphy, "but it doesn't bother me a bit to see an MP boot one in the backside if he gets within forty yards of a jeep."

The Lepers are used to seeing Koreans in their loose white clothing working on their mud-and-straw hovels, or tilling bean fields in the midst of an attack. One of the men in the company was on watch once and spotted movement in a shattered hut in front of the lines. He fired, wounding a Korean woman and child who were living and working there, completely unconscious of the war around them.

"We take a village and they smile at us and put up the Korean Republic flag and the American flag," says Dunphy, "but we know damn well that two days before those same smiles were for the Communists."

Outside of a printed statement from General Matthew Ridgway, nothing has been done recently about reminding men like Dunphy what he and his Lepers are fighting for. Perhaps the effort

Corporal Dunphy's War

Author Pierre Berton in Seoul.

would be fruitless.

"I know there's a lot of talk at high level about the liberty-loving Korean people," Dunphy says. "Maybe the guys on top really believe that. I guess that Triggie Lie comes over and says 'How're things going here?' and old Siggie Rhee says 'Well, we desire freedom' and all that business. But what in hell have they got to gain from freedom as long as they've got their rice? It seems you always got to take somebody's word for it that the Korean people are 'liberty loving,' I haven't met a gook yet who was."

In army parlance Dunphy's section is cheesed off with the country. The Pats have been virtually confined to barracks since they left Canada in November. In Korea there has been none of the sweet that usually accompanies the bitter of warfare. There is no leave because there is no place worth going to. There is no loot because there is nothing worth looting. Those who have cleverly managed to seduce Korean women have come down with venereal disease. The villages are riddled with smallpox and typhus and the commanding officer himself has come down with smallpox.

One wag in the unit has suggested that the country be divided vertically instead of horizontally so that the fighting can go that

309

way for a change. This about expresses the attitude of the fighting man in Korea. Few of them want to continue the "police action" warfare that seems so meaningless to them.

But, with the adaptability of soldiers of every age, Dunphy and his men have managed to keep their spirits up and their morale astonishingly high. They treat the war as if it were some colossal practical joke played on them by fate. When they tell how they crawled through wet soil fertilized by human manure they cannot suppress a smile. Dunphy chuckles when he explains how the MPs clobbered him. On the terrible night when he and Denne found themselves frozen to a slit trench they both burst out laughing. If the war is phony it is also funny: The country is a joke, the gooks are a joke, the Yanks are a joke, and the ROK army is the biggest joke of all.

If they have learned anything lasting from the killing climbs, the chilling nights, the long marches through the wretched ruined villages, and the straggling columns of expressionless refugees, it is that the country they came from is a far better place than they realized.

Dunphy, who is better at expressing himself than the others— after all, that is why he is section leader—is continually harping on this point.

"I thank Christ I live as well as I do in Canada," he says. "We all of us know how well off we are now after seeing this country. They can talk about democracy all they want but until you've seen this place you don't know what it means. No one can tell us anything more about it now we've been here. We know."

Karry Dunphy received the Military Medal for bravery for his service in Korea. After the war, Dunphy stayed in the army, becoming an instructor at the School of Infantry at Camp Borden, near Barrie, Ont. Later, he spent 29 years working for the Royal Canadian Legion headquarters in Ottawa before retiring to Peterborough in 1991.

Pierre Berton, a Maclean's assistant editor at the time, was the magazine's managing editor from 1953 to 1959 and continues to write from his Kleinburg, Ont., home.

CYPRUS

REPORT
FROM
CYPRUS

May 16, 1964

Ralph Allen

The well-trained and well-disciplined soldiers of the Royal 22nd Regiment of Canada have been learning only a limited amount about the art of war during their strange mission with the United Nations peace-keeping force in Cyprus. But they have had an unexampled opportunity to study another subject close to every Canadian's thoughts these days—the attractions, dangers and costs of separatism.

Whatever its labyrinthine past and whatever its dark and desperate future the war between the five hundred thousand Greek Cypriots and the hundred

Royal 22nd Regiment member and frightened Turkish child.

thousand Turkish Cypriots is, in its present phase, a separatist war. In 1960, while bargaining for their own independence, the Greek majority granted absurdly generous powers to the Turk minority, including the power of veto over all important legislation and all important government appointments. In 1963, having lived uneasily for three years with their clearly unworkable constitution, the Greeks proposed to wipe it out overnight. Almost at once the two communities were at each other's throats. By the time they got around to clarifying their aims they were both committed, by the sacred bones of their Christian saints and Moslem prophets, to positions from which the slightest retreat or compromise now seems not only craven but suicidal. The Greeks want nothing less than a virtually unconditional surrender of the Turks' minority rights. The Turks want nothing less than partition of the island; separatism carried to its conclusion.

When the Van Doos and their supporting light armor from the Royal Canadian Dragoons arrived last March to join the optimistically named United Nations peace-keeping force, there were already at least eight other armies on the ground or underground. The domestic Cypriot Army had split into its two main racial components; the Turkish soldiers were nominally in a state of mutiny but were also unshakably determined to protect their civilian communities from more of the small but brutal massacres of last Christmas. The relatively well-armed and well-trained regular army detachments from Greece and Turkey, which came here to defend the island against outside invasion, are now deployed to defend it against each other—although so far they haven't joined the serious fighting. All the island's police forces are playing a quasimilitary role and, like the Cypriot army, they're solidly divided on ethnic lines.

The last two non-UN armies are the irregulars of both sides. These include practically every able-bodied man who owns a World War Two or World War One rifle, or a family fowling piece, or knows someone from whom he can borrow one to go out in the mountains or up in the attic and take a few pot shots at the enemy or at some distant crag, boulder, tree or window shade that might conceivably conceal the enemy. And to add to the variety of the over-all war establishment—all of which is superimposed on a population about the size of Vancouver's and crammed into the area of the Niagara Peninsula—the United Nations force now includes detachments from Britain, Ireland, Canada, Sweden and Finland. Its commander is an Indian.

To say that the Van Doos are constantly preoccupied with the parallels between the separatist war here and the separatist manoeuvres back home in Quebec would be a serious exaggeration. Most members of the battalion are double-barreled nationalists—much closer to the spirit of Henri Bourassa than of Marcel Chaput. They are Quebec nationalists but they are also Canadian nationalists. They are intensely proud and generally pleased with both their homelands. "We would hardly be in the army unless we believed in Canada," a young lieutenant from Montreal remarked the other day while he listened to the gunfire from two nearby crests of the Kyrenia range. "We wouldn't be in the Van Doos unless we believed in Quebec."

Later on a sergeant and a corporal exchanged somewhat parallel reflections. "These guys," the sergeant said with an expansive wave that took in all the enfilading Turks and all the infiltrating Greeks, "are every bit as crazy as our own ALQ and FLQ. Maybe even crazier."

"Yes," the corporal reminded him. "But remember, these guys have had seven thousand extra years of practice."

The political mysteries disturb the Canadian contingent considerably less than do the military anomalies. Under its terms of reference the United Nations force has no choice except to wield a putty hand in a velvet glove. It cannot disarm any of the other armies on the island or even shoot at them unless the UN troops are shot at first or unless, by the movement of men as distinct from the movement of projectiles, one side threatens to engulf the other or wipe out the parlous lines of demarcation.

About all the UN commanders can do is play each situation by ear and rely on the devices of friendly persuasion. Major Phil Plouffe, whose company command post is in one of Nicosia's northern suburbs, has Greek pillboxes forty yards to one side and Turk breastworks sixty yards to the other. He has direct telephone

315

lines from his command post to the command posts of both the Greeks and the Turks and when they start shooting at each other, as they usually do at least two or three times a day, he gets on the phone to each position in turn and extracts an agreement from, say, the Turk that he will stop shooting in fifteen minutes if the Greek will stop too, then phones the same proposition to the Greek and usually gets a cease-fire sooner or later—even though one recent evening it took four hours.

Major Pat Tremblay, whose Charley Company has been doing a similar job largely by foot, helicopter and armored-car patrols in the Kyrenia hills, says with the imperturbable resignation of a good permanent force officer, "We don't order. We reason. We explain. We expound. Usually they listen." It takes no elaborate guesswork to divine that when a couple of weeks ago the Turks fired two rounds right past Tremblay's UN truce flag and came within a foot or two of hitting him, and Tremblay at last fired back, he gave the order not perhaps exactly in anger but most certainly not in sorrow either.

The fact is that the brief honeymoon between the Canadians and the Greeks and Turks is already a thing of the past.

The Turks particularly are growing increasingly contemptuous of the UN force. All the Van Doos took it as a grave affront to the regiment when one of the Turkish hill commanders was quoted as saying to an English reporter: "When British paratroopers were here they told you, 'Stop firing or we fire.' You knew they meant it. A UN patrol arrived by helicopter yesterday. They just behaved like court jesters, waving a flag and doing nothing else."

Now that they have been absorbed into the UN force, even the British troops on Cyprus have lost the privilege not only of talking tough but occasionally of acting tough. In the middle of a cease-fire near the sea coast the other day a Turk officer said disdainfully: "The UN is like a scarecrow in a field. It just sits there helpless."

Whatever fearsome offspring this beautiful island spawns next through its persistent cross-breeding of guerrilla politics with guerrilla war, it seems a fairly sage bet that the Van Doos will still be around for the accouchement. Originally they and the UN force were supposed to remain for only three months but now the prospect for any reasonable settlement seems as remote as ever. No doubt the Van Doos and the Royal Canadian Dragoons will eventually qualify for rotation, but from this highly compressed and bloodstained point of vantage it seems extremely probable that if the UN force is to make any lasting contribution its stay in Cyprus will be much closer to three years than to the original three months.

Ralph Allen, who died at 53 of throat cancer in December 1966, was editor of Maclean's *from 1950 to 1960.*

IRAQ

RISKY MISSION

—October 1, 1990—
Andrew Phillips

Three Canadian warships, the *Athabaskan*, the *Terra Nova* and the
Protecteur, entered the Suez Canal last week on their way to enforce
the international embargo against Iraq. *Maclean's* London Bureau
Chief Andrew Phillips boarded the supply ship *Protecteur* for a first-
hand look as the crew prepared for action.   —The Editor, 1990

Petty Officer Philip Manktelow says that when he ended his
two-year assignment aboard HMCS *Protecteur* in June, 1989, he
thought that he would never serve aboard it again. But in mid-
August, Manktelow, a 30-year-old native of Winnipeg, dropped by
his old ship, at anchor in Halifax Harbour, to see friends. And a
quick visit turned into an extended stay. The *Protecteur*, readying
itself to set course for the Middle East as part of Canada's contribution to enforcing UN sanctions against Iraq, lacked a radar specialist—Manktelow's area of expertise. "They asked if I'd go along,
and I guess I didn't want to see the ship stuck short," he recalled
last week as the force glided through the turquoise waters of the
Suez Canal. "You gotta do what you gotta do."

Last week, as the three warships travelled through the Red Sea
and around the Arabian Peninsula, Manktelow still had no clear
idea of how long his unexpected assignment would last. Commodore Kenneth Summers, commander of the Canadian task
force, told the 934 sailors, soldiers and airmen, including 27
women on the *Protecteur*, that they should be ready to spend six
months away from home. "I have mentally prepared myself not to
be home for Christmas," said Summers. "If we are back, then
great—it's going to be that much sweeter." But the crews at least
had a clearer idea of where they were going. The day before the

321

ships entered the canal on Aug. 16, Summers told them that they will be stationed inside the Persian Gulf itself, rather than farther from Iraq in the safer waters of the Gulf of Oman.

But even as they entered the comparatively calm Red Sea, tension heightened aboard the ships. During their 23-day voyage from Halifax to the southern end of the Suez Canal, the crews were busy with training exercises but relatively relaxed. They were on what the navy calls its "fourth degree of readiness," the lowest state of alert. Sailors wore shorts and navy-issue sandals under the broiling Egyptian sun. But when they entered the Red Sea, they went to the second degree of readiness—just one step short of preparing for imminent attack. They wore long pants and boots in case of fire, and hung gas masks from their belts. That, added to the knowledge that they were entering what could suddenly become a war zone, gave an extra edge to the hours of training that occupied their days. "You sure pay more attention to what you're doing," said Manktelow.

Even the *Protecteur* bore visible signs of the potential danger. The main role of the 21-year-old ship is to resupply its sister vessels with food, fuel and munitions. But before the force left Halifax, it was fitted with new defensive weapons: two rapid-fire Phalanx guns designed to knock incoming missiles out of the sky; two 40-mm Bofors guns; several .50-calibre machine-guns; and shoulder-fire Blowpipe surface-to-air missiles. "We're the best-armed tanker around," said Master Seaman Thomas McNeil, a 32-year-old naval weapons technician from Toronto.

The task force's heavy weaponry is loaded aboard the destroyers—the 4,700-ton *Athabaskan* and the 2,900-ton *Terra Nova*. The *Athabaskan*, which is 18 years old, carries Seasparrow surface-to-air missiles, while the 31-year-old *Terra Nova* is newly equipped with Harpoon anti-ship missiles. The force's five Sea King helicopters, originally built in 1962 and 1963, have been outfitted with new surveillance gear.

Although one helicopter experienced a failure in one of its twin engines last week and had to make an emergency landing aboard the *Athabaskan*, those aboard the ships insisted that the vessels are well equipped for any challenge. "We take care of them like vintage cars," said McNeil. "I've got no qualms about going into the area with what we have." Added Summers, the 46-year-old task-force commander: "Rust buckets they're not."

The Canadian contingent will join ships from more than a dozen other countries in monitoring all shipping in a central area of the Gulf. The vessels will use their radar, other sensor systems and the Sea Kings to determine the nationality, destination and cargo of any ships in their zone. If necessary, they will board any suspicious ones and make sure that they are not breaking the UN embargo on shipping goods to or from Iraq. And Summers said that that decision, when it comes, will not be referred to any other force in the area. "This is an independent Canadian operation under sole Canadian control," he declared.

Such a decision is still days, perhaps weeks, away. Meanwhile, the ships' crews are preparing for an extended stay in a harsh environment. All crew members were issued with Tilley cloth hats as protection from the sun, and along with its cargo of fuel, food and weaponry, the *Protecteur* carried cases of Factor 30 sunblock cream. During the hottest part of the day, when temperatures hovered near 40 degrees C, medical staff toured the decks ensuring that sailors smeared copious quantities of sunblock on exposed skin. Said naval Lieut. Kenneth Cooper, one of the *Protecteur's* medical officers: "The biggest threat to the sailors is not Iraqi Exocet missiles. It's the sun, the heat and dehydration."

Before the ships entered the Red Sea and the crews were required to cover up, Cooper encouraged them to wear long pants to keep the sun off their legs. But he had little success. "You're not going to get sailors to do that," he conceded. "They'd go nude if you let them." Some of the medical preparations were more ominous: the *Protecteur* has extra medical staff and a fully equipped operating room capable of dealing with bullet wounds and severe burns in case of injuries in combat.

The crews have taken morale-boosting measures, as well. They receive news from Canada radioed to the ships and then printed in a daily four-page newsletter called *The Gulf Gazette*. *Protecteur* carries plentiful supplies of Canadian snack foods, soft drinks and beer. And before the ships left Halifax, they stocked their video libraries. Air force Sgt. Richard Greensides, a veteran of 27 years with the armed forces, spent $4,000 buying 258 videotapes for the *Protecteur*, including *Robocop, Conan the Barbarian* and *Avenging Force*. "The captain said fill the shelves, it doesn't matter what it costs," said Greensides. "Only stipulation was no triple-X. It's a male-female ship, and I'm sure the girls wouldn't like it."

The 27 women aboard the *Protecteur* are housed in separate quarters, with their own washrooms. And some said that not all their male colleagues had adapted to the fact that women are serving alongside men in combat roles. "There is underlying tension," said 21-year-old air force Pte. Serena Richardson, the youngest woman on the *Protecteur*. "But they have to get used to the fact that we're here and we're staying."

Richardson confessed that she had mixed emotions when she learned about her ship's destination while she was visiting her parents in Burlington, Ont. "My first thought was 'The ship's going to get blown up,'" she said. "But my mom was real supportive. She said the chances of getting killed here or in a car crash are probably about the same."

Richardson, who helps to maintain the three Sea King helicopters aboard the *Protecteur*, left her husband of two years, navy cook Tod Richardson, at home in Halifax. "We had an all-out discussion," she recalled, "and he understands this is the reason we joined the military, to support our country." Facing the possibility of spending Christmas in the Persian Gulf was not a cheerful prospect, Richardson acknowledged. But she said that the crew had heard rumors that the Forces might tape messages from their families and send the videos to the ships. "That would help," she said.

Despite Richardson's concerns, other crew members maintained that they have few worries about the possibility of a shooting war. "It's going to be very boring," predicted McNeil. "We'll be lucky to see any Iraqis at all." Added Greensides: "With the power we have compared to what the Iraqis have, it would be like a fly taking on an elephant if they tried anything. The only way somebody's going to get hurt is going ashore, getting into trouble and being rolled by the locals." While that does not fit the dashing image of battle-ready warriors, their families back home doubtless hoped that they were right.

DOCTORS IN THE DESERT

—*February 18, 1991*—
Andrew Phillips

They have nicknamed themselves the "Dusty Beavers"—and with good reason. Around the temporary base housing a Canadian Forces medical team in eastern Saudi Arabia, the sand is a fine white powder that is whipped up by the hot, dry wind and penetrates almost everything. But the 75 medical staff and support crew, the advance party of a Canadian field hospital that will treat the wounded in the expected ground battle for Kuwait, were not complaining last week. Their base, a former camp for transient workers surrounded by a bleak landscape of construction equipment, piles of sand and assorted debris, at least has hot-and-cold running water and bunks with mattresses. Soon, probably by the end of February, Operation Scalpel will move north, even closer to the front line, and its staff will live in tents in the open desert. "That's when it will get tough," Master Seaman Robert McDougall, a 27-year-old medic from Beaverton, Ont., told *Maclean's*.

Military officials will not say exactly when the 100-bed Canadian field hospital, which will have a staff of about 550 personnel when it is fully deployed, will move north—or where it will go. That will depend mainly on senior British officers. They have been given what Ottawa refers to as "tactical control" of the medical unit—although it will remain formally under overall Canadian command. The Canadians will work alongside two British field hospitals near the front lines in an environment that is potentially more deadly than anything they have known before. None has experience treating battle injuries, but last week the advance team was getting down to business: attending lectures by British medical officers on how to treat victims of an Iraqi chemical attack.

By last week, two 16-member surgical teams had arrived in

Saudi Arabia, and the Canadians had erected a complete operating theatre in a tent at the site of their camp. Two more surgical teams are scheduled to fly in this week, while X-ray and lab equipment, supplies and other gear are on their way from Canada by ship. A 120-member company from the 1st Battalion of the Royal Canadian Regiment, equipped with 16 Grizzly armored personnel carriers, will also arrive to provide security for the medical staff. The entire team, officials said last week, should be fully operational by the end of February. The delay is providing extra time for training, which some medical officers said is still needed—despite the fact that a bloody land battle may be launched at any time. Even the unit's senior surgeon, Col. Claude Auger, a Quebec City native who celebrated his 40th birthday in Saudi Arabia last week, conceded that he had never performed an operation in a mobile operating room.

In the event of a gruelling ground war, the hospital's four surgical teams will be able to perform 48 major operations every 24 hours. And, medical officers insisted last week, they will not favor wounded British, American and other allied soldiers over any injured Iraqi prisoners of war who may be brought to them for treatment. "There are only medical priorities," said Col. Ian Creamer, commanding officer of Britain's 33rd General Surgical Hospital, to which the Canadian unit is attached. "The POWs will go straight into our system. Once an enemy is wounded, he is no longer an enemy."

Many of the Canadians say that they are concerned for their own safety during the expected ground war—but that they are even more worried about how their families back home are coping. Naval Lieut. Timothy Kavanagh, a 28-year-old health care administrator from London, Ont., said that he was particularly concerned about his parents because both he and his sister Margaret are serving in the Gulf. Margaret Kavanagh, 38, is a naval commander and the medical adviser to Commodore Kenneth Summers, Canada's commanding officer in the region. "Our parents were pretty upset when I came over," she said last week. "And they were really upset when Tim left. But they have calmed down. It's our job." Although Margaret Kavanagh outranks her younger brother, there will be no family friction, because she is based in Bahrain while her brother will move near the front with the field hospital. "We couldn't be in the same unit," she said. "It would be impossible."

Others also had their minds on Canada. Cpl. Frank Mio, a 26-year-old medic from Burlington, Ont., said that he phoned home on his second day in Saudi Arabia and learned not only that his wife, Sandra, had been in a minor car accident, but that she was pregnant, as well. "I was just shaking on the phone," Mio said. "But she's going to be all right." Before they left Canada, Mio and the other Canadians were told that their Saudi stint would last about six months, so Mio expects to be home for the birth of his second child. But, for those facing the prospect of setting up near the biggest ground battle in decades, six months could turn out to be a long time indeed.

MISSION ACCOMPLISHED

—March 11, 1991—
Rae Corelli

Refuelling a CF-18 in Qatar.

Maj. William Ryan says that he will long remember the limitless splendor at 30,000 feet above the Persian Gulf, watching the snowcapped mountains of Iran catch the first rays of the rising sun. Capt. Jeff Beckett will carry the memory of deserted Iraqi military airfields, which offered neither targets nor challengers. Master Cpl. Thomas Harrison will return to his base in Germany still wondering what happened to the only bag of clothing ever lost on his shift at the laundry unit. But, for Col. Romeo Lalonde, commander of the 750 Canadian CF-18 fighter pilots and support troops stationed in the emirate of Qatar since last October, the ceasefire in the Gulf War aroused expectations, not reflection. "I never look back," said Lalonde. "The fun's all ahead."

For the first Canadians to go to war in more than 40 years, what lay ahead last week was the imminent prospect of going home to tell stories of bombing missions over Iraq and Kuwait, of sunburn and souvenirs, of dusty boredom on the ground and apprehension in the air, of Scud missiles that fell harmlessly in the desert or into the sea. Troops left their gas masks in their quarters for the first time since mid-January, shopped for bargains in gold jewelry in Doha, the Qatari capital, or just lazed in the 25 deg. C sunshine. Some began packing or played volleyball on a makeshift court at the support base called Canada Dry One, eight kilometres east of Doha. At the airbase two kilometres from Canada Dry One, Canadian, American and French fighter planes were parked in silent rows. For the first time since last October, the only jets thundering over Qatar belonged to commercial airlines.

For the 36 Canadian pilots who flew 56 bombing sorties during the week's 100-hour ground war, there was time to talk of missions and morality. "We had trouble sleeping most of the week," said Ryan, 37, of Greenwood, N.S., a fighter pilot for 12 years. "We were probably a little anxious approaching the border into bad-guy country, but once we were across, we were too busy. But there was always a sigh of relief when we left." Relief was a common emotion among the pilots. Said Capt. Gerard MacKinnon of Windsor, Ont.: "I was really happy to be given the chance to do this sort of thing. But when you have been in the airplane for anywhere from two to four hours, you're anxious to get your feet back on the ground." In all, the CF-18s dropped 15 tons of high explosives on the Iraqi army's tanks, artillery emplacements and truck convoys. Because the weather was bad for most of the week, onboard computers and radar told the Canadian pilots when they should release their 500-lb. bombs. The pilots never saw the results. "Human life is not to be taken lightly," said Capt. Beckett, 32, of Owen Sound, Ont. "But our country called on us to do a job and every pilot, every ground-crew member, every soldier is ultimately going to have to reconcile within himself whether that is right, wrong or otherwise."

From last Oct. 9 until the outbreak of war on Jan. 17, the CF-18s flew combat air patrols north up the Persian Gulf to shield Canadian and other coalition warships. When the war started, they began flying sweep and escort missions as well, covering other allied aircraft that were attacking targets in Iraq and occupied Kuwait. But the first shots that Canadians fired were actually on a Gulf patrol: pilots Maj. David Kendall and Capt. Steve Hill strafed an Iraqi boat. Beckett, who took part in the first sweep and escort mission and the first air-to-ground attack, said that the Canadians never encountered an Iraqi fighter. "To be perfectly honest," he said, "there is some degree of disappointment that the Iraqis didn't give us the chance to test ourselves." Said Ryan: "Maybe it would have been nice to have that challenge. But it's also nice to come back alive every time."

The families of the two pilots live at the Cold Lake, Alta., airbase. The slight, sandy-haired Ryan said that although he had wanted to go skiing when he got home, his wife, Ruthann, "appears to have had enough of the cold weather, so I guess we're going to take the kids and head down to Disneyland—that's the plan, so I've been told." Beckett said that he and his wife, Lisa, would "drive to the mountains for three or four days—some place that's not flat." That eagerness to get home was also evident among the groundcrews and support troops of the Canadian contingent. Sgt. Robert Fiander of Halifax, an airframe technician, sat watching a cribbage game in a recreation shack and said: "What I miss most, besides my wife, is the freedom of being on your own—your own car, your own time schedule, your own refrigerator. And I miss the harbor." At Canada Dry One, the laundry unit's Harrison, of Courtney, B.C., said that his daughter was born at the Canadian Forces base in Lahr "just before I took off." Harrison, 28, has helped to supervise the handling of 220 bags of laundry and 120 sheets a day for the past six weeks. "We only lost one bag and it's a mystery to me where it went," he said.

Capt. Diane Whitney of Cambridge, Ont., a 28-year-old physician, said that what she would miss the least was "getting wakened up in the middle of the night by another air-attack siren."

Mission Accomplished

There were a lot of sleepless nights. Iraqi missiles launched towards Dhahran in eastern Saudi Arabia set off more than two dozen air-attack warnings at Canada Dry One and the neighboring airbase during the first three weeks of the war. Then, at 1:30 a.m. on Feb. 26, some five hours after a Scud attack on a barrack near Dhahran killed 28 Americans, the sirens sounded again—and this time, Qatar was the target. One Scud dug a 20-foot-wide crater in the desert 40 km north of Doha, and a second sailed over the city to land in the Gulf.

Not surprisingly the Canadians took every opportunity to relax after President George Bush had announced the end of hostilities in the Gulf. On Friday night, the Canadians threw a party for the pilots of the U.S. air force F-16s, with whom they had shared the airbase, and for various other Westerners: Canadians living in Qatar, local diplomatic personnel and oil company officials. Although alcohol is publicly forbidden in Moslem Qatar, non-Islamic embassies and other enclaves can obtain private licences from the government. The Canadians obtained their licence through the British Embassy, and the beer, flown in from Germany, flowed freely.

Earlier Friday, Lt.-Col. Donald Matthews of Calgary, commander of the CF-18 squadron, met reporters to review the four-month mission. Said Matthews: "Every time our planes took off, I said a little prayer. And every time they came back, I said another one because there were people out there trying to kill us." His pilots, he said, frequently had to take evasive action when their radar warned that Iraqi surface-to-air missiles and anti-aircraft artillery were tracking their planes. During the week, Matthews said, allied ground forces had moved so rapidly that they had often overrun targets by the time the 1,200-mile-an-hour Canadian fighters had reached them. In those cases, the pilots had to seek out secondary targets. Matthews and other pilots openly discounted published reports in Canada that took note of some public opposition to their role in the Gulf War. Said Matthews: "We had letters and messages of encouragement from all kinds of people—veterans of other wars, church groups, police departments, even an employment agency." Beckett added: "I'm incredibly proud of the way the Canadian people have rallied behind us." There was ample evidence to support their claims: the walls of the trailers at the flight line were covered with valentines, crayon drawings, letters in childish scrawls and other messages bearing scores of signatures.

For Lalonde, sending the fighters and the support crews back to bases in Germany and Canada may very well be the easiest part of the withdrawal operation. His biggest task will be to decide how to dispose of the prefabricated living quarters, the portable trailers and tons of equipment and furnishings. Lt.-Col. Dennis Roberts of St. Catharines, Ont., Lalonde's deputy commander, said that the Qatari military had expressed an interest in buying everything, including the sandbagged weapons bunkers used by the 150-man Royal 22nd Regiment security force that guarded Canada Dry One and the airbase flight line. But the leftover beer, the pilots said, was not for sale.

SOMALIA

COMING BACK TO LIFE

—January 18, 1993—
Mary Nemeth

Four months ago, long after bandits had looted her family's herd of cattle, goats and camels, Habibay Eden Ibdow left the village of Golol with her husband and 10 children in search of food. They walked 30 km to Baidoa, to the heart of Somalia's worst famine zone, a city of 15,000 swollen to more than three times that number of desperate refugees from the countryside. Only 43-year-old Ibdow and two of her boys, aged 14 and 21, survived the famine. They now live in the corner of a filthy room in the stripped-down shell of a once grand building on the

---

Guarding food supplies in Baidoa.

city's outskirts. Among the weeds and the stench of human feces in the garden, three small mounds of dirt mark the graves of her youngest children. A frail woman wrapped in rags, Ibdow said that she does not know where the others are buried. "God has condemned me to be a widow without a husband and children," said Ibdow, her face lined with sorrow. "I am unable to forget their faces." Somalia is slowly coming to life again. But years of drought, famine and civil war have decimated the population and left a legacy of personal tragedy, fear and bitter clan hatreds.

In the capital, Mogadishu, buses and cars jostle with U.S. marine tanks and donkey carts along roads crowded with roadside hawkers selling everything from Chiclets to chunks of camel meat covered with flies. A Somalia women's organization and several foreign aid agencies are beginning to open schools for children traumatized by three years of bloodshed. And soldiers from 20 countries—including 1,262 Canadians—serving as part of the U.S.-led operation to deliver food to Somalia, have begun escorting relief shipments to rural areas long cut off by violence.

Still, more than 150,000 of the country's estimated population of 4.5 million people (there has been no accurate census for decades) remain badly malnourished, and another two million need constant feeding. "It's not over, not even nearly over," said Lt.-Col. Don Young, chief of staff at the Canadian Forces headquarters in Mogadishu. "If we left now, I think it would revert to exactly the way it was before."

Even with 31,500 foreign troops stationed in Somalia, there is looting and tribal conflict throughout the countryside. The situation in Mogadishu remains especially volatile. Last week, while 14 of Somalia's warlords met under UN auspices in Addis Ababa, the capital of neighboring Ethiopia, where they agreed to a ceasefire and to convene a "national reconciliation" conference, clansmen from the capital's two major factions fought street battles and took potshots at American troops patrolling the city. The International Medical Corps (IMC), which is working in Mogadishu's Digfer hospital, received up to 10 patients with gunshot wounds each day. But no one seems to know how many victims died before reaching a hospital.

Coming Back to Life

As the death toll continues to climb, Somalis are clamoring for U.S. forces to disarm the population—a monumental task in a country where perhaps hundreds of thousands of people carry arms. Somalia is a lawless society, so heavily armed that even hospital patients hide guns and knives under their beds. Mary Lightfine, an IMC nurse from Tampa, Fla., who began working at the Digfer hospital three months ago and now runs the agency's medical logistics, says that she once found an ill man lying in a hospital corridor. "He had diarrhea and smelled bad, so other patients on the ward pulled guns on him and forced him to leave," said Lightfine. "They say the gun situation is better now. But I wouldn't want to piss off anyone. If you argue too much, you might get shot."

In Belet Huen, 330 km north of Mogadishu, Canadian soldiers last week located what may be one of the largest single weapons caches discovered by coalition troops: an armory that included more than 3,000 hand grenades, 300 rocket-propelled grenades and 27 long-range multiple-rocket launchers. With no place to store the cache, which belonged to a local faction of one of Somalia's largest warring parties, the United Somalia Congress, the Canadians simply padlocked the building. But Lt.-Col. Carol Mathieu, commander of the 845 Canadian and 55 American troops stationed in Belet Huen, pointed out that rival forces loyal to deposed president Siad Barre, in areas not pacified by coalition forces, are not being disarmed. "If we disarm these people, they will just be more vulnerable to attack," said Mathieu.

Meanwhile, the Canadians are finding themselves drawn into a complex political landscape. Mathieu asked local elders to form committees from local clans to deal with security, relief, politics and reconstruction issues. At last count, there were at least 15 clans or sub-clans demanding representation—and the number is rising. As well, says Col. Serge Labbé, the commander of all Canadian Forces in Somalia, "the concept of neutrality is one that they find foreign, and they are convinced that we are not." When the troops rented three trucks from members of one clan last week, said Labbé, Somalis from the other side of town viewed that as evidence of partiality.

Officially, the mandate of the coalition forces is to establish a

337

secure environment for bringing food supplies into Somalia. American military officials have insisted that their role does not include disarmament, and that they will only seize weapons that pose a direct threat to their troops. But there were indications last week that the Americans were becoming more aggressive. On the morning of Jan. 6, after coming under sniper fire from a cantonment area where forces loyal to one of Mogadishu's warlords, Gen. Mohammed Farah Aideed, had agreed to store their heavy weapons, marines attacked the compound in a nearly hour-long barrage. There were no reports of casualties among the Somalis, who may have withdrawn from the building before the assault.

Still, it seems almost certain that American forces will hand the Somalia operation over to the UN peacekeeping troops before the country is disarmed or any lasting political solution to the tribal conflicts is achieved. And that prospect worries many Somalis, who blame the United Nations for failing to act more swiftly to halt the famine. "The United Nations has failed before and if they try again, the Somalis won't accept them," argued Michel Clerc, a 32-year-old information officer working with the Doctors Without Borders (MSF).

The depth of hostility was evident on Jan. 3 when UN Secretary General Boutros Boutros-Ghali arrived in Mogadishu. A scheduled visit to the headquarters of the United Nations Forces in Somalia (UNOSOM) had to be cancelled when hundreds of stone-throwing demonstrators besieged the compound. Col. James Cox, a 45-year-old Toronto native and veteran of three peacekeeping tours in Cyprus who now serves as UNOSOM's deputy commander, called the criticisms "a bit unfair." Noting that Somali gunmen are now firing on American soldiers with increasing frequency, Cox added: "There is a period when the honeymoon is over. Anyone who is here and does not produce as much of an improvement in the country as the people of Somalia expect will become unpopular. The task force has been successful in exactly what it wanted to do, but the overall problem of Somalia and its complexities is still here."

In fact, some aid workers claim that by undermining the power exercised by the country's often brutal warlords, the foreign troops have created a vacuum—with its own set of uncertainties. "We're very happy that the military are here," said Cynthia Osterman, a spokesman for CARE. "But this intervention has turned everything topsy-turvy. Before, we sort of knew the ground rules. If there were problems, we knew who we could go to. Now, there's no real structure in place and everyone feels kind of afraid."

Those dangers were made tragically clear on Jan. 2, when a foreign aid worker was assassinated for the first time since the marines landed in Mogadishu a month ago. Sean Devereux, the 28-year-old officer in charge of UNICEF's office in the southern port city of Kismayu, was shot in the back of the head as he left the organization's compound. The motive for the killing remains unclear, although Devereux may have annoyed the wrong people a week earlier when he was widely quoted in the media denouncing local clansmen for massacring their opponents. There were also reports that Devereux had provoked the ire of his own guards by cutting their salaries.

The killing sent tremors through the foreign relief community. Clerc of MSF said that aid agencies have been reassessing their presence in Somalia since Devereux's death. "It's not because we're afraid," said Clerc. "We know we are saving lives. But if there is no improvement in the situation, if a patient gets back on his feet but there is nothing for him to do but pick up a gun to get food, what have we achieved?" Added Dutch aid worker Frank Theunissen: "You get so used to the violence, you don't think it can happen to you. This brings it close to home."

Aid workers, who generally live in special compounds guarded by paid Somalia gunmen, form part of a tightly knit community of expatriates that operated virtually under siege before coalition forces arrived in Somalia. Danger is not the only common denominator. Many expatriates express frustration at Somalis who charge the aid organizations exorbitant rates for their services—some drivers charge up to $350 a day—as well as with the Somali gunmen who steal food from their own people while foreigners put their lives on the line. And many of them say that Somalis' demands always seem to outstrip whatever the aid agencies can achieve. "Sometimes it's frustrating because it seems Somalis are always expecting more," concedes Cindy Pettersen, a 26-year-old nurse from Peterborough, Ont., working with World Vision in Baidoa. "I don't think you can blame them though. I think with all they've been through, it's become every man for himself. I'm not sure what I would do either if I was in the same kind of desperate situation."

Certainly, there are thousands of Somalis toiling in food kitchens and hospitals, many of them working without pay. It is equally clear that the situation is improving. In Baidoa, where as many as 400 people were dying each day in September, the daily death toll has fallen to about 30. Most of the victims are people weakened by malnutrition who fall prey to disease in an over-crowded city with no government, no order, no sewers and little sanitation. "Forget AIDS—malnutrition is the world's leading cause of immune deficiency," said Ric Price, a 28-year-old MSF doctor who has set up a tent hospital for the most severe cases. "Measles is a killer here; so is hepatitis, dysentery and chest infections."

Last week, at a World Vision feeding centre in Baidoa, Pettersen began inoculating children against measles. Most of them appeared to be thin, but not starving, as they lined up stoically for their injec-tions. "The kids have all either died or they are improving," said Pettersen. "They go down really fast, and they come back fast too. But you still see teenagers and older people who are very skinny."

Mad Kerow Emet, an emaciated 16-year-old boy, is among them: four feet, 11 inches tall, he weighs just 84 pounds. His mother died of malaria eight years ago, he said as he sat on the floor at the feeding centre, drinking a cup of milk. His father was shot dead by clansmen from a neighboring village during the civil war. Five of his nine brothers and sisters died of starvation before Emet left his village of Sarman for Baidoa. He got as far as Ashogabo, about 15 km away, before being stricken with measles. "I was too weak to walk any farther," explained Emet. "I stayed alive by eating the skin of animals after toasting them on a fire." He finally arrived in Baidoa last week. "I feel better now, as I have porridge and milk and everything necessary to live," he said. "Now, I intend to stay here. I want to study the Koran and law, something better for the future. I've never been to school before."

Coming Back to Life

Half a year ago, starving children could hardly have expected to fulfil such dreams. But even schools are slowly becoming a reality in Somalia. Last week, as torrential rains bathed Mogadishu, water cascaded down the stairwells of an unfinished building that serves as both kitchen and school, nearly drowning out the voices of children chanting the Koran and their ABCs. It is one of 30 schools opened two months ago by a Somali women's organization called the Kitchen Committee, with assistance from the International Committee of the Red Cross. It serves students like Maktar Dero, an eight-year-old orphan from Baidoa, whose parents were shot to death nine months ago, and 14-year-old Mumin Jilani Aweys, who lives across the road in a refugee camp of twig huts. "We sold all our jewelry to buy books, blackboards, chairs," said Asha Dirie, the Kitchen Committee's 41-year-old chairman. "We made a big investment. Otherwise, the children would have no place to go."

The rains and the delivery of food aid into the countryside have also made a difference, drawing some of the urban refugees back to their fields. A food convoy, escorted by U.S. marines last week from Baidoa to the village of Abuurow, drove past green fields of sorghum—the first crop in years. In Abuurow, aid workers read off more than 500 names from a list provided by local chiefs, and gave each family a 50-kg bag of wheat. Occasional arguments would erupt over who could claim the portion allotted to absent families. And, as the day wore on, the jostling and pushing crowd grew increasingly restless.

There were about 50 people left by late afternoon when the last of the names had been called. But someone noticed one severely emaciated youngster—clearly the weakest person in Abuurow that day—and gave him a leftover bag. The boy sat down on the sack while aid workers and marines prepared to leave. Suddenly, in the melee, a teenager pulled the bag of wheat out from under the starving boy and ran off into the bush. It was just one more obscenity heaped onto the desperate tragedy that Somalia has endured—another sign of just how hard it will be for the country to ever overcome its legacy of violence, famine and war.

CANADA AT WAR

Carol Mathieu was twice found not guilty by a court martial of negligent performance of duty and retired from the military in October 1994. Serge Labbé was posted to NATO headquarters in Brussels in August 1996.

YUGOSLAVIA

COURAGE UNDER FIRE

—July 13, 1992—
Andrew Phillips

In the haze-shrouded hills surrounding Sarajevo airport last week, heavy machine-guns sounded out their death rattle. On one slope $2\frac{1}{2}$ km away, the muzzle flashes of a gun could be seen in the bright sunlight as it fired repeatedly from the lush green foliage. Down below, Canadian soldiers, who had just arrived at the airport as the largest contingent of United Nations peacekeepers to relieve the city, evaluated the threats around them with practiced eyes. The regular sound of gunfire made the potential dangers clear, but the soldiers appeared

---

Maj.-Gen. Lewis MacKenzie (far right).

relaxed and calm under the hot sun. One young corporal casually shaved using a mirror hung on the back of his armored personnel carrier (APC), and then slung his wet towel over the casing of a spent Yugoslav tank shell, one of dozens littering the tarmac. His commander, Lt.-Col. Michel Jones, a native of Montreal, puffed a cigarette and gazed out at the hills. "As long as they're not shooting at us," he said, "I'm happy."

The Canadians, a regiment of 800 troops, drove to the Bosnian capital in two convoys of 300 vehicles from their base in Daruvar, in neighboring Croatia. Their presence gave the United Nations badly needed muscle to add to its moral authority. Until they and 160 French troops arrived last week, the United Nations had just 34 soldiers in a city that civil war had turned into a deadly camp of rival militias. With the blue UN flag raised over Sarajevo's battered airport, camouflage-painted Hercules transport planes from half a dozen nations finally began to fly in with badly needed food and medical supplies for 300,000 civilians trapped by three months of fighting.

The planes are vulnerable to attack from all sides, and the threat to the city's new lifeline is evident. Maj.-Gen. Lewis MacKenzie, the Canadian with overall command of the UN forces in Sarajevo, acknowledged the hazards as he welcomed a Norwegian plane arriving with 15 tons of syringes, antibiotics and medicines last Thursday. "There are no guarantees," he said. "The people who fly in here have to have some nerve. But the UN can't just get involved where it's peaceful and comfortable and you take Saturday and Sunday off." As if to illustrate his point, the next day a ricochet from a sniper's bullet wounded Capt. Michael Rouleau of the Royal Canadian Horse Artillery. MacKenzie said that Rouleau suffered a slight graze on the face, but resumed duty shortly after the incident.

For MacKenzie, the opening of the airport and the arrival of the Canadians was both a relief and a personal triumph. Since he arrived in Sarajevo in March, the 52-year-old career soldier had been tied down by the crossfire of a war that spiralled downward into increasing violence and bitterness as Serbian forces fought to seize control of territory from the republic's mainly Muslim and

346

Croatian population. With a tiny staff, almost no firepower and a limited UN mandate, MacKenzie found his hopes of bringing relief to the city repeatedly dashed. At one point in late June, he said that he had eliminated the word "optimism" from his vocabulary.

But the dramatic six-hour visit to Sarajevo by French President François Mitterrand on June 28 helped to focus world attention on the suffering in the city and put political pressure on both warring sides. Mitterrand flew in on a French helicopter, mingled with local people in central Sarajevo and visited the site of a murderous May 27 mortar attack by Serb militiamen on a group of people lining up to buy bread. Mitterrand described his visit as a humanitarian gesture to a city that had become a worldwide symbol of suffering, and he promised to send aid even if it had to be protected by force. The visit was a security nightmare for MacKenzie, who acknowledged in an interview last week that he was only able to relax when Mitterrand left safely. "I was delighted when I saw the helicopter become a small black speck on the horizon," he said.

But Mitterrand's visit also marked a turning point in the Sarajevo standoff. The next day, Serbian forces finally left the airport and UN forces raised their flag. Then, MacKenzie ordered his troops to leave their base in Daruvar, where they had been standing by impatiently for 17 days, and start for Sarajevo.

The troops began the $2\frac{1}{2}$ day, 300-km trip in the 4 a.m. darkness of June 30. For Jones, the lieutenant-colonel who commands the regiment, it was a challenging trip. A Serbian militia commander known as "the Warlord" refused to let the Canadians pass through his territory in central Bosnia and threatened to open fire if they tried. Jones said that the man was clearly too drunk to conduct negotiations. "He stood in front of us with two bodyguards who pointed their Kalashnikovs [assault rifles] at us," said Jones. The Serb's forces also included two tanks, and a confrontation would almost certainly have resulted in deaths. As a result, Jones retreated about 20 km and he and his convoy settled in for the night.

The next morning, July 1, the Canadians met the Warlord again. And again he refused to let them pass, but Jones used what he later called "diplomacy and force." He recalled: "I said, 'At 2 p.m., I'm moving. And if you shoot, we'll return fire.' " Jones

347

deployed his troops in a combat stance, putting out snipers and bringing up his TOW armor-piercing missiles, antitank weapons and APCs with 50-calibre machine-guns. During a final meeting, the Warlord told Jones that the Canadians would have to retreat far back up the road. "I said, 'No way,' folded my map and said, 'I'm leaving,'" Jones recalled. "Then he said, 'No, sit down, we'll work it out.'" Within half an hour, the convoy was on its way—but it had lost almost a full day.

When they finally arrived in Sarajevo on July 2, dirty and unshaven after spending two nights sleeping in their vehicles, the Canadians found the city in ruins. Smashed and burned-out cars littered the streets; abandoned streetcars blocked roads, their broken overhead cables dangling menacingly; many buildings were burned out. Drivers raced through the city at high speeds, trying to minimize the risks from snipers who were targeting exposed cars.

City residents, after three months of fighting, had found ways of carrying on their lives while adapting to the dangers. They strolled casually in protected areas but darted nervously across open spaces exposed to sniper fire or stray bullets. And at the checkpoints that mark the boundaries between Muslim or Croatian areas and mainly Serbian neighborhoods, young men in a bewildering variety of uniforms cradled automatic weapons and struck macho poses as they interrogated nervous drivers.

Even amid the terrors of a war without a front line, the people were finding ways to survive. One afternoon last week in the heart of the city's once-picturesque old quarter, under red-tiled roofs and minarets, they lined up to buy ice-cream bars, T-shirts and cigarette lighters. Children still played outdoors—although they sometimes adapted their games to the degree of danger surrounding them. MacKenzie recalled seeing children playing soccer in a vacant lot until the shooting in their area became too intense. "They just picked up the ball and played basketball against the wall where it's safer," MacKenzie said. "When firing died down they went back to playing soccer. People are amazingly flexible."

For many local people, the arrival of the Canadian and French troops was a welcome sign of international concern. On the peacekeepers' journey south from Daruvar, people cheered the Canadian convoy. Some cried and others offered coffee and slivovitz, the fiery local plum brandy. In one small city, recalled Gilles Trembley of the Royal Canadian 22nd Regiment, the fabled Van Doos, "It seemed like the whole town was on the streets cheering and waving." The warm reception, said the 23-year-old Ottawa native, was a welcome change from the boredom of waiting for more than two weeks at their base in Croatia for orders to move. "In Daruvar, the people were getting tired of seeing UN troops," he said. Recalled Sgt. Christopher Johnson, 32, from New Glasgow, N.S.: "In a few towns we stopped and we were just mobbed. The streets were all lined with people, some of them were throwing flowers. It gives you a real good feeling."

Johnson said that the dangers of Sarajevo did not particularly trouble him or his comrades in Six Platoon, November Company of the Royal Canadian Regiment. As he sat beside his APC in a parking lot in the centre of the city, watching Serbian tanks on a distant hill firing at an unseen target, Johnson recalled a nighttime mortar and artillery attack on his platoon on April 13, shortly after they moved into their positions in the Croatian town of Sirac. "So far, this is nothing compared to Sirac," he said.

But some Sarajevo residents remain deeply pessimistic about the future. On Vase Miskina street in the city's old town district, flowers cover the spot where Serbian mortar shells killed 22 people lining up to buy bread in May. Posters on the walls nearby commemorate the incident with a blood-red poppy symbol and proclaim that the thoroughfare should be known from now on as "the street of defiance." Several passers-by last week voiced skepticism that opening the airport to relief flights would do anything to improve their lives as long as fighting continued. Said Osman Music, a 46-year-old engineer: "It's not good enough just to give us food and let us still be killed by these murderers in the hills." Asked if he wanted a more powerful UN force to intervene directly to stop the fighting, Music said quietly: "Wouldn't you? Wouldn't you?"

His companion, 35-year-old Slaki Faruk, another engineer, was equally angry at the outside world's powerlessness in the face of the fighting that destroyed his home in a Muslim neighborhood. "Everything I had has been burned and destroyed," he said. Tugging at the sleeve of his green cardigan, Faruk added: "Even this is from someone else, given to me. Now, I am like a charity case. I don't even have any pictures from my childhood. Even that has been stolen from me by those terrorists." And he stabbed his finger towards the outskirts of the city where Serbian gunners are dug in.

MacKenzie told *Maclean's* that he is fully aware that many Bosnians are disappointed in what the United Nations has done so far. Many do not understand that his peacekeeping force has only a limited mandate: to secure the airport and ensure the safe delivery of relief supplies to the city. That may do little to stop the sniping and shelling that still claim lives every day in Sarajevo. Canada's chief of defence staff, Gen. John de Chastelain, told *Maclean's* that MacKenzie was not equipped to operate beyond the peacekeepers' constraints: "If the aim of the operation was to get both sides in Bosnia-Herzegovina to stop fighting, and use force to do it, it could take thousands of troops and large numbers of heavy weapons and aircraft." He added: "But UN Secretary General Boutros Boutros-Ghali has talked about going beyond the humanitarian assistance. He is talking about limited action to ensure that no one interferes with the humanitarian relief effort, but he is not talking about stopping the fighting."

Last week, some people in the Sarajevo suburb of Dobrinja, a Muslim area near the airport that has been hit hardest by the fighting, published a letter in a newspaper in Zagreb, the Croatian capital. Said MacKenzie: "They got 1,800 signatures of people who want to try me as a war criminal because they are dying in shelling and fighting, and who else are they going to turn to, to stop that, if not the UN?" He added: "We are a victim, if you want to call it that, of the limitations of our mandate—something every UN force is used to. It lacks a bit of impact if you respond that you don't have the legal authority to get involved."

In another incident last week, MacKenzie said, a Serbian man whose brother had just died in an ambulance tried to attack the general, but other Serbs restrained him. "He looks at me and he thinks I'm to blame, because who else is he going to blame?" said MacKenzie. "He comes charging at me to seek revenge. And you understand him. These are not exactly good moments."

Courage Under Fire

The strictly limited UN mandate presents a dilemma for the peacekeepers. "Nobody had time to educate the two sides on what peacekeeping means," said MacKenzie, Canada's most experienced officer in such missions. "There is an anomaly here because there is no peace. Normally, we go in when there is an established peace and a demilitarized zone to park in and observe. Here, there's no ceasefire and no ceasefire line."

On Friday morning, Canadian troops positioned their APCs at strategic points along Sarajevo's main street to make sure that supplies travelled safely from the airport to the city's main distribution centre. By week's end, cargo planes carrying more than 150 tons of food, medicines and other emergency aid arrived from France, Britain, the United States, Italy, Norway and other countries. At one point during the day, three planes landed within 15 minutes, transforming the airport into a hive of activity for the first time since the war broke out in March. Indeed, UN officials even voiced concern that relief organizations might jam the airport with supplies that could not be distributed quickly enough to the beleaguered city.

For the Canadian peacekeepers in Sarajevo, the work may soon be over. Last week, Boutros-Ghali announced that they would soon be replaced by 1,500 troops from France, Egypt and Ukraine. The Canadians, he said, will return to peacekeeping duties in Croatia. "Our guys have performed magnificently," MacKenzie told *Maclean's*. "I've never been prouder of Canadian soldiers." His admiration was widely shared. Said President George Bush: "I think the Canadians who have stepped forward deserve a great vote of thanks from the entire world for what they're doing."

MacKenzie says that peacekeeping missions are likely to increase in the future. Declared the general: "Peacekeeping is a growing industry. It is not going to go away as long as countries, and organizations within the countries, pursue their own agendas." The veteran Canadian soldier was calling on all his peacekeeping experience last week as elements of the old Yugoslavia furiously pursued their agendas all around him.

ON
DEADLY
DUTY

July 1, 1994

John Howse

"Don't get any closer to Greg and me. If we blow up, we don't want to wet your clothes." The remark was a typical display of gallows humor by Cpl. Mark (Izzy) Isfeld who, along with Sgt. Gregory James, was leading a Canadian mine-clearing team on an early June morning in southern Croatia. It was also tragically prophetic. On a similar operation last week aimed at clearing areas for United Nations patrols, Isfeld, 31, was killed and James, 35, seriously injured when their armored personnel carrier (APC) tripped a mine. The blast also wounded another

---

Cpl. Mark Isfeld in southern Croatia.

On Deadly Duty

Canadian, 31-year-old Sgt. Paul McMillan. By coincidence, Maclean's correspondent John Howse had accompanied Isfeld, James and their team on two mine-clearing operations just two weeks earlier near the town of Kakma—the same area where last week's tragedy occurred. He filed this report. —The Editor, 1994

It was a hot morning, almost 40 deg. C, and the Serb guides arrived more than an hour late to lead the Canadian peacekeepers into their territory. Claiming there were no antitank mines on the route, the Serbs led the way in a heavy truck, past abandoned villages with burned-out, roofless houses to a dirt trail that the Princess Patricia's Canadian Light Infantry (PPCLI) had selected for patrols of its 50-km-long protection zone separating Serbs from Croats. Not taking any chances, James and Isfeld followed slowly on foot, scraping with their bayonets at suspicious mounds of earth, pushing gently into the trail's rocky earth with their hand-held probes. Behind them walked two more "sappers"—combat engineers—with mine detectors that buzzed constantly because of the many pieces of shrapnel and spent bullets littering the ground. A 31-year-old Canadian APC followed, bulldozing an inch or two of trail surface to make sure the men in front had missed nothing. Bringing up the rear was an ambulance, which followed the procession all day.

After about a kilometre, James turned to Isfeld. "What do you think?" he asked the corporal. They agreed that it felt safe enough to move on. The four other members of the crew concurred—with combat engineers, decisions are consensual, not necessarily from the top down. "What we do has a lot to do with the obvious," explained James, who has 16 years of experience with explosives. "We ask everyone on this team how they feel. If one of us thinks the place is mined, it means a very slow approach from us all." Since April, when they arrived in Croatia with the PPCLI Battle Group, James's 40-man unit has cleared more than 400 km of trail.

There is never a moment when the mines are forgotten. During a break, while the soldiers swilled mineral water and ate boxed rations of German biscuits, rice and canned pork, some of the troops talked about the dangers they face. Like many peacekeepers,

Cpl. Terry O'Leary, a medic, has cultivated a healthy skepticism of the Serbs. "They told us one day there were no mines," he said, "and the engineers found 30 antipersonnel mines just off the road."

After their arrival in southern Croatia from Chilliwack, B.C., 1 Combat Engineer Regiment worked 21 days straight. Now, to reduce fatigue, the sappers rotate two days in the minefield with one in camp. "The tension builds up," said Isfeld, who did a six-month tour of duty in Croatia in 1992. "You feel a climax coming. It gets spooky." He explained: "The Croats and Serbs lay different [mine] patterns and there are different terrains. Some days you feel, 'Damn, there are mines here.' You can't see them but you know. I once walked over an antitank mine—I wouldn't be here if it had gone off. But we're not psychic." Added James: "All of us some-time have felt our testicles leap into our armpits. You look at a map and see no reason to put mines there. But that doesn't mean they're not there. And you can't go back to the books when you're in the minefield. You must not be afraid."

One of the biggest frustrations for the sappers is that they have no UN mandate to confiscate mines—an estimated two million are scattered across the former Yugoslavia—from the combatants. Instead, they usually turn them over to the side that put them there in the first place. Said James: "We BIP [blow-up in place] a few, but the politics is that if they want to take them, they do. That's the worst thing about this job."

As the Canadians proceeded up the trail, now overgrown with high grass, everyone scanned the ground for hidden trip wires. "All of us have touched a wire with our ankles," said Isfeld. "We know how much tension it needs to break it." The high grass soon ended and the trail appeared clear. The Serb guides said that it was well used and were eager to drive on. James surveyed the area and agreed that the trail seemed safe. Besides, he'd seen signs of activity in the area recently. "You saw those empty mussel shells and sheep shit back there," he said. "It's the little things like that which help."

Eventually, one of the Serbs wandered over to report that their truck was low on fuel. James readily agreed to supply them with a jerrican full, as well as some food rations. "We're not going to lose a Canadian boy to a mine because we were too cheap to give these

354

guys some gas and food," he explained. "No point in pissing them off." James urged his men to take their time. By late afternoon, they had completed seven kilometres without incident. Then it was time to return to the engineers' base, a comfortable, two-storey building formerly used as a brothel.

The next day, Isfeld led the crew to a windswept battleground in the shadow of the Velemit Mountains. Immediately, the Canadians spotted danger—lines of antipersonnel mines mounted on stakes. Activated by a sharp tug on the trip wire, the mines can kill anyone within a 40-metre radius and seriously injure within 100 metres. As a sapper deadpanned, "Definitely, it would ruin your day." A Serb helpfully pointed to mounds of earth surrounding a small blood-soaked crater where a cow had recently been killed. "Don't step there," he warned through a UN interpreter. The Canadians found a cowbell in a nearby bush.

Isfeld was not impressed with the way the Serbs walked around the minefield. "It's a little unnerving," he said. "They're tugging away at those wires. My call is that it isn't safe to go in there with them." He ordered the crew to clear the road shoulders but not to accompany the Serbs deeper into the minefield. The Serbs picked up 40 mines and stacked the fuses, stakes and spools of wire before loading them into the back of their vehicle. It was a bigger haul than the Canadians expected. But without the power to confiscate the munitions, they were well aware that the mines could soon be replanted elsewhere.

Back at base camp it was barbecue night, and Isfeld cooked steaks for his men. They would have the next day off, so some of the troops relaxed with cold beer. Isfeld, a nondrinker, abstained. He recently wrote home to reassure his mother, Carol, and his wife, Kelly, after an earlier mine incident seriously wounded two Canadians. "We are being careful," wrote Isfeld, "not letting complacency set in."

The young corporal, who had no children, had been scheduled to return to Canada in late June for three weeks of home leave. Instead, his body was flown to British Columbia for burial, a grim reminder of the high price some Canadians have paid for trying to keep the peace in a blood-soaked land.

355

CALLING THE SHOTS

—December 19, 1994—
Bruce Wallace

There seems to be only one thing that scares a Bosnian Serb these days. "We call it 'mouse fever,' because it seems to be carried by the mice living in garbage dumps," says Lyle Pleasants, an RCMP officer who just concluded a six-month tour with the UN's civilian police force in the encircled Muslim enclave of Gorazde. "If you catch it, your kidneys fail and you're gone within a couple of days," says the broad-shouldered Edmonton policeman. "If you want to get through a Serb checkpoint, just tell them you're carrying a passenger with mouse fever. They won't even search the vehicle. It's just: 'No problem,' and they wave you through."

It is said that elephants fear only mice and, in Bosnia, the Serbs are undisputed leviathans of the ethnic jungle. In their showdown with the world's great powers this fall, the world blinked. Unable to force the Bosnian Serbs to stop their assault on the onetime "safe haven" of Bihac, unable to muster more than pitiful pleas for peace, world leaders came to the conclusion last week that the Bosnian Serbs cannot be ejected from the lands they hold. There will likely be no more NATO bombing runs. "That is the very strong signal coming from the world body," says Col. Jean Trepanier, the Canadian who is in charge of the United Nations Protection Force (UNPROFOR) Land Operations based in Zagreb, Croatia. "It may not be fair, but it is a fact of life."

On the ground, where it counts, the Bosnian Serbs call the shots. Witness their disdainful treatment of UN soldiers, including 55 Canadians, held as hostages to deter NATO air attacks on Serb positions. The Canadians were finally released last week, many of them going right back to work manning checkpoints behind Serb lines. But more than 300 peacekeepers remained hostage, and UN commanders admitted that their troops could be taken and held at Serbian will. Meanwhile, the Bosnian Serbs and their allies in the Krajina region, a Serb-occupied swath of Croatia, primed surface-to-air missiles to shoot down NATO patrol planes.

With the situation becoming ever more dangerous, UNPRO-FOR commanders had little option but to step up preparations and plans for a withdrawal of their 23,000 peacekeepers. The United States indicated its willingness to commit 25,000 ground troops to protect UN soldiers, who may be forced to fight their way out of Bosnia. Retreat was about all that the allies were doing in concert last week. The 52-nation Conference on Security and Co-operation in Europe, meeting in the Hungarian capital of Budapest, could not even agree on wording to appeal for a ceasefire in Bosnia. And the impasse continued to drive a wedge between the United States and its NATO partners. Declaring that Bosnian policy was at "a total dead end," France's Foreign Minister Alain Juppé criticized the Clinton administration by slamming governments that "teach us lessons daily and have not lifted a little finger to even put one man on the ground."

Its NATO backing revealed to be all lip and no muscle, UNPROFOR began to make policy on the run. Western diplomats said that, for the first time, the United Nations was refusing to provide humanitarian aid to Serb-held areas unless convoys were allowed to pass into Muslim towns first. That breaks from the traditional UN practice of unconditionally feeding everyone in need, regardless of political allegiance. The quid pro quo tactic worked: the Serbs finally allowed a desperately needed convoy into Sre-brenica, a safe haven protecting mainly Muslims in eastern Bosnia, and the beleaguered battalion of 500 Bangladeshi peacekeepers in Bihac were also resupplied.

But as long as peacekeepers remained hostages, UNPROFOR commanders sweated over the possibility of confrontations between the Bosnian Serbs and NATO. On the one hand, the emboldened Bosnian Serbs were vowing to shoot down NATO planes using surface-to-air missiles. On the other, NATO's rules of engagement require pilots to take out any missile batteries that electronically "lock on" to their aircraft. UN officials worried that

357

such an exchange could occur even by accident, resulting in hostages being killed in reprisal. So desperate was UNPROFOR to avert such a confrontation that when a British patrol came under attack near Gorazde one day last week, the soldiers chose not to call for NATO air support to help them escape.

Indeed, there was broad acceptance that, although the siege may be long, a Serb victory in Bihac is unavoidable. The enclave is almost surrounded by a horseshoe-shaped assault force, and the Serbs appear content to keep squeezing the pocket until it surrenders. Their aim, said UN military commanders, was simply to disarm and neutralize the Bosnian government's once-vaunted V Corps based there. Few observers believed that the Serbs were prepared to try to take the city, street by bloody street. "They have refrained from going in there and having atrocities against women and children shown on American television every night," said Trepanier. They have even left a way out for the V Corps soldiers to escape—provided they leave their weapons behind.

But although the Bosnian army was on its heels in Bihac, the fighting in the rest of the country may still have a long way to run. "The Bosnian government army is very much alive," says Maj.-Gen. Ray Crabbe, the Canadian who is UNPROFOR's deputy force commander. "They are constantly hitting, probing and jabbing along the confrontation line, forcing the Bosnian Serbs to redeploy troops all the time and to use up crucial fuel supplies." UNPROFOR officers also acknowledge that they are extremely worried about the prospects of Croatia re-entering the fighting to try to regain territory lost to the Bosnian Serbs in the 1991 Serb-Croat war. The Croatian government continues to insist that if it does not get conquered lands back through negotiation, it will try to retake them by force.

But whether Croatia can convince its citizens to back another war remains to be seen. The country is enjoying the fruits of peace—international financial credits and a prospering investment climate—which would be swapped for pariah status if it resumed its war with Serbia. UNPROFOR's Trepanier says that the first signs of war fatigue are emerging on all sides; even Serb soldiers are now deserting in greater numbers. "Everyone says that they are tired of the fighting and just want to go home," adds the RCMP's Pleasants. "Then again, the Muslims in Gorazde still say that they must have their villages back, and that they will fight to the death if they have to." No one wants more war; they just want peace on their terms.

To the Bosnian government, the West's shifting policy in dealing with the Serbs amounts to betrayal. "The Bosnians were sincerely convinced that UNPROFOR was here to defend them," says Trepanier. "It may take a week, or two, or three, or a month," he says, but the Bosnians will eventually wake up one day and see that they are on their own, and their military situation is dire. "The West will not fight for Bosnia," added one Western diplomat last week. "This is their fight, and the sad fact is that one party is stronger than the other, and is going to get its way. That, unfortunately, is the way of the world."

A SOLDIER'S STORY

June 12, 1995

Luke Fisher

During a seven-month tour of duty in the former Yugoslavia, Sgt. Michel Sartori was detained by the Bosnian Serbs three times for a total of six days. A section leader in the Royal 22nd Regiment (the Van Doos), based in Valcartier, Que., Sartori served in the region from November 1993 to May 1994, and is scheduled to return there in September. Sartori, 32, who is married with two children, spoke about his experiences with *Maclean's* Ottawa Bureau Correspondent Luke Fisher. —The Editor

Sgt. Michel Sartori.

A Soldier's Story

The day I arrived in Sarajevo, I was scared because there were snipers all around. I wrote a letter to my family telling them I didn't think I would survive. Then, as soon as we got to Visoko [site of a UN observation post], the Serbs bombarded us with mortar fire. My God, it was crazy. I never, never felt safe.

There weren't many people who wanted to serve in the Serb areas, so they sent the Van Doos because the Serbs respected us. After an attack on a [Serb] hospital in Visoko, we showed up and cleaned the place. Everybody was sick, people were lying in excrement. We were supposed to leave after we finished, but I refused and we ended up staying for another two months to help out. Things like that made the Serbs respect us. Whenever they tried to provoke us, we would put our weapons down and talk. The Serbs were amazed and would say, "We're not used to soldiers acting like that."

In December 1993, Lt.-Gen. [Michael] Rose, the British commander of UN forces at the time, said he was tired of Serb heavy weapons causing trouble in one area, and he sent the Canadians to take the weapons. That's when we were taken hostage the first time. The Serbs surrounded us, saying that everybody had better give them their weapons or they would fire. Then they said that if we weren't gone in two hours, they would drop mortars on our heads. We received orders to move into the hills. As soon as we did, the Serbs put mines around us and took us hostage. The commander came to me and said, "Sorry, Mike, but we don't like the way you're treating us." There were 16 of us. He said we'd probably be released the next day and that we shouldn't be scared. But we were ridiculed by the other Serbs for allowing ourselves to be handled so easily. They released us three days later, after making their point.

The Serbs, Muslims and Croats play the same games. The Muslims took hostages in Visoko—they didn't want us to leave because then they would be killed by the Serbs. The Serbs took us to protect them from NATO aircraft. And the Croats took us in Srebrenica because they feared being killed by the Serbs. It's a crazy country.

At first when we were detained, we were frightened, but I

quickly grew to know that the Serbs weren't going to harm us. The more important problem was the NATO bombing. We were worried that bombs would be dropped on us.

In fact, the Serbs treated us pretty well. My guys didn't like the food, so we asked to bring in some Canadian food. The Serbs said, "No problem." The French and British hostages did not get their food brought in, but we had a better relationship. We also spent a lot of time chatting with the Serb commander. We talked about the war and tried to understand each other's points. We never disagreed with them.

The biggest problem was that so many of the Bosnian Serb soldiers were drunk. They were drunk through the night, and drunk in the morning. When you go to talk to these people you must take some alcohol or nobody will talk to you. So everybody is drunk, and for the Serb commanders it isn't easy. It's not like the Canadian or British army. They are mercenaries, and lots of soldiers don't want the war to stop because when it stops they have nothing to do.

My response to NATO air strikes is, "No, no, no." Every time it happens, I turn to my wife and say, "Tomorrow we're going to have hostages." We should stop the aircraft now, apply diplomatic pressure and get our guys released. It was very stupid to have the air strikes on May 25 and 26. The Americans may love bombing, but remember that they don't have any GIs on the ground. The only way we can solve things is by talking, not with weapons.

When I saw that television footage of Capt. [Patrick] Rechner, I wished I could say to his family, "Don't be nervous." The Serbs did it for TV, and everybody knows that. I doubt he's being held like that [handcuffed to a pole] all the time. They wanted to make a point. This is a weapon of theirs. The Serbs are not nuts—they're fighting a war. I don't think it's a good way, but it has worked for them.

When it came time to return to Canada, I told my commander I wanted to go and say goodbye to some of the Serbs. He said no, because he was worried about us being taken hostage again. I wish I could have said goodbye to that Serb commander who treated us so well. I was disappointed.

To be honest, the first month I came home I cried all the time.

A Soldier's Story

I don't know why, exactly. After that, I talked to my friends and family about the children and the old people I saw. In my section, one guy felt suicidal and another actually tried to kill himself and a third had his wife leave him. We have problems, but I'll be glad to get back there in September. I feel my place is in Bosnia, helping the people.

AFTERWORD

IT ALL STARTED with D-Day. In 1994, when *Maclean's* began researching a special issue marking the 50th anniversary of the invasion and the end of the war in Europe, the pages of the magazine from that era yielded intimate stories of the challenge and the heroism. At home and abroad, it was a time of heartbreak, bravery and, ultimately, triumph. Then, during the celebration of our 90th year as a magazine in 1995, we ran excerpts of several other wartime articles. The response to both efforts was so enthusiastic that we soon were planning a collection of war stories from the pages of *Maclean's*, the bylines a roll-call of famous writers. The project was headed by Michael Benedict, *Maclean's* Editorial Director of New Ventures, who brought to the effort a keen eye and a genuine enthusiasm for breathing life into Canada's proud past. It is our sincere hope that the exploits of Canadians at war will not be forgotten as the nation faces the daunting challenge of keeping peace in the family.

Robert Lewis
Editor-in-Chief
Maclean's